Praise for *Keeper*

"By writing so skillfully and personally about Alzheimer's, [Gillies] has given caregivers and families a gift. Gillies weaves one family's story with various medical theories about the care and treatment of patients, accounts of well-known people who have been stricken with this disease, and musings on the meaning of memory and the self. . . . It's not an easy book to read, but it's impossible to put down."   —*Minneapolis Star Tribune*

" 'Alzheimer's' is the health-care word that can freeze a pleasant dinner conversation. Maybe it's spoken in a whisper; maybe it's left unsaid. . . . Alzheimer's [is] a debilitating, devastating terminal illness. If it affords few moments of grace, at least Gillies has said that honestly. And out loud."   —*Los Angeles Times*

"Forthright, smartly researched, and warmly recounted . . . Gillies writes with a novelist's eye for detail, and her unflinching rendering of Nancy's excruciating loss of self is skillfully and tenderly drawn. . . . An invaluable resource."

—*Publishers Weekly,* starred review

"With an economy of expression, an eye for detail, and a storyteller's knack for dialogue, Gillies charts Nancy's terrible course from doddering to vicious and her own decline into caregiver dementia. . . . An unvarnished cautionary tale."

—*Kirkus Reviews,* starred review

"The key to Gillies's personal strength resides in the numerous literary and philosophical observations she frequently quotes and from which she draws inspiration in this awesome chronicle."   —*Booklist,* starred review

"Overflows with history, literature . . . [a] compassionate account."
—*Times Literary Supplement*

"A painfully honest account." —*Daily Express* (London)

"The most poignant aspect of *Keeper* is the way Gillies traces the increasingly unbearable pressures that are placed on carers as patients progress from memory lapses, not remembering important life events and no longer recognizing family members, to the final advanced stage that Gillies calls the 'darkest shadow.'" —*The Lancet*

"Andrea Gillies's account of living with Alzheimer's is the perfect fusion of narrative with enough memorable science not to choke you. It's a fantastic book—down to earth and darkly comic in places." —*The Psychologist*

"In *Keeper* there is hope and humanity and the warmth of sacrifice." —*Catholic Herald*

"Deeply moving." —*Daily Mail* (London)

Keeper

ONE HOUSE, THREE GENERATIONS, AND A JOURNEY INTO ALZHEIMER'S

Andrea Gillies

Broadway Paperbacks

New York

BROADWAY

All rights reserved.
Published in the United States by Broadway Paperbacks, an imprint of the
Crown Publishing Group, a division of Random House, Inc., New York.
www.crownpublishing.com

Broadway Paperbacks and its logo, a letter B bisected on the diagonal, are
trademarks of Random House, Inc.

Originally published in slightly different form in Great Britain by
Short Books, London, in 2009, and in hardcover in slightly different form in the
United States by Broadway Books, an imprint of the Crown Publishing Group,
a division of Random House, Inc., New York, in 2009.

Library of Congress Cataloging-in-Publication Data
Gillies, Andrea.
Keeper: one house, three generations, and a journey into
Alzheimer's / by Andrea Gillies.
1. Alzheimer's disease—Patients—Care—Scotland.   2. Gillies, Andrea.
3. Caregivers—Scotland—Biography.   4. Alzheimer's disease—Patients—
Scotland—Biography.   I. Title.
RC523.G476 2010
616.8'31—dc22   2010006659

ISBN 978-0-307-71912-6
eISBN 978-0-307-71913-3

Printed in the United States of America

Book design by Lauren Dong
Cover design by Laura Duffy
Cover photograph: © Claire Morgan / Trevillion

10 9 8 7 6 5 4 3 2 1

First U.S. Paperback Edition

To C and the children,
And with love and gratitude to my family and friends

I am—yet what I am, none cares or knows;
My friends forsake me like a memory lost:
I am the self-consumer of my woes:—
They rise and vanish in oblivion's host,
Like shadows in love's frenzied stifled throes:—
And yet I am, and live—like vapours tossed

Into the nothingness of scorn and noise,—
Into the living sea of wakeful dreams,
Where there is neither sense of life or joys,
But the vast shipwreck of my life's esteems;
Even the dearest, that I love the best
Are strange—nay, rather stranger than the rest.

—JOHN CLARE (c. 1840)

Keeper

Introduction

You have to begin to lose your memory, if only in bits and pieces, to realize that memory is what makes our lives. Life without memory is no life at all. Our memory is our coherence, our reason, our feeling, even our action. Without it, we are nothing.

—LUIS BUÑUEL

It is singular how soon we lose the impression of what ceases to be constantly before us. A year impairs, a luster obliterates. There is little distinct left without an effort of memory, then indeed the lights are rekindled for a moment—but who can be sure that the Imagination is not the torch-bearer?

—LORD BYRON

THE PROCESS OF WRITING THIS BOOK, THE PHYSICAL act of putting it together from diaries, scribbled notes, books about the mind, and concentrated bouts of introspection, has proven an illuminating exercise for me, demonstrating just what it is that dementia takes away. (Answer: everything; every last thing we reassure ourselves that nothing could take away from us.) The way the brain works, the supercomputer folded modestly into every human head, marshaling its forces, making connections, prompting and synthesizing, is dazzling and extraordinary and yet seems every day perfectly unexceptional and ordinary to us. There's nothing we take more for granted. In recording the decline of somebody with dementia, and seeing her preoccupations grow narrower and narrower, and her intellectual pathways block off, I've found myself preoccupied with unexpected things, more and wider things, my mind disappearing down all kinds of unforeseen alleys, which has been exhilarating but also poignant. I'm left feeling a profound gratitude to the life of the mind, how associative it is and how rich, in its leading on from one thing to another, into that whole interior landscape of yoked-together and often incongruous thoughts that adds up to a self. This book has turned out to be as much about the unraveling of a caregiver as it is about the person cared for, but its starting point was wanting to write about Alzheimer's and about life with an Alzheimer's sufferer, my mother-in-law, Nancy.

We spent many years looking after Nancy at one remove from us, a responsibility made more stressful by distance, and then at closer range—in a big Victorian house in a remote part of Scotland, with Nancy and her disabled husband, Morris, living with us and our three children. The house was not an ordinary one and, in a way I didn't anticipate, became another character in the story. It was an imposing, drafty mansion on a wild, near-treeless headland. We moved there specifically to attempt an extended family; when that failed, we had little choice but to leave. The official gloss put upon this exit is of the "phases of life" sort: job done, time to go. The private verdict is soaked marrow-deep in defeat.

I'm aware that in many ways this is a story about privilege. We could afford (could convince the bank we could afford) the big house and the part-time help, and when push came to shove (and it did, literally), my in-laws could come up with the fees for a good nursing home. But there are monetary consequences to caregiving, above and beyond the obvious weekly bills, and there has been a real financial hangover that we're still working through, brought on by months and years of having no choice but to put work second.

Well, so what, you may be thinking. *You took in your husband's parents. Boo-hoo. Big deal.* Across other, more populous continents, three-generation households are the norm, after all (the Asian three-generational photograph is lodged reprovingly in my brain), and they will likely become more commonplace here, as the care crisis bites harder. It's pretty clear that it *will* bite. The world seems to be in the grip of a dementia epidemic. Here in Britain, there are 820,000 people who've been diagnosed with dementia, two-thirds of them women, and the figure is rising sharply. In the United States, it's more than ten times that number. Of these, according to the Alzheimer's Association, 5.3 million have Alzheimer's disease. There are estimated to be more than 35 million dementia sufferers across the globe, with over 65 million forecast for 2030 and more than 115 million for 2050: the figures near doubling *every twenty years*. That's why the phrase "dementia time bomb" is beginning to be used. The devastating extra sting of dementia is that, unlike heart disease and cancer, it doesn't shorten life. It's a cruelly lengthy business. The changes in the brain can begin twenty years before a formal diagnosis, and the average life expectancy afterward is eight years.

Alzheimer's disease is only one of many varieties of dementia, though by far the commonest. Over 60 percent of diagnosed dementia sufferers have Alzheimer's disease. Back in 2002, BBC News reported that more than 40 percent of UK home caregivers of someone with Alzheimer's had been forced to give up work in order to look after the person. In the United States, 10 million people act as caregivers to someone with dementia and millions more offer support. About the same percentage of American caregivers are not employed, and two-thirds of those who can manage to hold down a job report major disruption to the workweek. I quote these statistics as a roundabout way of answering my own question: Why write this book at all? There were several reasons. One of these was to share in my own revelation, hard-earned, that Alzheimer's isn't just about memory loss; that *memory loss* isn't just about memory loss, but leads to disintegration. I wanted also to kick the system ineffectually in the shins; to give a glimpse into the dementia abyss; to show that for every "client" in the statistics there are one, two, four, six others (aka the family) whose lives are blighted in addition; in short, to give a little insight into the reality that ensues from the apparently noble idea (the noble, and for the country's financial bottom line, far preferable idea) that the elderly ill should stay at home whenever possible.

Question: Do governments understand just how dehumanizing Alzheimer's is? (A rhetorical question. Answer: no, or they wouldn't withhold good drug treatments or limit research programs on grounds of cost.) Question: Does anybody who hasn't been through it understand just how dehumanizing caregiving can be? (A rhetorical question. Answer: no, or there would be proper nursing home provision and it would be free.) As things stand in the United Kingdom, dementia patients in nursing homes, unlike cancer patients in hospitals, are regarded as "social care clients" and charged hotel rates, and if they have savings and houses must give them up to pay the bills. We British may regard ourselves as two steps ahead of the United States in the matter of universal rights to health care, but when it comes to dementia, the two systems are very alike. Medicaid will step in and pay for residence in a nursing home only if the ill person's own assets have dwindled away almost to nothing, and it's pretty much an identical situation in the United Kingdom. Once the money runs out, the ill person's house is likely to be sold to pay for care, unless a spouse or dependent is still living in it. Even if American houses can be placed out of risk in the short term, certainly they are at risk after the owner with dementia has died, via *estate recovery* (the rebate of nursing home fees in arrears to Medicaid—a policy that's pursued energetically in most states). Advice about loopholes in the system that allow a family to hang on to a loved one's home long term has grown into an industry, and almost every American Web site that talks about costs and rights to do with dementia suggests consulting an attorney. It's a system that's good for lawyers: in other words, bad law.

There's also a selfish answer to the why-write-the-book question. I'm one of those who have found work incompatible with caregiving, even work that I have always done at home, sitting at a table by a window, or slouched uncomfortably on a sofa, laptop at a precarious angle, mediating children's interruptions—work that you might assume would be ideal in the circumstances. It's more than economics in my case. Writing is more in the way of a compulsion. It may even be a psychiatric disorder. If days pass dryly—that is, without sentences being made and remade—I find that I begin to drift into the arena of the unwell. Throughout my years of caring for Nancy, the drive was there to produce something salable, but other than the occasional article, the content wouldn't follow the impulse. Following an early career producing sensible nonfiction and then a long hiatus while having and raising children, I was supposed to be cutting loose and writing a novel—and, on the face of it, I was immensely productive, almost manically so. I wrote two and a half novels. I wrote them in a rush, thinking, I can make some money at this (almost a guarantee of failure). The two finished ones were bad, superficial, studded with frustrations like cloves in an orange. The half is still a half, stopped, stalled. The muse left me. She did it quite abruptly, though things had been sticky between us for a while. After that, all I could seem to write about with any passion or conviction was my mother-in-law. Writing about her was sustaining through the dark days of creative roadblock. It was, to be blunt, a way of not cracking up.

This might also be the moment to tell you that names in

the account that follows have been changed. Nancy is beyond minding or even registering the fact that she's the subject of what you might call an unauthorized biography, and changing names provides only a tissue-paper-thin layer of anonymity, but it feels right, nonetheless.

A lot of what follows is taken from unedited diaries, which accounts for the use of the present tense and also for the emotional rawness of some passages. While filling the diaries, I used some of the entries in a newspaper piece I wrote about Nancy. It was straightforward and at moments graphic about her problems (and ours), and this didn't go down well with on-line commentators. Their chief complaint had to do with my having written intrusively about my mother-in-law without her consent. Even by then Nancy was long past the point of being able to consent to anything; she found the choice of Weetabix or cornflakes baffling enough. Intellectual competence aside, the argument remains that whatever the truth about rights, it's in bad taste to write in such unsparing detail about another's decline. The daughter of former British prime minister Margaret Thatcher has been pelted with rebukes since disclosing her mother's dementia. Her critics insist that the disease should be "kept in the family," which is only a short hop from suggesting that it's stigmatizing and shameful. Tony Robinson, the actor who played Baldrick on the popular BBC show *Blackadder,* was accused of something similar when he let UK Channel 4 make a documentary about his mother's last weeks. His response was robust: no, quite the opposite; he was proud of the program. There's a public service element to allowing media access, even if it might appear to the viewer to be cloaked in voyeurism. Those of us who have loved ones embarked on the dementia journey—and it *is* a journey, with clearly defined stages—publicize the details of their decline not despite our love, but in large part because of it. In some cases, the love is shared with the nation at large. In the case of Ronald Reagan, the announcement of his Alzheimer's disease by means of an open letter in 1994 (a poignant and brave last message that marked the end of his public life) prompted a whole new national surge of affection for the former U.S. president.

SCIENCE STILL ISN'T sure precisely what triggers Alzheimer's, though things are moving so fast that the mystery may be solved by the time you get to read this. (In fact, the pattern in the last few years has been that they move fast and get nowhere much.) What's uncontroversial is that Alzheimer's brains show the presence of two weird and provocative things: (1) a wild overproduction of beta-amyloid, a naturally produced and usually soluble protein, contributing to sticky blobs called *plaques* and (2) the knotting and snagging of the tau protein that forms the "rungs" in the communication ladders within brain cells into *tangles*. The race is still on to determine what the definitive cause is.

An adult brain has about 100,000 million nerve cells, individual *neurons* that each look rather like the branching root of a tuber pulled out of the ground—tubers of different shapes according to flavor. A good analogy, put forward by the Oxford professor Susan Greenfield, is to think of the brain as the Amazon rain forest inside your head. In the Amazon rain forest's 2.7 million square miles, she says, there are about 100,000 million trees. Imagine all that foliage condensed into the size of a cauliflower within your skull: 100,000 million tiny trees, making a dense neuron forest. Our memories and our thoughts travel through the forest as encoded electrical signals. The "roots" of the neuron are called *dendrites* (from the Greek for *treelike*), and its stalk (trunk) is called an *axon*. The information comes in to the neuron via the dendrites, into the *soma* (cell body)—that's the front door—and then goes out the back door, travels up the axon, along parallel lines of communication called *microtubules,* and out the other end at branches called *synaptic terminals.* This information moves, in tiny leaps, from axon to dendrite, from one neuron to the next. How does it do that? For a while there were two camps of conjecture, spark versus soup. The sparkers, who believed in an electrical leap, lost out in the end to the soupers, who thought that the constituency of the soup was key. The spaces at which the crossing is made are called *synapses,* though they're more like ports than spaces—ports at which clusters of *neurotransmitters* are waiting as a chemical transport system. Subsequent research has shown that there are indeed electrical as well as chemical synapses in the brain, though the electrical ones are heavily outnumbered. The number of dendrites and synapses varies hugely according to the neuron's function, but on average a neuron is thought to have around 7,000 synaptic terminals. Multiply that by 100,000 million and the mind begins to boggle.

In photographic comparison, a normal brain resembles a freshly peeled chestnut, pale and fat and glistening, and a brain with advanced Alzheimer's disease looks rather like a walnut, shrunken and shriveled with bits apparently eaten away. The disease takes place as a physical invasion, involving the progressive destruction of the neuron forest. Under the microscope, the damage is theatrically obvious: there are plaques—fuzzy, rust-colored accretions of protein fragments—which interfere with the transport network, and tangles, which look rather like strands that have grown over the neurons, like bindweed in a garden, though in fact they're a distortion of the neuron wall itself, its microtubules having collapsed into knots. As cells wither and die, gaps form in the tissues, leaving characteristic holes. American researchers working with the new generation of scanners, and thus able for the first time to look into the brains of living Alzheimer's patients, have found that the disease starts in or adjacent to the hippocampus (the memory-processing zone) and moves farther into the limbic system (our emotional nerve center); around eighteen months later, it has crept into the frontal lobe (site of the thinking, reflecting self). The disease always starts in the same place and takes the same general route, but proceeds unevenly in its spread. Some sections of the brain will be decimated, but neighboring ones might be unaffected and normal. It's rather like a forest fire in which clumps of blackened stumps sit adjacent to trees that seem oblivious to the disaster, untouched, their green canopies intact.

The term *dementia* (from *de mentis,* "out of the mind") was coined in 1801 in the asylums of Paris. Today it is used to mean brain failure, and in just the same way that heart failure is a condition caused by a whole host of problems, brain failure has many sponsors. One in fourteen UK citizens over sixty-five has some form of dementia and one in six over eighty, but for UK citizens reaching the age of sixty-five in 2010, the risk of developing dementia is one in three. Almost one in six Americans aged sixty-five will go on to develop dementia, and more than one in five aged eighty-five. And that's the trouble with it, in terms of PR. It's an old person's disease, by and large, and elderly ill people aren't easy to "sell." The issue is confused by our muddle about what's normal in old age—the idea that senility is an ordinary part of the human condition, that it is aging itself made manifest, and thus can't be cured. Progress is slow.

Research funds aren't generous, despite the fact that currently dementia costs the United Kingdom about £23 billion a year and the United States a staggering $148 billion just to deal with damage limitation and long-term care. Unpaid caregivers, their lives transformed into a round-the-clock vigil, are saving the British government about £12.4 billion. In just one year (2008), the economic value of unpaid caregiving in the United States was estimated to be $94 billion. Two-thirds of UK citizens with late-onset dementia are living in a family home; about 70 percent in the United States. Both figures are probably higher when undiagnosed cases are taken into account.

In the United Kingdom, only £61 is spent on research per Alzheimer's victim, though the amount is £295 per patient for cancer. In the United States in 2008, $5.6 billion was spent on cancer research, but only $0.4 billion on dementia science. Cancer has higher cultural status, even, perversely, a twisted, dark kind of glamour. Plucky young people get it, pop stars battle it, pretty wives and dashing young husbands die of it, and their pictures are spread across the newspapers. Cancer is a disease that journalists get and write about on the premise that if life hands you lemons, make lemonade. People with dementia don't write about it much because writing isn't something they do— or wasn't, until recently, when the very-early-diagnosed patient lobby sprang into being and people like the writer Terry Pratchett began speaking out. The much-loved author of the *Discworld* novels, a man who's sold 55 million books worldwide, allowed a BBC TV crew to follow him for twelve months. The resulting television program (*Living with Alzheimer's*) charted unsentimentally the beginnings of his decline, his defeat by the attempt to tie a knot in his tie, his having to pause in giving a reading because he found that a "shadow" was falling repeatedly across the page. This is the kind of cultural event that introduces people to the idea that dementia has something to do with them. It will be a long road. In general, the Alzheimer's demographic and its symptoms have meant that it's very low caste—something that, even now, we associate with decay and the cabbage-and-disinfectant scent of the geriatric ward.

There are widespread misconceptions about the disease.

Uncertainty is the midwife of misconception. The trouble is, nobody knows for sure what triggers Alzheimer's. All we can hope for is that keeping fit, doing crosswords, and eating well will spare us. They don't, necessarily. The illness of writer and philosopher Iris Murdoch attracted so much interest because people were amazed that someone like that could fall prey to Alzheimer's, someone so clever, articulate, affluent. We live in an age-defying, mortality-denying culture. We don't believe in ourselves as elderly. We're interested in cancer and the carcinogenic because those are words that might turn out to apply to the thirty-eight-year-old as much as the seventy-eight-year-old; cancer afflicts the young and rich and fit. If Alzheimer's equals old age, then that's something we'll deal with later . . . though we'll be fine, because we drink soy milk and do Sudoku and play tennis on the weekend. The most widespread misconception is that dementia's a good way to go: "They're in their own little world and pretty happy" the misconception goes, and "they've no idea they're going to die of it right up to the very end, which doesn't sound too bad to me." Very occasionally and exceptionally, in the online Alzheimer's community, sweet-tempered-to-the-last is reported; the slow-fade sweetie who was never any trouble and died smiling in bed before indignity could take hold. But that isn't the norm. That hasn't been Nancy's fate, alas.

IF I HAD to pick one catchall descriptor for Nancy's life in the last few years it would be *misery*. Profound misery, unceasing and insoluble. She knows that something is wrong, very wrong, but what is it? She's had a series of terrible daily encounters with herself and her environment that might have come directly from an amnesiac thriller: waking to find she has aged fifty years overnight, that her parents have disappeared, that she doesn't know the woman in the mirror, nor the people who claim to be her husband and children, and has never seen the rooms and furnishings that everyone around her claims insistently are her home. Time has slipped, gone seriously askew. Every day for her is spent in an ongoing quest to put things right. The trouble is, she can't seem to concentrate on the question or on possible clues to it. She can't navigate the problem. When she left us for the nursing home, she was daily engaged in a very protracted, slow-motion form of panic. It's been over eight years now since the formal diagnosis and eleven years at least since symptoms began, but even after all this time, she's only at stage 6 of the disease. Stage 7 looms, the cruelest and last phase, with its loss of continence, motor control, speech, and ability to swallow. Eventually her lungs will forget how to breathe, her heart forget how to beat, and her quest will come to an end.

I have thought, said, and probably even written in here somewhere that Nancy has lost her self. That at least is the impression anyone who knew Nancy twenty years ago would have if they spent a weekend with her. The things that made her herself are all but gone now, I say, but what does it mean to say that? Obviously she is still herself, isn't she? She isn't anyone else. It's just that the self is changed. Disease has changed it, or else, in some vaguely science-fictional manner, overlaid it with something new. But what exactly is the self, anyway? Must it have unity, continuity, in order to be authentic? Does it exist beyond and beneath the health or otherwise of 100,000 million neurons? Is there something else that encapsulates the self, something extra, indefinable, that we call the soul? If, as some philosophers of the mind argue, being conscious can't be said to be without content, that it has to do with being aware of not only your own person but also your past and future, your place in the world, your culture and context, your hopes and fears, then where does that leave Nancy? John Locke may have come up with the notion of "consciousness" specifically to spike Descartes's idea that we are thinking all the time, even when sleeping, but Locke also thought that we are only ourselves in having our memories, and defined personhood accordingly. Locke's definition, being antique, is easy to forgive. It's surprising, though, to find much more recent definitions that agree broadly with his. As late as 1973 an American philosopher named Mary Anne Warren demanded of *persons* that they be conscious, rational, capable of abstract thought, able to communicate, able to exercise free will, and have self-awareness. Under this severity, nobody with brain damage is a person, and Alzheimer's, so often misreferred to as a mental illness, involves a catastrophic form of brain damage.

Materialists would contend that there is no soul, that we are only a kind of organic machine, our notion of a unique self misguided. It's difficult not to be convinced by this idea, seeing Nancy's selfhood warp and flicker and wane as the disease colonizes her. It's not good—not even for privileged bystanders, counting their blessings—to see a self under attack. We prefer to think of our *selves* as something original in the world, inviolate, independent of our physical bodies. The idea that we are biochemistry, and that's all, that thoughts and feelings are produced by neurons, that neurons can die and our selves die with them . . . that's a deeply undermining idea. It's far more comforting to contend that Nancy's soul, her essential self, remains intact beyond the reach of her struggle to think and express herself, and will be liberated and restored by immortality. I try hard to believe this when I see her, alone in the dayroom in the nursing home, sitting rubbing her hands together and muttering. I can't help wondering what she's thinking. *Is* she thinking? Is she having a dialogue with her disease, negotiating with it in some way, aware of the great buried store of memory, her past, her self, glimpsed under the tangles of Alzheimer's like a ruined house under the suffocating grip of ivy?

Now that she's at one remove from us again, it's easy to love her, and where love falters, guilt is primed and ready to fill its place.

Chapter I

NANCY IS STANDING AT THE WINDOW AGAIN, THE ONE with the spectacular view, worrying about how the oil tanker will manage to get out of the bay. She is making her anxious hands, rubbing each palm against the back of the other in turn, brisk and rhythmical.

"I just don't think it will get out of the space, it's too big," she says, rubbing harder, her eyes full of concern. She is wearing all the cardigans she could find in her bedroom, in layers, having insisted on doing up all the buttons on each and tucking each sleeve under at the wrist. Her mood has improved since breakfast time, when she woke with the now-characteristic belief that she was newly discharged from hospital into the care of strangers: "But where is my family? Are they coming for me?"

"We are your family, honey," I soothe.

She laughs disdainfully, shaking her head. "Either you're a liar, or I'm going mad." Most mornings, there are tears. Tears and confusion. Dressing is hard. She wants to do it herself, but bras and trousers go on backward. If we don't get to her quickly enough, she wanders the halls in her underwear. She looks younger than seventy-nine, everybody says so, and this is especially evident in her near-naked wanderings. Physically she's amazingly good for her age: unstooping at five foot seven, well proportioned other than a mild potbelly, determinedly upright.

Her legs are strong and shapely. She can walk for miles, has thick silvery hair cut in a bob (it was sandy colored once, set into soft curls at the local salon once a month) and a charming smile, her pale face barely lined, though her blue eyes are rheumy now and her nose growing hooky. She's acquired a prickly white beard under her chin, which my husband, Chris, shaves off every now and then. She won't always let him at it. She can be protective of it, sitting stroking it in her chair. Some days it horrifies her. "Who put this here? Where did this come from? Take it away!" Or she thinks it's a wound, a scab. "I must have tripped and fallen. But it's getting better now." Nancy's at a good-days-and-bad-days stage of Alzheimer's, and on bad days she accuses Morris of having given her the stubble, perhaps because she recognizes that beards are properly the province of men.

She returns to her little sitting room, her coal fire, her husband, and sits in her pale blue winged armchair. She asks, now, if it's hers and if she can sit there. She hasn't had it long enough to remember it. Only the very-long-term memory is functioning. Morris is sitting in the chair beside her, is always sitting in the chair beside her. His is electrically powered, tips back, is upholstered in orange tapestry. He was stout once and, with his square face, mischievous dark eyes, dark hair combed over, and mustache, resembled a rather better-looking Oliver Hardy, and was just as likely to suffer fools gladly. He's mellowed. He appears to have shrunk, in all dimensions.

I've known Morris and Nancy for twenty-two years. When I first met them, brought home by Chris from university, I thought them old-fashioned, thrifty (furnishings and appliances had remained unchanged over decades), sociable, hardworking, right-wing. They were *Daily Mail* readers, natural conservatives, but generous about our student leftiness. I don't recall anything much in the way of ideological standoff. They were all hospitality, bailed us out when we got into financial hot water, let us stay with them on an indefinite basis when work plans went awry. Despite finding our postgraduate ideas about office jobs and steady security highly provoking (we didn't fancy either of these much), they were nothing but kind. Kind but unforthcoming, opinion withheld. This has been a pattern in our relationships.

Nancy and Morris moved here with the rest of us this summer. We have a lot of latitude in where we live. Latitude and longitude. Chris is an internationally known-in-his-own-niche expert on a specific use of new technology, and he consults widely, mostly from his home office, though there are bouts of meetings and flying. We have two teenage girls—Millie, sixteen, who's tall and dark like her mother, and Caitlin, fourteen, who shares her father's ash-blond coloring—and a boy called Jack, ten, a senior at primary school, tall and lanky and Italianate, with a scruffy dark shock of hair.

Moving, it turns out, isn't good for Alzheimer's patients. Leaving behind the familiar, having to adapt to the new. Nancy's disorientation is ongoing. "I don't know where I am," she sobs, "I don't know what I'm supposed to be doing."

I've been reading about memory. In cases of transient global amnesia (total but temporary memory loss), people ask over and over where they are and what they should do, how they got there, what they should do, *what should they do now?* Doing is a big preoccupation. They don't ask what might seem to be the obvious question: Who am I? That doesn't seem to be a question the self asks of the self. Instead, it looks for clues from context: where, how, what.

Chris and I have different responses to her anxiety. He takes her hand and is tender, explaining that they weren't coping, she and his father, and have come to live with us. I go for a jollier approach. "Well, lucky for you you're retired now and you can sit in this chair by the fire and eat biscuits and watch the afternoon film on the telly," I say. "Not like poor old me, I've got washing to see to, dogs to walk and vacuuming, the dinner to sort out, and you should see Jack's bedroom." Jack is proving dedicated to the acquisition of stuff, particularly electronic stuff (gadgets, dead laptops), as well as guns, swords, and lighters. Sometimes I worry about where these interests might lead.

"Oh, poor you, having to do all that," Nancy says, fleetingly lucid, playing along, and I'm embarrassed at being caught out talking to her in this nice-nurse fashion. But the moment passes and she's back at the window. "Look at all that water." Her voice is astonished.

"Yes. We live here, out on the peninsula; the sea's all around us. Do you remember coming here with us to live? We came last month. Do you remember?"

"Edinburgh," she says under her breath.

"You used to live in Edinburgh, years ago. But then you moved up to Speyside, near our old house. Do you remember the bungalow? By the river?" She looks blank. "And now you live here, with us."

She looks at me, grim-faced. "That's all very well, but they laugh at me, you know. Not you, I'm not talking about you, but the others. They look me up and down in the street and I can see that they're thinking, Who the hell does she think she *is*?" Paranoia, an Alzheimer's marker, is just beginning to get its grip on her. But she's been lovely to the children all summer, which is reassuring. Her face lights up when they go into her sitting room. She pats her knee, like she used to; Millie's five foot ten and can't help laughing. "Now come and tell me all about it," Nancy says. About what, she doesn't specify. The girls are good with her, as Morris is always telling me. They're patient, tolerant, don't rise to verbal bait. They do things at Granny's pace, taking her arm in theirs. "Come on, Gran. Let's go and make Granddad some tea," talking her through the operation step by step. "Put the tea bags in the pot now. In the pot, not the mug. That's it. Right. Hot water next, can you manage the kettle okay? That's the kettle. Yes. Here, let me."

Morris prefers television to conversation, or indeed any-thing, and it's been this way for a long time. Depressed and immobile, he is master of the remote and flicks between chan-nels with a desperate air. It's like he can't look away. Things are too awful in his present to contemplate them squarely. Because he's so focused on his television day, Nancy's life is frequently lonely. She can't follow a television program any longer. She's more interested in being with me, because—when running the household, at least—I appear to be doing things. She's less keen on me when I'm writing or reading. "The men just sit there," she tells me scornfully, unable to distinguish between one kind of sitting and another: one at his desk on his laptop and phone, consulting and earning, and the other in the armchair next to her, absorbed fifteen hours a day by the flickering screen. She follows me around. She wonders half a dozen times a day where *the friends* are, and if they are coming.

"I don't want the friends to know I've been ill," she says, as we pick tomatoes in the greenhouse. She eats the ones she picks or puts them slyly in her pocket, thinking I haven't seen. Or just picks the dried-out leaves from the plants and puts those in the basket, smoothing them carefully. Then she takes them out again. "I don't think these are ready," she'll tell me, trying to fix them back on the trusses.

The friends—imaginary friends—visit us sometimes, and she has days when she worries about how they'll get here and how they'll get home. In truth, her real friends have long de-serted her, had deserted the two of them long before their move north. *Desertion* is a strong word; the truth is the process wasn't so premeditated—it was a more gradual loss of atten-tiveness, a social slippage, the kind that happens when people get sick and have little to talk about other than their problems. Three from their old circle telephone from time to time, but it's us they want to speak to, for reports.

"I need to say good-bye," Nancy insists, twisting her hand-kerchief. "I need to see the friends off."

"Don't worry," Chris says, trying to ease her agitation. "They've gone already. I saw them leave earlier." And then, seeing her expression, he adds, "But they said to tell you they'd had a lovely day."

"Gone already? But they didn't say good-bye."

"They did, don't you remember? I think you might have been asleep."

"They haven't gone."

"They have. I saw them; they left on the bus."

She looks indignant, draws her shoulders up tight. "*They didn't come on a bus.*"

She appears to be having hallucinations. These are new, have arrived quite abruptly, and it occurs to me that our moving her here has aggravated the decline somehow, has accelerated it. Guilt is something I'm going to get used to, but for now it's fresh and new. I take Nancy into the drawing room and we look through a stack of interiors magazines, me commenting and Nancy cooing. My laptop's open on the table, and my attention is 80 percent diverted while I trawl the Internet for answers. Temporal lobe damage, it seems, can cause autobiographical hallucinations. Does she see the friends striding toward her across the lawn, looking just as they did twenty years ago or more?

Sometimes I think I can see them myself. The house doesn't feel haunted—some big old houses do, but this one doesn't—though there have been sightings, I'm told, in years past, of Victorians paused on the stairs, their eyes oblivious to the present. The first day we were here and went to the pub for supper, a fisherman propping up the bar asked how we were getting on with the spooks. I haven't seen anything or heard spectral footsteps, but the whole property is soaked in what I can only describe as pastfulness. It's pastful, and sometimes, even though I know it's just this, I've half believed there are women in rustling silk frocks in that part of the wood that was once the rose garden, have half heard brief melodious laughter in the paddock that was once a tennis court. Who are these people, the friends Nancy talks about? It's occurred to me that the altered perceptions of Alzheimer's might allow people to see ghosts.

The house sits out in near seclusion at the neck of the headland, at the point where the neck joins the shoulder of a second, bigger peninsula, two miles from a village, fifteen miles from a small town, and far, far away from everything. It's a great, four-square Victorian house with sash windows, crenellations, and crowstep gables, its overgrown walled garden framed in lichen-covered stone. It's the kind of house that, while not grand enough for Manderley or Gothic enough for Walter Scott or English enough for Jane Austen, might serve as the scene of a death at the vicarage in Agatha Christie. It sticks up high on the low, gently undulating profile of this wind-scoured green promontory like a church, the sea rushing up the cliff faces around it. Building upward in this climate is an act of faith, almost of defiance. The architectural vernacular hereabouts favors single-story longhouses, long and low and hugging the ground, though a good many of these have been weathered into rubble, with kit-built bungalows parked alongside. After the longhouses fell from fashion, the local style favored one-and-a-half-story cottages, high enough to be provided with an upper floor snuggled into the eaves, low enough to brace themselves against the weather. The eighteenth-century terraced housing that lines the two principal streets of the village is fully double story, held in a self-protective loop around a deep harbor.

The house and neighboring farm were once one property, and together they owned all the land that can be seen from the single third-floor window, the attic window that leads out onto a precarious half balcony. The original farmhouse is two hundred yards down the hill, across the lane, enfolded by its barns and cattle courtyard into a wind-resistant square. The building of the big house in 1860 marked the achievement of wealth and status, a move up from the cottage to a grander residence on higher ground, one gleefully elaborate in its luxurious details. All that remains of the estate are the four garden acres inside the high wall, the privacy-giving wall, marking off the domestic world from the working one, separating peasant from gentry, keeping the bullocks and harvest workers in the adjoining fields out of the sight of the strolling, tea-taking, tennis-playing manor dwellers within.

The house layout is ideal for an extended family. The kitchen has two doors: one into Morris and Nancy's sitting room, and one into the rear corridor, where their bedroom and private bathroom were converted from two former maids' rooms. Off their sitting room in the other direction is a small lobby, which leads into their private daytime bathroom. So Nancy and Morris have, in effect, their own suite of rooms, with only the kitchen shared, and even that is two-family friendly, having two stoves and two full-size tables along its double length. The original thinking was that Nancy and Morris would self-cater, up to a point and with our assistance. They were keen, Morris said, to have as much independence as possible. They brought what remained of their marital past in packing crates, everything that had survived successive years of downsizing: their 1960s crockery and pastel-colored kitchenware; tarnished silver cutlery with worn bone handles; old pillows, duvets, blankets, marital linens smelling of cedar wood; boxes of clothes and miscellaneous items dating back forty years; old toiletries, socks, lamp shades; wallets and watches, belts and business paper.

With the exception of a daily excursion into the conservatory for coffee, their world has shrunk into this little sitting room by the kitchen: its two armchairs, a 1960s coffee table, a partner's desk, a television, a dresser laden with ornaments—unused steak knives and ancient paperwork idling in its drawers—and a book-case scantily furnished with photograph albums, thrillers, *Reader's Digest*s, the *RAC Guide to Great Days Out,* 1970s cookbooks whose pages are stuck together with cake mix.

Nancy's Alzheimer's seems to advance in phases, as if we're mining underground, into the unknown, toward obliteration. Currently we've hit the seam of lost prepositions. Morris gets exasperated with her lapses, her confusion, her failure to recognize what's ordinary and deal with it in the old ordinary way. He has his own health problems: replacement hips that have worn out, poor circulation, numbed legs and feet. Walking is a struggle, and in the past he's relied on his wife to be his legs. She has trouble with this role now.

"No, no!" we hear him shouting. "The cup! The cup! In front of the book! No, not under it, in front of it! Now put the spoon in it. In it! In it! Not behind it! That's a book! Not a book, a cup! Oh, for god's sake, woman!" She can't seem to distinguish between cup and book. Parietal lobe damage is responsible for this, apparently; for failing to match objects with words in that apparently simple but sneakily complex two-hander we call recognition. But telling Morris so and asking him to be less irritable makes no difference. Occasionally Nancy gets fed up with being yelled at and gets her coat and handbag. On one such day she finds me in the kitchen making soup.

"Excuse me." A plaintive little voice. She can't any longer remember my name. "Excuse me, lady. I think I should tell you that I am going to have to find other accommodations." This formal way of speaking is new. Perhaps it stems from uncertainty: her being a stranger in a strange land, needing the help of good Samaritans and needing to be polite to them. If you're unsure who anybody is, or indeed who *you* are, come to that—their rank, your rank, what your relationship might be—then you're likely to be deferential. Either that or bolshie, asserting your position. Bolshie will come later.

When Nancy's upset, distraction's the only way out. Everything else, and especially *reasoning,* only escalates and intensifies the trouble. I take her outside, where flowers and butterflies and birds and trees do the job like nothing else, all upset forgotten. We go down to the road, down the long driveway between looming dark hedges of fuchsia, and stand between the entrance pillars and admire the view. She runs an appreciative finger over the house name, indented in brass set into the stone, and I'm shocked to find that she can't read the word that's the house name. She can't recognize the letters and, even when I tell her what they are, can't vocalize them into a run of sounds. She's interested in them, though, as in something half remembered, on the tip of her tongue, running her fingers over the brass a second time, frowning and with concentration. Shocked, I go back to Chris in his office. "Your mother can't read; she can't read anymore," I tell him. It's stunning because it's so absolute, so concrete a loss. Parietal lobe damage is to blame again, it seems, in that zone of the brain where visual impressions are organized and reading and writing are ordered and understood. I read about this on the Internet, which has become my personal guide, dementia caregivers' network, MD, and hospital rolled into one handy package.

It isn't, any of it, a linear progression. Damage, or at least the symptoms of damage, can appear to waver like flickering wiring. Some days Nancy has vocabulary, some days not. She's wandering the house looking for her shoes, and when I ask if I can help, she looks down at the floor, offering me a lifted socked foot. "The things, the things that go on the . . . that go on the things. I want to. I want the things that go on the end." Perhaps this is a sign of parietal lobe damage again, failing to match word and object, or perhaps it has to do with the plaques/tangles invading Broca's area, a patch on the left side of the frontal lobe that was named after Pierre-Paul Broca (1824–1880), who had a patient in 1861 who could say only "tan." It's the zone charged specifically with talking. It's fascinating, this physical loss of abilities in the departments of self, but in tracking Nancy's neuronal failure, I face self-accusations of ghoulishness.

Random stream-of-consciousness nonsense has become a feature in the mornings. Miscellaneous phrases from the past, from the long-term memory, fall out of the box in random order.

"I'm so glad you're here," she says, "because I was worried about that."

"About what?"

She looks at me appraisingly, as if making a decision about whether she can confide, before launching in. "It's been a long time, and I didn't always do it that way, oh no, don't you believe him when he puts it off, because I can tell you, it's all the other way, really, to be quite truthful, and he knows it is, and I could strangle him sometimes, but the woman said I was to go that way, so I went, and it wasn't there. Did I tell you that? I said that before and you haven't got it. I know that. I do know that. I'm not really as stupid as I look, but she says—oh the things I could tell you about her, but I won't because you shouldn't—and I have got to find the thing now or I won't hear the end of it."

"Her?" I ask.

"The woman," Nancy says, rolling her eyes.

"But it's just you and me here," I say. "We're the only ones."

"No, no, no," Nancy says briskly. "Not you. The other woman."

TAKING ON NANCY'S care, full time, seven days, twenty-four hours, has been . . . I wish I could find a better word than *shock*. It's been a shock. The thesaurus offers "trauma," but that isn't remotely it. It hasn't been a "blow" or an "upset," a "bombshell" or a "jolt." It's more like the kind of experience that leaves you staring into space openmouthed. *How on earth did I get here?* you think. *And how am I going to extricate myself?* There's no adequate preparation for the physical demands, the physical hour-after-hourness of full-time caregiving. It hadn't occurred to me that I would need to dress and undress her, for example, and get her toileted and into the shower, and would find myself, in consequence of this, adopting the nice-nurse-ish patter that theoretically I hate. "Righto, Nancy, let's get you sorted for bed, shall we? Cardigan first." When I get her into her nightie and take her trousers off, her feet are bluish: white and blue and mauve, her toenails thickened, opaque and yellowed like smokers' fingers, her shins crocodile-skinned. *Proximity.* That's the key word. Up close and disturbingly personal. There's emptiness behind her eyes, something missing that used to be there. It's sinister. It seems sometimes, in fanciful moments, that it's Nancy who's missing, though her body continues to live and breathe and walk around in the world, redundantly.

I HAVE A new role, a new identity. Mothering somebody's mother, and being thanked for it effusively. Nancy comes into the kitchen when I'm cooking and wants to help. I find something for her to do and then she bursts into tears.

"Oh no. What on earth is it?" I put my arm round her and she cries harder.

"It's just that you're so-o g-good to me," she blubbers. "You're so good and kind and you do everything for me. I wish I could do something for you. Tell me what I can do. I want to give you something. A present. Will you take my money out of the bank and get yourself a present?"

"There's no need, really. I don't need anything. Really," I tell her.

She goes back into her sitting room.

"Oh god, what is it now?" I hear Morris asking.

What exactly is my new relationship with my in-laws? I am their housekeeper, something approximating their parent, their perpetual hostess, but also a servant. I send Morris a pot of Earl Grey and a warm Victoria sponge, feeling as if I have visitors and need to provide afternoon tea, and in return he gives Jack a penny and says, "Here, give this to the waitress."

We begin to integrate ourselves a little into peninsula society. First into commerce, then into other people's kitchens. Professions here are often of the multiple kind. Paul, the gas fitter, installs an eight-burner stove in place of the inherited curly-plate electric, then makes new stable doors for the yard, and is turning out to be a very nifty tiler. Though tradesmen aren't easy to find. At the end of the week I scissor the local paper, cutting out announcements for the pinboard. The newspaper's being read everywhere we go on publication day, by shopkeepers, office and health workers, people at the wholesalers and in boatyards, people in tea shops. Ordinary routine comes to a halt. There's a piece about new Neolithic finds made farther up the coast. Someone has been shooting seals and the public is appealed to for tip-offs. Wrecks have been plundered by treasure seekers, and a diver's brought up dead. A man's airlifted from an uninhabited island, injured while birding. A skipper's been charged with being drunk in charge of a boat. There's been another suicide, someone who came from England on holiday and leapt off our cliffs to his death. There's been a country dance, and intoxicated teenagers hospitalized. All this is absorbing enough, but I'm more interested in the advertising. The advertisements are a godsend. Not every trader has a shop or even a sign, and lots of the smaller businesses are done anonymously from home. Thus it is that we find ourselves in a barn one morning, choosing tiles, while being watched intently by heifers.

We take afternoon walks on the beach, going down in the

car so that Morris can come. He can't make it over the strip of pebbles, nor manage the low grassy dune, so he sits in the car with the door open, watching and smoking. I take the dogs to the water's edge and throw sticks toward America, the retriever plunging in after them and the Jack Russell barking at him from the shallows. Chris walks his mother up and down the length of the sand, Nancy holding on to his arm and striding along. She's happy, just for this moment, radiant, smiling into the sun. Sometimes a change in the weather is enough to restore our optimism, and this seems truer for those with Alzheimer's than the rest of us. Nancy's world is re-created every minute. She lives in the moment, and therein lies the problem. The minute we get back indoors, she's lobbying to go out for a walk. The walk she's just had is rendered down into an idea, one that persists and nags at her. Perhaps the best thing for Alzheimer's sufferers might be nomadism of a kind. A permanent ambling trek in talkative company, with pauses only for meals and to sleep, would make her happy, I think. Everything, every moment, would be new, and everybody in her party would be on a more equal footing of constant change.

It's our wedding anniversary at the end of the month and Chris and I go to the village restaurant to celebrate, leaving the children in charge. We eat crab cakes, a fish and crustacean stew, a lemon tart with marmalade ice cream, delighting in everything but preoccupied with home, two mobile phones winking on the tablecloth.

"The fish is wonderfully fresh," Chris tells the owner. "Is it caught in the bay here?"

"Actually no," the owner says. "We can't get the quality here. All the good stuff goes south. All our fish comes down from Shetland."

Chapter 2

Inspiration may be a form of super-consciousness, or perhaps of subconsciousness, I wouldn't know. But I am sure it is the antithesis of self-consciousness.

—AARON COPLAND

W E HAVE ALWAYS HAD A TASTE FOR SEMIREMOTE-ness. The short-drive-for-milk, long-drive-for-olives model is one Chris and I have honed and perfected. We thought we knew all about backwaters. But this, the peninsula, is a backwater in a different manner. Living here makes you question the terms of your disengagement with the Big World, something that thus far has been merely instinctive. In this society, almost as far north as it's possible to be in Britain, the Big World becomes a catchall for everything that is wrong with life. The Big World is referred to as *south*. The question of whether, for instance, children will have to go south for work is much discussed, in worried terms. South is corrupt, spoiled, feared. We have a little kingdom here, a far-flung corner that prides itself on difference. It's a Roman outpost. The barbarians are talked about partly with pity and partly with scorn. It's Shakespeare: "This other Eden, demi-paradise, / this fortress built by Nature for herself / against infection and the hand of war. / This happy breed of men, this little world, / this precious stone set in the silver sea."

It's easy to assume that there'll be a natural camaraderie between those who choose the edge and not the center. It isn't always true. The physical edge is easy to achieve—you just take up your bed and hand it to the furniture removal company. But what about the metaphysical edge? Edge dwellers are no more likely to be readers, to be articulate, to be interesting people with fulfilled creative impulses—all the usual stuff we hope for in our neighbors—than anyone else. They're just as likely to watch bad television and talk about it. They're just as likely to be unhappy. More so, probably. Unhappiness has driven a good number of the edge dwellers edgeward; unhappiness that morphs into reclusiveness. Utopianism brings others, and intense sociability, an aptitude for running things, starting things, galvanizing all of us disparate souls into community.

Aside from the spatial demands of a two-family setup, Chris and I came here for the usual material reasons (big house, smallish price), for the particularly privileged reason that we work at home and can choose our location, but also, certainly in my case, looking for a new relationship: one with the Sublime. I came looking for inspiration (for work, yes, but also for life) as something concrete (the quality of the view), something engulfing and omnipresent (the quality and shape of clouds)—all of which is just outside the door and there at whim. It wasn't really about clouds, of course, or views. It's always about engaging with elementals. Mail-order catalogs find their sales rise if they choose backdrops of beaches, meadows, hillsides, riverbanks, and forests. Our visitors' book is bulging with remarks about the spirituality of the location. If these things are emblematic, then we on the peninsula are emblem rich, emblem saturated. We have house, meadow, wood and wall, a vast panorama of sea and sky, steep drops and long beaches; we have weather and the tides at our disposal. Those with a lot of geography in their lives are envied. A person at one with geography is admired—the more extreme the geography, the more extremely.

The landscape here is people dwarfing. A succession of headlands rise vast cliffed. The Sublime is here if it's anywhere. Wordsworth is its chief prophet, in my library at least. I have tried to look at my surroundings with his eyes, feel bolstered in his near-supernatural manner. Look at this, from "Tintern Abbey":

> *And I have felt*
> *A presence that disturbs me with the joy*
> *Of elevated thoughts; a sense sublime*
> *Of something far more deeply interfused,*
> *Whose dwelling is the light of setting suns,*
> *And the round ocean and the living air,*
> *And the blue sky, and in the mind of man:*
> *A motion and a spirit, that impels*
> *All thinking things, all objects of all thought,*
> *And rolls through all things.*

We expect this of wild places, because we are all Romantics in our way. We still live in the Romantic age, the age of will and the individual, seeking some anthropomorphic godlike power in immensity, perhaps, as we park the car at the cliff-top walk and stand, coat blowing, looking out at nothingness, everythingness, somethingness: whatever it is that rolls through all things, it's ill defined. Or something more mysterious. Here's Wordsworth in *The Prelude*:

> *. . . and I would stand . . .*
> *Beneath some rock, listening to notes that are*
> *The ghostly language of the ancient earth,*
> *Or make their dim abode in distant winds.*
> *Thence did I drink the visionary power.*

Visionary power. That's what I came looking for. For writing, but also as a corrective to the person that caring for the in-laws might make me; a balance, a bulwark, a reasserted sense of perspective. But what is it, this *spirit that impels all thinking things*? It might be God, it might be Gaia, or it might be the effect that immensity, despite its inanimate nonconsciousness, has on the mind, and that's what I take the Sublime properly to be. Whatever the case, people come to live here with just the same kind of impulses, expectations, needs. The wilderness knows nothing about us. Self-reinvention isn't only possible here; it's provoked, nurtured, made flesh.

The Sublime, it turns out, is disappointingly elusive. Which is to say that I don't often feel it, almost never; I more often find I'm feeling nothing, and I know I'm not alone in this. There are things that stop us from being properly present in the landscape, that stop me, at any rate. The self intrudes on the Sublime; the past and future intrude, and worse, much worse, the banal considerations of domesticity, the *lists*. The lists follow me out to the cliff tops and onto the beach. I go there hoping for, at the least, the experience of a kind of self-dilution, but instead the strip of sand becomes just another venue for the things that bothered me at home. In addition to which, I'm cold, it's too windy to breathe easily, my ears hurt. My feet are wet from the thick dew of the dunes I had to cross to get here, my ankle turning painfully on the smooth pink landslip of pebbles. I'm distracted. The risk, now, is that the landscape will become peopled by my own mind. The sea, its restlessness. The wind, its stubbornness. The gulls, their superficiality. The Romantic poets went out into the Sublime, sublimity bagging, as a response to the encroaching materialism of their times, the Industrial Revolution and the mystery-extinguishing age of science. I go in order to feel stronger, strong enough to deal with Nancy and Morris and their constant neediness. Wordsworth would have enjoyed the peninsula. He'd have been out all day, returning unhungry, unthirsty—he was possessed of extraordinary unworldly stamina—and would have settled in a fireside chair to write about it, barely aware of numb fingers, cold ears, wet socks. The experience would have suffused him with his reportedly "lofty thoughts"; it would have convinced him that despite the "dreary intercourse of daily life . . . all which we behold [i]s full of blessings." Which is how we all want to feel.

Wild and desolate beauty is, it turns out, not a backdrop to life that works for Alzheimer's. Nancy seems barely to register the landscape, and when it's pointed out to her—a stunning lighting effect over the hills, a sunset over the bay—she seems not to notice, or at least not to see it properly. Her admiration comes across as forced, something done to humor me. Perhaps beauty, aesthetic sense, is lodged deep in the memory, and for Nancy that memory is lost. Perhaps beauty is something we're taught and must remember, and now that Nancy's lost her bearings intellectually, she's also lost the idea that a golden hill is preferable to a cloudy one, a red sun prettier than a yellow one. Perhaps our aesthetic sense is as much autobiographical as innate. Mistakenly I'd thought that the Sublime would make itself felt in Nancy's circumscribed life, that its primitive kind of language of symbols and feelings (the feeling, simultaneously, of being nothing in the universe and at its dead center) would speak to her, digging deeper in than language can, or that at the very least she'd find the wildness stimulating. I thought she'd love the cliffs and the views, the walks and the seabird colonies, the seal families pulled out on the estuary rocks. But Nancy sees the hills and headlands, seas and skies, as a backdrop to nothing happening, an absence, a stage set where no play will take place. Only people interest her now. Alzheimer's sufferers like cities, bustle, noise, a person-made world. Or at least this one does.

We made the decision to take Morris and Nancy in some six months before it happened. We decided that the answer to the problems proliferating with their living alone was that we should find a much bigger house, one with an annex or a cottage, a project Nancy and Morris would make a contribution to, an agreement put on a formal footing with a solicitor. It was either that or get them urgently into residential care, and Morris was miserable about that prospect (this is an understatement—throat cutting was mentioned, as I recall). But all the contenders that came up in our own area were way out of our league. They were the kind of houses that had their own brochure. Nevertheless we went to see some of them. The ones we could almost (but not quite) afford were in grotty surroundings, by main roads or cheek by jowl with stalag-style chicken farms, encircled by council estates and dead cars. Realizing that this was the reality of our budget took a lot of legwork and a lot of driving. We drove a long way and made Nancy very carsick. Then we spent two months almost buying a ruined farmhouse, drawing up plans for the conversion of outbuildings, but the projected costs spiraled out of control and we abandoned the plan.

Faced with a dead end, I cast the Internet net wider, including anything big in any location. And that is how I came to see the house, on a Web site, and send the fateful e-mail to Chris, who was working in the next room.

The answer flashed back.

"Far too remote. How would I get to meetings? Need to be practical about this." And then hard on its heels, another e-mail. "Had a look at the flights situation. Possible, if not exactly cheap. And I could get a little boat for weekends. Tempting. But the running costs will be horrendous."

"Well, I could turn part of it into a bed-and-breakfast," I replied. "There's a separate apartment, up a separate stairway."

WE MADE THE family visit to the house on April 1 and a second visit the following afternoon, invited to tea by the charming eighty-year-old owners, last of the line. Not literally the last of the line, in fact, but the last who could countenance *living* here, a long way from proper jobs and department stores. The house set its trap with care. It was a perfect spring day, warm, with barely a breath of wind. The beach down the lane shone out yellow and blue. Spring birds were all atwitter. Children romped around the garden, their distant shouts brought closer by the reverberating of voices off old stone. Away from the formal lawn, down the drive toward the sea, wilder areas of garden beckoned, tall grasses mown into paths, and a secretive wood, where sycamores stunted by wind, venturing only tentatively above the line of coping stones, huddled, heads down, arms linked above their heads like a rugby scrum. Pools of sunlight fell among them. I sat on a mossy bench and the sun was warm on my face. A tame turkey sat at the base of a tree looking back. Once the heart is lost, the head can only throw in the towel.

Perhaps this should be known as the Lichen Peninsula. Lichen's everywhere in pale green mats, curly fingered, densely layered. The air smells different here. Linen fresh, ozoney, briny, undercut by something earthy and sappy. When the tide is out and the sun is warm, there's a rank drying seaweed note. In summer—and summer is short, sweet, cherished—the air is full of dry grass aromas, sweet hay scents mixed in with the brine, and the light, sea bounced, is dazzling, jabbing in unprotected eyes. Everything seems vividly colored. There's a soaring pale wash of blue above, with a quality about it that's nostalgic: the kind of soft and summery depth that childhood skies had once, the kind that small airplanes leave trails in. The grass is the brightest kind of green. The sea is clear and painterly: the royal blue and azure and turquoise marking shallowness on clean sand, the dark green and brown patches indicating depth and weed. There are three beaches within a five-minute walk, all different: estuary and pebble and sand. The sand beach is closest, just down from the house, and the pebble beach is at right angles to it, round the corner of the headland. The estuary, on the road toward the village, is huge and golden and puddley. Comical oyster catchers stride briskly about on drinking straw legs, then stand together crouched over, round-shouldered in black coats like old men in a bar.

I'd thought that Nancy might respond to the history of the house. It was a foolish thought. But I've always liked buildings with a strong sense of identity. Houses that don't need you, their character already made and set by other, more interesting people who pushed their experiences, their thoughts, into the stone of walls and wood of floors, the faded wallpapers and paneled doors. That's what original features have always signified, to me at least. It's relaxing to feel yourself peripheral to another era, a ghost from the future in a house where the past is still present. I had a peculiar idea that Nancy would respond to this. Her early life was spent at a castle—a real one, with acres of lawns and walled warm corners where pineapples and peaches were grown under glass. Her father was head gardener at a great estate, one that's now a hotel, wedding venue, and conference center with depressingly corporate Web pages. Added to which, Nancy's early married life and her child-raising years were spent in Victorian city surroundings. I thought she'd feel at home.

On our second day, excitedly, I take her on a tour of the outbuildings. The main yard has an L shape of them, incorporating tractor shed, coach house, garage, stables, a quaint row of low outhouses bordering the drying green beyond. The gardens are charming, though romantically gone to ruin, with wide herbaceous borders, extensive shrubbery areas with paths behind, and elephantine hummocks of *Escallonia* and *Hebe*. Generations of family dogs and cats are buried in the wood and in the vegetable garden, with headstones and names and dates.

I take Morris on the tour, too, and we move at his slow, stick-aided pace round the grounds. Morris had been typically gung-ho about the move. He was going to learn to sea fish, and go sailing with Chris. He was going to get one of those electric buggies. He was going to plan and oversee the planting of the kitchen garden. But the truth is that he's no longer good with outdoors. Outdoors taunts him with everything that he's lost. His life today consists of the achievement of selfhood through television. Pictorial absorption. Mind meld. A domestic annihilation that invokes Nancy's presence, perhaps, in healthier and younger days, when all the adult comings and goings of television pictures mirrored their own busy lives, their powers, their choices, and was restfully vicarious. Now it's as if he disappears down a wormhole out of the present. Nancy's presence is preferred, the two of them driving the spaceship together, like they did in their heyday at the family house, when they converted a tiny study into a private TV room, two armchairs and a television squeezed into a pod. But now that she's ill, Nancy isn't content any longer to sit in her armchair all day with the TV on, and why should she be? There has to be more to life. Even she, standing at the doorway that leads from moderate to severe Alzheimer's disease, can see that.

Morris wants to be indoors, and Nancy wants to be out. She comes into the garden with me half a dozen times a day, and every time we go I point out the view. Ordinarily she'll say "Oh, ye-es," drawing the word out as if impressed, but her attention flickering. I'm not convinced she really sees it. So I persist. "Look at the next headland, Nancy—do you see the lighthouse?"

"It's wonderful. Look at that! And really not very much traffic at all." She's pink faced because it's humid today, and because she isn't good with the heat.

She seems to know what I'm thinking. "I'm not good with the heat at all, never have been to be quite truthful."

The short-term memory is shot. The long-term memory is failing, but parts of it are still intact. Fewer of these memories— records stored up on the higher ground, the flood waters lapping against their green hillock—present themselves as autobiographical lately, though random instances of likes and dislikes remain, and rise casually to the surface at unexpected moments.

"You're hot. Maybe you should take some of your cardigans off, then," I tell her.

She looks down, holds her arms out from her body. "Oh. Yes. I didn't think of that."

I help her to take the three extra ones off. But when I see her a few minutes later she's got them all on again, and is just in the act of buttoning the top one, badly and askew.

WITHIN A FEW short weeks we fall into a sort of pattern that we should probably call a life. It's my in-laws' life, at least. The challenge for us is not to let it be all of ours. For now, there is optimism. The new life is full of structure. Structure and comforting sameness, that's what The Book says Nancy needs, and I am, at least for now, keen to do things by The Book. We get Nancy and Morris up once the children are off to school, put them back to bed at night when Morris is ready, and in between the days unfold almost identically. Only meals remind them of the time—meals and the television, their lives parceled out in programming. The day begins with the delivery of breakfast to their sitting room. Morris announces his arrival and his readiness for the teapot by means of several penetrating coughs. He'll stay there all day, politely accepting lunch and supper like a passenger on a long-haul flight. They've elected to eat all their meals there, on lap trays with padded bases.

Nancy will sit down for short periods, but the rest of the day she follows me around. She comes with me to walk the dogs in the morning, dawdling along and bending to look at things like a young child does.

"Don't pick that up, Nancy. It's dirty."

"What are you talking about? It's perfectly clean."

She brings sticks home, the tops of ineptly picked flowers, sprigs of dried grass, a stone, a leaf she liked the look of, and puts them on the table. Within five minutes, she'll be complaining about them—"Who left these horrible things here?"—and ferrying them individually to the wastepaper basket.

After the dog walk, we come in and have a cup of tea and deliver one to Morris with cake. Cake's become a big part of the day. The dishwasher's kept busy with teacups, and I am learning to measure out my life in coffee spoons. The chirpy drone of a home-improvement show burbles through the kitchen door. Nancy helps load the dishwasher, handing me things one by one, wiping the jam from knife to hands to trousers. We put some washing on, and then, because Nancy loves housework, we zip round the ground floor vacuuming and dusting. Nancy is delegated little jobs. She gets to tidy the newspapers and magazines and does this conscientiously, glancing at me to ensure I'm happy. She is given a duster and some spray polish and sings as she polishes: "When Irish Eyes Are Smiling." This is her song. Since we got here she's sung nothing else. The trouble is, she doesn't know the words and fills her own into the stanzas, experimentally.

"When all the things are lovely, dee dee, dee deeee de dee, And I am a milkmaid and I have a car, de dee, de deee, de deeeeeee."

OUR MEMORIES FOR music are stored in a different part of the brain from the ordinary language memory, and tunes survive longer in Alzheimer's than words do. Capitalizing on this, dementia singing groups are springing up around the world. One reports great success with the Beatles songbook. What's interesting is that the music memory appears to bring the words along with it, unlocking the language block. These groups have reported success with quite advanced dementia, citing cases of people with very little residual language who find, after a few sessions, that they can recall and sing lyrics without trouble.

Music professionals with dementia make for interesting case histories. The American composer Aaron Copland (1900–1990), who died of Alzheimer's, seems to have had a slow fade, having first developed symptoms in the early 1970s. He didn't compose much after 1973 other than for reworking a couple of old pieces, but was still conducting his best-known work, *Appalachian Spring,* almost to the end—though critics complained that he lost the thread in the very last performances. Conducting is done from a different part of the brain again—squirreled away in the cerebellum, where our highly practiced, automatic gestures are delegated and stored. The cerebellum is one of the last places reached by Alzheimer's disease.

Copland seems to have had a lonely end. He was dropped by old friends as dementia took hold; two such who ventured to his home on his ninetieth birthday, three weeks before his death, expecting there to be a gathering, a party and a cake, found there were no other visitors. People are afraid of this disease. I know of people who find that when their parent becomes demented, the rest of the family and all the old friends cut them off. One of the people I have "met" on Internet Alzheimer's forums, an American who's returned from her city life to live with her ill and widowed mother, tells me that not only have people stopped calling or visiting, but when challenged about it they grow hostile, pointing out that it's her mother's "bad behavior" and "madness" that are to blame for their absence. People act as if dementia were contagious, she says, and the social stigma is as strong as ever. It can't help if you're a gay man, like Copland, without even the grudgingly given support of family. When things get difficult for old colleagues and fans, it's easier for them to turn away, untroubled by duty.

Nancy begins to sing variants of "When Irish Eyes Are Smiling" all day, on and off, for days at a time. I know what it's like to get a song stuck in your head, one that seems to be there in the background of thought, unbidden, like Muzak playing in a shopping mall. But it's possible that Nancy is suffering musical hallucinations. This isn't just music that's imagined but music that's heard, as if by the ears. PET scans have shown that in hallucinators all the same areas of the brain light up as they do when people listen and pay attention to external music, other than for the principal auditory cortex that does the listening, and in this respect the inner music is exactly like a visual hallucination. The brain is "hearing" (again and again) music that isn't coming in at the ears but is in every other way perfectly replicated. It doesn't seem able to turn it off. Nancy, I suspect, is stuck in a hallucinatory loop, and is singing along to hers. I try her on some other songs I think she might remember, with no luck, though she can hum some of them, in snatches. *Three blind mice, see how they run. . . .* We start together, and sing the same line again, and then we both come to a halt, look at each other, break out laughing. Neither of us can recall what comes next. Farmer's wife, carving knife, but how does it go exactly?

Chapter 3

*A memory is what is left when something happens and
does not completely unhappen.*

—Edward de Bono

We're a month in to the experiment and I decide that for now at least, I'll give up the struggle to
work. It's the school holidays and for now at least,
the pressure can justify itself in being off. I kick to the back of
my mind the persistent question: What will Nancy do all day
when you're busy? That isn't really the question, of course.
The question, the real question, is: How will you get any work
done with Nancy in the house?

I go out into the hallway and see Nancy rubbing away at
the same table I left her at ten minutes earlier, sweeping her
cloth over the table legs and round the rim. The spray polish
isn't consulted. It's too difficult to use the push button. The
squirting stuff comes out at unpredictable angles. She places
the tall can at the other end of the room, under another table,
so it can be overlooked. I rescue it. I hover with it, my finger
on the trigger.

"Shall I spray a little for you? It makes the furniture shinier."

"No, no, don't bother. Don't bother yourself. I don't like it.
I don't like any of it."

"Oh dear. What's the matter? Are you tired? Would you like
to go and sit down?"

"Certainly not. I'm fine. I'm in the prime of life. I'm not
going to let a little thing like the woman get me down."

"Woman?"

"The woman. She comes here. She tells me what I'm to do and I've to do it if there isn't to be trouble."

She's talking about me. Doubt surges in. I thought she liked to clean. I thought it made her happy. That's the only reason I bought the spray.

"Stop then," I tell her, taking hold of her hand. "It doesn't matter. It doesn't really need doing again. You did it yesterday. It's fine."

She throws the duster across the hall. "This is not my job. I wasn't brought here to do all the work and I'm not doing it."

"Come on. Let's go and find Morris."

"He's a lazy bugger, that one. Old buggerlugs. All he does is sit there."

"Well, he has bad legs, Nancy."

"I know. I know that. You don't need to tell me that, thank you very much." She stalks off, disappearing into her sitting room and banging the door. There's dark muttering from within, Morris saying, "What? You're not making any sense at all!"

Nancy helps me get the lunch ready. She butters the table, puts the bread together at odd angles, picks ham off the pile with grimy fingers and eats it, hungrily and a slice at a time.

"I thought you were making Morris a roll."

"No, no. Not for him. He doesn't deserve it."

"Here. Let me." I take charge of the buttering knife. "Let's take him a chair picnic and go into the garden. We can hang the washing and have a walk."

"Ooh lovely. I like a walk."

AFTER LUNCH WE make soup for tomorrow. Nancy wants to help and spends ten minutes scraping a carrot. What's left of it when it's scraped collapses into three weedy bits. I have sympathy for the carrot. The carrot and I have a special spiritual connection. I need to get away from Nancy and her wittering for a bit. I can't stand any more. I am missing my laptop and silence and words that come biddably out of finger ends. I am beginning to feel, quite suddenly, rather desperate. I jump up.

"Well," I say, "that was great, but I have to do some work now, on my computer."

"Oh dear," she says without feeling. "You'd better not be late." Her face has a customary betrayed look. Betrayed and stoical. I know which way this mood will lead and have a silly tactic at hand. It's called Can You Walk Like This?

"Can you walk like this?" I cry, putting my hands over my ears, sticking my elbows out and my knees, losing a foot or more in height and walking like a robot, making nerp-nerp robot noises.

"Oh no! No! I can't do it!" she screams with laughter. I glance round and find her wiggling her fingers and moving her head from side to side, and laugh, too. Then I take her firmly by the shoulders from the back and maneuver her into her sitting room and put her in her armchair, still in robot character, Nancy giggling, Morris looking puzzled.

I go to the drawing room and swoop on the laptop, sinking into my customary chair, my customary spot by the window, with a happy sigh. This is where I should be. This is home. But then I find I can't work. I'm listening for Nancy. And sure enough, there she is. I hear her wandering the house, trying each door in turn.

"Oh look, look at this one. This is a nice one. A bit dark. Very big. They don't know how big it's got lately. Somebody should tell them, to be quite truthful. I think they might come and see it and be surprised. Hmmm, hmmm, hmmm." The singing starts up. "When all the place is ready, and the place is fine and free, and the man isn't there and the man isn't there, and that is all for me."

She can still rhyme. She butters the table but she can still rhyme, can still come up with lyrics that scan, can, in effect, still write poetry. This is a very peculiar disease.

I hear her rattling the conservatory door. "Nancy?" I call out, expectantly.

She doesn't answer. More rattling. The rattling grows louder, as does the muttering. I jump up to go see. "Nancy?"

"What?" Now she's rattled, too.

"Don't let the dogs out, remember."

Paddy is a reddish gold golden retriever, dim and soppy and mildly bowlegged. Left to himself, he'd be happy to carry paired socks round the house all day and wag things off tables. Unfortunately he's easily led astray by his little white friend, Sparky, a Parson Jack Russell, who's long legged and well muscled, has adorable cupped ears, is formidably cunning and a merciless killer. Sparky is quick to learn and Paddy quick to follow. Paddy is his friend's dopey apprentice. They hang around the outer doors waiting for Nancy to let them out.

"Oh doggies. Hello, doggies. Nice doggies. You want to go out? Here, off you go." Whoooosh: a flash of streamlined white and an ungainly portly ginger thing cantering gamely behind are seen disappearing into the horizon line. So this is how it is. About the dogs, we are dogmatic. They can't ever go out on their own. Our neighbor has eight cats. Beyond the lure of feline sniffs, the mesmerizing cat trails leading through the wood, there's an open gate, miles of quiet roads and open fields. There's trouble out there. Farm dogs to get into fights with. Unsuspecting pet rabbits. Plus, and here's the clincher, they've proven not completely trustworthy with sheep.

IT'S A BEAUTIFUL day and Nancy wants to be out in the garden. Nobody has the time (at least Chris and I don't) or the inclination (Morris doesn't) to be in the garden with her in the way that she wants: attentive, lazy, gossiping, devoted to her amusement. But it's a really beautiful day and I have to face the fact that I'm not going to get any writing done. I go out to do some weeding and take Nancy with me. Every inner piece of wall has a herbaceous border, and every border is overgrown. It's the myth of Sisyphus, horticultural version: I push the wheelbarrow up the hill and it just rolls down again. Dandelions see extermination as a challenge: lop their heads off and they'll grow twice as many new ones overnight. But it's a beautiful day and the heart wants to be outdoors. The heart wants it and Nancy is determined. Nancy and I go out singing, each our own versions of "When Irish Eyes . . .". Hers, I note, involves a pudding and a gate. I give her the two gardening cushions to hold and a rug to sit on, and I fetch the trowel and the shears and a scarf for my head. We go to the border beyond the north lawn, which is wide and full of white and yellow flowers of uncertain parentage, and the whole dishearteningly grassy. I kneel and have the trowel poised and sense Nancy standing behind me. She's right behind, leaning forward to touch my shoulder.

"Do you want to help?" I ask her.

"I'd love to help. Nobody ever asks me, though. They're not nice people here. They don't let me out."

"Well, you're out now."

"It's the first time in about five years, I can tell you that."

"Here. Kneel down next to me." She can't, of course. She's almost eighty and her weeding days are over. But she's already bending, apparently effortlessly, to pull dead flowers from last year's *Potentilla* and secreting them in her palm. She makes a heap on the rug, and then she pulls a tulip out, bulb and all, holding it aloft like a sword and looking vaguely triumphant.

"Let me tell you what needs doing," I say pleasantly.

"You should because I'll make a terrible mess of it otherwise. I can't remember things anymore."

Is it memory that's returned to her, in this gobbet of self-awareness, transitorily, almost freakishly, or is it language, allowing her to express thoughts she can't ordinarily articulate? Has the singing done its work?

"I haven't been very well lately," she tells me. "But I can't quite put my finger on it. What it is that's wrong. Something's wrong, I know that. But I can't . . . I can't seem to find it."

She knocks the heel of her palm against her forehead and her eyes fill with tears. "My memory doesn't work. I can't remember things. Even quite little things. And they tell me it doesn't matter. At the hospital, they tell me that. But it does matter. It matters to me. They say I'll get better. The doctors, they do say that. I have to be patient. But it's difficult, you know. And I know that something is very badly wrong."

There's a shout from behind and Jack's there. "Hey, Mum. Hi, Gran."

"Hello, hello, hello," she says to him. "And how are you today? How's my little man? You look very smart in your jacket."

"I'm fine, thanks. Well . . . I'm just going in. Starving," he says, turning and loping away.

"You must be, yes, you must get something nice to eat," Nancy sympathizes. She runs her fingers through her hair. She looks at her old hands and shakes her head.

"Nancy, you have an illness," I blurt. "In your brain. It's the illness that makes you lose your memory." Why do I feel so urgently that I want to make her aware of her predicament? There's no point in it, truly none, when I know that the waters are about to close over her again.

"They told me in the hospital that I would get better, though," she says. "The doctors said to me when they sent me out, 'It will take a while but you'll get better slowly.' 'Slowly, but you'll be fine.'"

"You won't get better," I say. What am I doing?

"Well, that's what they told me, that's what the men said."

"You'll get worse. You won't be able to remember any-thing. And eventually it will make you ill and you'll die of it." I hate myself. I do.

"We all have to go sometime," Nancy says. She sits down on the rug beside me and we look at each other. I find myself taking her hand, which is gnarled and blue veined and ruched with age. She's wearing eight rings. There's a large wart on her knuckle.

"Tell me what you remember," I say.

"Not very much at all and that's the trouble," she says. Her voice is warbly with emotion. She has a look of great concen-tration. "My father. My father worked in the garden when I was born. We lived in a big house, you know, huge. It was ab-solutely beautiful. So many flowers and trees. Then I got sent away in the war. He was so clever, such a good gardener, you know. My brothers were always busy. They got whatever they wanted but I didn't. I minded that and I've minded all my life."

She keeps talking about the "brothers." But she only has one—doesn't she?

"What's your name?" I ask her.

"Nancy. But I've always hated it—ugh! It's a horrible name."

"Do you know your married name?"

"Oh, that. No. Old buggerlugs just sits there."

"He has bad legs, Nancy."

"We all have bad legs sometimes. There's people a lot worse off than him. But he won't get up. He needs to walk about a bit. It doesn't do him any good just sitting. I tell him and I tell him and it doesn't do the first bit of good. He won't listen to me. He doesn't hear a word I say."

"Do you remember living in Edinburgh? Meeting Morris?"

"Oh yes, of course."

"And working at the company? You were the office dynamo,

you know. You ran the place more or less single-handedly. Morris and the children never saw you. Worrying over your computer system. . . ."

"Oh, those were such good years. Such good years."

"Do you remember getting the babies?"

"Of course I remember, course I remember."

"What are their names?"

"Oh, it was such a long time ago. I've forgotten all about it."

"You adopted them, didn't you? A boy and then a girl. I'm married to the boy baby."

"Are you? That's wonderful. Oh, they were lovely. What wonderful days."

It's The Book—one of the many books that tell the caregiver how to care—that instructs me that I should be straightforward with Nancy about her illness. The Book says that acceptance is the key. It makes two assertions: (1) those who accept the truth handle the situation better and (2) dementia sufferers don't have to be violent and unmanageable. No explicit connection is made between these two remarks but I sense there may be one. Caregivers, in this psychotherapeutic view, are like parents of potentially unruly children. The same scary nanny woman who haunts British TV, who diagnoses faulty parenting in almost every case of trouble, might have a parallel, a scary caregiving expert, sent around to three-generation households to watch, diagnose, prognosticate. She, no doubt, will pronounce *bad caregiving* as a self-fulfilling road to trouble. Like being a parent, being a caregiver is fraught with expectations, duties, and blame.

The Book says that dementia sufferers should be told what's wrong with them. Trust is vital, The Book explains; it is of paramount importance between caregiver and care-receiver, and there can be no trust without disclosure. If a person has

Alzheimer's, she should be informed it's Alzheimer's. She has a right to know and to plan accordingly (to kill herself while still able, I think they mean). A doctor on the Internet writes quite candidly that he would plan for suicide if he were diagnosed with dementia. Suddenly, this approach is commonly talked of in Web land. It's boosting the social respectability of self-inflicted death in the United States, one of my forum contacts tells me. There's quite a bit of it about, she says: the stockpiling of pills, and unemotional discussions about the best, most reliable, and least painful methods. But Alzheimer's has a different profile in the United States—an additional profile to the one we know in the United Kingdom, I'd say, from reading around American forum culture. The sheer numbers of dementia sufferers and much earlier diagnosis: put these together and what happens is that a lobby group grows up. That's what has happened in North America. Articulate, professional, early-diagnosed dementia sufferers, as yet showing few signs of the disease, able to talk and write and head up campaigns, are lobbying for better drugs, for widespread scanning, for more and better research. There is a good deal of humor in the mix: black humor and self-satire. If these new stars of the dementia lobby seem impressively to "go gentle into that good night," it's only because they've been diagnosed years earlier than used to be the case. Their good night is likely to be a ten-, fifteen-, twenty-year event, and they are engaged in a long journey through a gradually encroaching twilight.

The Book says planning is crucial. They make it sound like investing in stocks and bonds. Get organized, they implore. Do the research early, and get the nursing home of your choice sorted out in readiness for the inevitable day. (How do you do that, then? Join a waiting list, presumably. If the home of choice doesn't operate one, it's difficult to plan anything. And how do you coordinate the timing of your relative's need and his or her getting to the top of the list?) In their world, that of the writers of The Book, whom I'd guess to be city-medical or psychiatry-southern-suburban in type and origin, nursing homes are as plentiful and local as boarding schools; the client is king and cost isn't an issue.

The Book expects us to be saints. Make Alzheimer's fun, they exhort. Give it your all as a caregiver. Stay upbeat. Get help. Make tasks with the sufferer as lively as you can. Learn coping strategies. Manage the behavior in imaginative ways. Keep score so that bad days can be analyzed and caregiver behavior adjusted. Assess your approach and change it. Keep notes. Make sure you're not inadvertently making things worse. Don't punish the demented, ever, or reproach or scold; these are all forms of abuse. Remember, the demented are no longer responsible for their actions. Keep calm. Step back. Ignore bad behavior. Don't try to reason with them. Distraction is more effective. Reward good behavior. Above all, create tranquillity. Keep reassuring them. Look at things from their perspective and adjust your pace and attitude. Create routines they enjoy and can relate to. Keep them busy, involving them in home life where you can. Create an environment that makes them feel safe. Give them space, light, warmth, activity, companionship, love. Find somewhere to take exercise safely indoors and out. Adopt child-proofing techniques around the home. Don't allow change—it will upset them. Minimize new things, new situations, new people, noise. *Basically, caregiver, your life is over.* (My italics. My conclusion.)

In general this caregiver manifesto holds true across the media, other than for the first point, about telling the sufferer what's wrong with them, which it turns out is an out-of-date approach. Nobody any longer seems to advise the telling of hard truths. The buzz phrase in dementia now is *person-centered care.* Person-centered care takes its cue from the misapprehensions of the ill person and plays along with her, joining in with the delusions that dementia unfolds. In the United States, a process related to this way of thinking has been called "validation."

I try this with Nancy, try living in her reality unquestioningly, but the present keeps intruding, rearing inconsistently into view. I have a go at providing some props for her as Nancy the office worker. I set up the computer for her and some pens, files, a stapler, and she fiddles with these, opening drawers and making piles and pressing buttons, for all the world like a preschooler at a play group. But the absorption is short-lived and very soon I'm asked who the hell I am and what I'm doing there, as this isn't my office. Then, instead of evicting the interloper, it's Nancy who storms off. I go after her and try to steer her back with some guff about a meeting, and our being late. I take her to her bedroom and help her pick a jacket, but she bursts into tears and demands Morris, and shuts the door on me, and is inconsolable. It's as if the two worlds, mine and hers, are ocean liner and iceberg and can't come together happily for very long. She goes for her nap unhappy and wakes full of confusion, and I redirect her to her lunch, but she wonders where her work colleagues are and I stumble over my responses, watched by a baffled Morris. I hold a warning finger up at him as he begins to say, "You're not in the . . ." and take Nancy into the hall. She wonders when the children will be home and I ask about them and she tells me they're lost. I suggest we go and make biscuits ready for their coming back from school, and she sits and watches me make them, looking forlorn, not wanting to join in. I give her a bowl of her own and some flour and butter and a cutter, and then because she's lost and anxious, I mix the sugar in for her and roll the dough, and my cheeks burn with shame. She dips her hands into the mixture and is happy for a few minutes but then she isn't sure what to do next and nothing I say and nothing I do can stop the tears from coming back, her head bent low over the bowl, her fingernails full of mixture and her nose streaming. When I say that it might be time for her to go back to the office, my own voice is cracking.

"They don't want me there," she tells me.

"Course they do. Let's go now or you'll be late."

We go, hesitantly, back to the office in the house and she pauses at the door. "This isn't it. Where are you taking me? Why are you lying to me?"

After three or four days of effort, Nancy more unhappy than ever and her humiliation complete, I determine to take the days as they come. I'll try to engage her in real-time activities. I will join in with her if she insists on being in the past, though I won't try to lead the action or develop it. That seems to take us to a place where we both feel patronized and unhappy.

Chapter 4

Lulled in the countless chambers of the brain,
Our thoughts are linked by many a hidden chain.

—ALEXANDER POPE

UNLIKE THE HEART AND LUNGS, THE HUMAN BRAIN doesn't look from the outside as if it's *for* anything in particular. It doesn't appear to have moving parts. It looks very like an inert lump, silent and motionless. Ancient peoples tended to underestimate its importance. From our brain-savvy, brain-centric world, it's easy to scoff at this, and at why it was that the heart, so obviously merely a blood pump, should once have been thought the seat of the moral self. Plato was considered radical in his idea that the brain might be its real location, as was Hippocrates, who declared, in the manner of a man who expected to be contradicted, that "from the brain and the brain alone comes pleasure, happiness, laughter, as well as sorrow and pain." The ancient Egyptians discarded the brains of those they were mummifying, removing them in bits through the nose with long hooks and binning them, though they preserved the hearts of their kings for the kings' later use.

The brain is a big thing and heavy. It can weigh three pounds. The outer layer, the cortex (from the Latin for *tree bark*), is wrinkled so as to cram more surface area into the limited space. The cauliflower shape is actually a twinned half-cauliflower pair, two halves, left and right, with functions allocated, divided, and shared. People who've had the connection between the two halves severed medically experience a troubling dual consciousness in which one hand really doesn't know what the other one's doing.

Brain use is tiring work. Whether purposely trying to think or not, conscious or unconscious, the system takes a lot of energy. Up to a fifth of food energy is dedicated to fueling brain functions. Glucose is the brain's gasoline, and brain glucose levels plummet in Alzheimer's; one of the newer diagnostic tests measures these levels in living subjects. Aside from the 100,000 million neurons, there are ten times as many *neuroglia* (from the Greek for *glue*), cells that form the support network, feeding and repairing the lead actors. This support network also suffers devastating cell loss in the Alzheimer's forest fire.

They're gray, these neurons, Hercule Poirot's *leetle gray cells*—gray with white axons. And so many of them: 100,000 million is a big number. There are fewer than 7,000 million people in the world. I read somewhere that the phone system covering the whole planet, with all its connections and interconnections, parts of it at rest and parts of it firing with calls, is nowhere nearly as complicated as the interior of one human brain.

While neurons are different shapes according to function, those illustrated in neurology texts are generally star shaped. Neurons are microscopic, but an axon can be as much as half an inch long, directing its communications network in particular sequences, though most stay very local, passing information along like firemen passing water in buckets (albeit huge numbers of firemen and buckets), passing water too fast for the naked eye to see.

The neurons are packed tight in the cortex, and the cortex divides into four main areas, or lobes. The *frontal lobe,* the front third of the brain, in and behind the forehead, is where we think in the most obvious, self-conscious sense, plan, imagine, debate, decide. It's the area that develops last in the growing child. It's the area that best distinguishes us from the rest of the animal kingdom. It's our executive center, the seat of the executive I. It has vital secondary roles in all kinds of brain function and is crucial in the retrieval of memory.

The *temporal lobes,* worn like earmuffs at the sides of the head, are memory banks and instrumental in language and the comprehension of language. They analyze sensory input and, with the auditory cortex, interpret sound. The temporal lobes work in emotion as well as memory. The so-called God spot is here, the mysterious brain area that may give us our sense of the divine. In an experiment done with nuns, it was the same small location in the right temporal lobe that lit up within each, shown on a scanner, when they were asked to focus on communication with the Almighty. Richard Dawkins, the biological theorist who wrote *The God Delusion,* thinks that this God spot, in evolutionary terms, has to do with belonging to a tribe and the socially unifying effects of tribal genuflection. The bishop of Oxford thinks it's provided by the Lord as an interface.

The *parietal lobe,* at the upper part of the back of the head, helps orient us, giving us spatial awareness, our three-dimensional sense of the world, our own detailed body map, and our orientation to left and right. Number recognition, and the ability to manipulate numbers, is worked on here also.

The *occipital lobe,* at the lower rear of the head, is responsible for vision. Vision takes up a lot of space and energy. Other centers in the brain collaborate to process visual information. Among its visual tasks, the occipital lobe helps interpret writing.

Across the top of the head like a stretchy headband runs the *motor cortex,* and behind it lies a second headband-type strip, known as the *somatosensory cortex,* where messages from the nerve endings in the body arrive for processing and analysis from the spine.

Deep beneath the cortex, the *limbic system,* folded away in its own compartment, includes the hippocampus and amygdala and our sense of smell. A dulled sense of smell (like Nancy's) may be a predictor of Alzheimer's and contributes to problems with appetite. The amygdala has been described as the fear zone, the seat of primitive emotions, instinctive, fearful, and aggressive. The egglike thalamus, at the center of the system, acts as mediator between the limbic system and the cortex, between instinct and abstract thought, and may be the brain area that most specifically corresponds to the experience of consciousness. The hippocampus processes short-term memory, which may or may not then be laid down into long-term memory. It's called hippocampus because it's supposed to look like a sea horse.

The *brain stem* is in evolutionary terms the original organ and resembles the whole brain of simpler animals like lizards. It handles all the basic regulatory functions, the heart rate, hormones, sleep, breathing, blinking, blood pressure. It's a bulbous small area at the top of the spine.

The *cerebellum,* at the base and back of the skull, is an onion-shaped organ that's thought to be a minibrain in itself, a minicomputer, and may be a sort of backup generator for the rest. Traditionally, its main responsibilities are thought to be for movement, coordination, posture, balance. It's also the seat of our most secure, most deeply embedded memories. How to walk, for instance. Automatic actions, the kind we don't need to think about anymore—cleaning our teeth, riding a bike—are handled from here. The cortex learns things and then delegates, once we have the thing mastered. Forty million fibers connect the cerebellum to the cortex.

The romantic view of the brain as an interior landscape predated the Romantic movement by over two thousand years, in its using cave and weather and smoke metaphors. "Caverns there were in my mind," Wordsworth writes, "which sun could never penetrate." Coleridge's "intellectual breeze, / At once the soul of each and god of all." Erasistratus, born three hundred years before Christ, talked about "vital spirit," the *pneuma,* a liquid life force flowing around our bodies like blood. The second-century doctor-scientist Galen thought the cerebrospinal fluid to be the pneuma and discounted the hard-boiled-egg-consistency, gray-and-white matter that surrounded it as merely protective.

J. K. Rowling uses this antique idea of selfhood as something vaporous, silvery, swirling through the caverns of the mind like mist. In the Harry Potter books, memories can be decanted, studied, held in a *pensieve.* The dying Snape's memories emanate with his final breath and are caught by Harry in a flask, to be reviewed later. Nurses on intensive care wards open windows to let the souls of the just-deceased escape the walls of the hospital. Absurd though the idea of memory as a silver mist might be, it's in truth far closer to our own idea of the workings of our thoughts than the actual mechanism is. The actual mechanism has all to do with electricity made by the body. How can a body make an electrical impulse? Chemistry provides the answer, down at the cellular level—the fact that chemical molecules carry electrical charges that react with others. Your body may be a temple but it's also, far more intriguingly, a laboratory within which chemical reactions are ongoing.

The *resting potential* of a cell is created by potassium leaking out of it. There's a high concentration of potassium inside cells, and a weak solution of it outside, where there's a high concentration of sodium. The potassium flowing out of a cell creates a negative charge (−70 millivolts). That's the resting potential of a cell. Along comes electrical information—from a pain in your leg, say, or something seen, or something learned, or a memory—and astoundingly, it seems that the information in every case is of the same order; it's just the question of where it comes from and where it's directed in the brain that translates it into pain, vision, knowledge, recall. What happens is that the sodium outside the cell flows in through a hinged gate, creating a wave of positive charge, which happens to be 110 millivolts, so that the balance from the original −70 is +40 millivolts. Sodium flows in, potassium flows out: It takes about a thousandth of a second. The electrical charge passes to the next excited cell, and onward in waves, at fantastic speeds. After the sodium/potassium exchange has occurred, a protein inside the cell is responsible for ushering out the excess sodium, chaperoning back the potassium, so that the cell is reduced to its usual state, ready for the next impulse (which is called an *action potential*).

All this was confirmed, incidentally, by Alan Hodgkin and Andrew Huxley's research using the squid, which has a giant axon, a millimeter thick and visible to the naked eye. They were awarded the Nobel Prize for their work in 1963. Hodgkin commented that the prize should have gone to the squid.

Chapter 5

OUR FIRST BED-AND-BREAKFAST GUESTS ARRIVE, A foursome of young friends, three Scots and an Australian. It is a perfect golden day, windless and warm, and I serve their afternoon tea in the garden. As I'm handing out cups and setting down a plate of warm scones, I'm wondering what to say about Nancy. I may be guilty of being defensive about her. Should I warn people who come to stay about the potential for encounters with Alzheimer's? That's what is going through my mind as I pour tea. Nancy may well want to meet them. She's at an insistently sociable stage. I put the teapot down, take a steadying breath, point out that I made the rhubarb jam, and leave them to it, Nancy's name unspoken. It's too difficult to pitch it. I need to give some thought to this.

Later, I find the visitors gathered in the hall, looking very much as if they want to waylay somebody with a query. A question about eating: How do I rate the pubs in the village? Before I can answer, a hesitant voice says, "Hello?"

"It's all right, Nancy," I say, "just houseguests." And then, to our visitors, "This is Nancy, my mother-in-law."

"Hello, Nancy," they chorus.

"And how are you today?" the Australian asks her. "You have a beautiful house here. We're just admiring the plasterwork."

Nancy, beaming, shuffles forward. Some days she has an old-lady gait, uncertain of her footing. She has her arms outstretched as she comes, grinning. "Oh, it's you! Hello!" she cries to the Australian, and for a horrified moment I think she's going to kiss him.

"Let's go into the morning room; this is where you'll be having breakfast," I say, taking Nancy's hand and yanking her forward.

"Oh, you'll be comfortable in here," Nancy assures the visitors. "This is my house, you know. I was born here. I've always lived here. My father is here, too. He's in the garden. He doesn't mean to be rude." She smacks her lips together. "Well, I don't know, actually. Perhaps he does." She's giggling now.

The visitors are looking at Nancy in a new way. Wondering. I'm wondering, too. She's determined that her father's here, and perhaps he is.

"So is there anything you'd like or don't like for breakfast?" I ask them. "Eggs, bacon, baked flat mushrooms, baked tomatoes, black pudding?"

"Oh, I don't like black pudding," Nancy says gravely. "I hope that won't put you to too much trouble."

"I'm not sure I know what black pudding is," the Australian pipes up.

"It's horrible," Nancy tells him. "But I like tomatoes."

Everybody laughs. It's going to be fine.

AT BREAKFAST TIME, though, Nancy is having one of her restless mornings. This is difficult when I'm trying to cook the Full Hot Scottish. I come down at seven thirty and find her in the hall, stock-still in her pink nightdress, with a pensive expression and one shoe. I put her back to bed—she's cold and has probably been wandering for a while—and go and start the cooking. Then I go and check on Nancy. She's lying in bed flat on her back with her arms crossed over her chest like a medieval marble tomb effigy, eyes open and unblinking. I return to the kitchen. Apples are fried up in butter for the black pudding eaters, and then I go and check on Nancy again. She seems to be asleep. Chris swings into action, cooking up pancakes and collecting the eggs. I take dishes of grapefruit salad through and encounter the guests, who are just coming down. "Good morning," they bellow, and I wince, because they'll wake her. I go to make the coffee and when I come back, I see Nancy, naked other than for a large pair of lilac-colored underpants, coming out of the dining room, followed by a suppressed burst of laughter.

"She's quite a character, isn't she?" the Australian says.

BY THE END of the first summer we have the measure of the house. It is only late in August, as the light begins to fail and the first cold snaps descend, that measuring announces itself and the charming dark green of every inner wall is revealed as algal, the invoker of Stygian gloom. When it rains, water comes into the library. The chimneys are blocked by decades of nests. There are three kinds of heating, all expensive and inadequate. When the wind blows in a certain direction, the rain is driven under the roof and the children are called to bucket duty. When the wind blows in a certain direction, the kitchen stove and central heating are snuffed out and all the fireplaces puff out choking smoke. Needless to say, the wind blows in that certain direction quite a lot. And before you wonder aloud what all this has got to do with September, believe me, even August can be cold. Not cold as in chilly out of the sun. Cold as in *hailing.* Summer happens on about May 20 (with the occasional parting of clouds, an increase in the temperature of the wind) and if you're lucky will stutter through, notwithstanding the occasional storm, a surprise snow shower or two, the odd monsoon, until the final week of July. August marks the start of autumn. On the twelfth, when ice cream's dripping down the hands of children at the southern English resorts, the north of Scotland's putting on its tweed for the beginning of the field sports year.

Despite this hard-won knowledge, the peninsula agricultural show is held in August. It doesn't always rain. It isn't always freezing. The show's sprawling and immensely competitive, whether you're entering a bullock, a Labrador, or a bouquet of onions. Also, Boots the chemist runs out of hair dryers. I know this because I went to buy two for the B and B rooms. "You'll not get one in show week," the assistant told me. I must have looked blank. "They wash the beasts, you see, and then they need to dry them." And indeed, when idling round the stalls on Saturday afternoon, the penned-up, fed-up-looking sheep are unnaturally white and fluffy, fat clouds anchored on legs.

Among the promotional goodies on offer there's free local steak and also rather good beer, in unlimited, plastic pint-glass quantity. I join the steak queue and Chris gets in line for the beers. We notice that some people are eating steak and drinking beer while queuing for another. I, not driving that day (a nondriver, in fact), get back in the beer queue three or five times. After this, I am fearless about breaking the ice. And this is how we come to order the chickens.

We've never kept hens before and I expect to be able to take them home immediately, have already wondered aloud whether they'll stay put on the backseat or, like a Jack Russell, indicate a preference for driving, but alas, the chickens on view are representative only of style and color: *display* chickens, not for sale. We order six: two Dutch Blacks (good layers, we're told), two Marans (delicious brown eggs), and a pair of French Bluebells (pretty), plus henhouse and accoutrements.

Two weeks later they arrive, dealt out from a vanload of identical hole-punctured cartons. There inside are murmuring little chicken bodies, fluffed up and warm and faintly disgusting smelling. Poor Audrey, a Dutch Black, dies on day three, found slumped on the henhouse floor, and is buried with full state honors in the wood. As in Hollywood, so in the henhouse: Ava and Bette are sworn enemies, plotting behind each other's backs. Doris is chirpy, Lauren sardonic, Marilyn the one that can't find the door (ouch). Nancy enjoys the chickens. Ava turns out the tamest and will crouch low to be stroked, or consent to be tucked under an arm and petted. Nancy bends to touch, her gnarled hand strikingly discolored as it moves very softly and with concentration along the dark feathers of Ava's back. For a few minutes after this triumphant rural experience, I feel vindicated in bringing Nancy here and confident in everything that semiremoteness can offer her.

I DECIDE I need to crack on with the garden, which now, as summer's turning, is gloriously profuse, though the weeds are as profuse as the flowers. There are thistles, docks, a firm infiltration of giant dandelion, and even—horrors—abundant patches of nettle lurking at the back. Morris is supposed to be helping with the garden, if only in an advisory capacity. He kept an allotment for thirty years. But Morris seems to have lost interest. The August wind is shockingly cold, but at least in the separate pair of formal gardens, high walled and south facing, it's still possible to work without a coat. I help him outside, and take chairs out, and make a point of asking his advice about the care and pruning of various shrubs. I'm hoping that sitting in the flower garden will engage him a little. There's a lot to do here, its former grandeur overgrown and tatty, but it could be wonderful.

"It could be wonderful, couldn't it?" I say.

"Uh-huh," he agrees.

Poor Morris seems more depressed than ever. Nothing we do to try to cheer him up—outings, lunches, tea parties, lavish amounts of grandchild attention—seems to make any difference. Several times I almost embark on a conversation designed to let him talk about his sadness—about how he feels now, deprived of his last remnants of independence, brought into our lives and his own effectively over, the two of them smothered by our inept attempts at kindness, unable to salvage anything meaningful from it all. Nancy, her condition, her deterioration, must be overwhelming for him, and it's inescapable that his role now as husband is to accompany her with as much strength as he can muster to the end. He must feel like the oarsman directing the rowboat across the Styx. What would you wish for in his situation, that the current would pull faster or that it would linger longer? It's an impossible question. The impossibility of things getting better, ever, of this being the final slow descent to the end of time—that must haunt him every waking minute, mustn't it? Though I don't know if that's how he feels. We don't have the conversation. I'm not sure why. I can only suppose it is out of some instinct that he wouldn't be glad of it, would find it intrusive and final. Once darkness is admitted, self-consciously, to our situation, then all hope of lightness will be lost. I can't bear to introduce this intensity to all our lives. And so I talk to him about the garden.

Morris must see that the garden could be lovely. It's just that he's found himself on holiday in the valley of the shadow of death and so, understandably, can't speak enthusiastically of such temporal things. Loveliness may offend him, and our happy, irreverent family silliness offend him also. He does, increasingly, seem to offer an unspoken opinion that our continuing, apparently undaunted and unaffected, to be a cheery child-parental group is somehow a failure of tact. Pushing this to the back of my mind, I press on with discussing the planting. The bare bones of loveliness are all here. The walls are of the most beautiful old stone, patina-rich in grayish cream, luxuriant in places with ivy. The trees along the west wall are twisted and furry with lichen. In the center of the garden there's a horseshoe-shaped pond, green with weed, and four borders bracketing it in an interrupted circle, each of them matted tightly with grass. There's a lot to do. The Victorian greenhouse has broken and jagged glass, its roof open to the weather. The grapevine inside has tiny pips of grapes, and its interior raised bed is dense with shell-pink poppies. I am trying to talk to Morris about the plants, but it isn't easy. He is gray, sullen, chain-smoking, and much more interested in what Nancy's doing. It reminds me of conversations with a girlfriend in my then-kitchen, way back, when our children were small and she couldn't focus on anything but toddler discipline.

"What do you think about this *Pulmonaria*?" I say to him.

Nancy offers him six blades of grass in her hand. "What do I do with this?"

MORRIS: It's just a bit of grass, you silly woman! Put it down! Put it down, Nancy!

She turns to me, holding the six blades at arm's length as if they will bite. "What will I do with it?"

ME: Just put it in the wheelbarrow. Look. Over there. See? Wheelbarrow. With all the grass in it.

She looks around helplessly and I take her to the wheelbarrow. She starts to rearrange the weeds, talking to them. "Now you're a nice yellow one. And, oh look, you have a friend."

I return to the digging. After a while I see that Nancy has gone to the paved area by the greenhouse and is moving stones about.

MORRIS: Nancy, will you stop doing that! Leave the gravel
    alone!

NANCY: I'm just tidying it; it's my day to sort it out.

MORRIS: What are you talking about, your *day*?

ME: Morris, do you think these primroses will survive if I
    move them over there?

NANCY: The people who live here want me to do it so I'd
    better do it.

MORRIS: What are you talking about? You live here. We *are*
    the people who live here.

NANCY: Don't be silly. I never heard such nonsense. You
    say that to all the people but they know who you really
    are. (She stalks off, through the archway and out.)

ME: I'll fetch her. Shall I get you some tea? A hat? The sun's
    quite warm.

MORRIS: That would be lovely, dear. I really don't under-
    stand what Nancy was on about.

ME: She has Alzheimer's, Morris. You do know that, don't
    you? You know what Alzheimer's is?

MORRIS: Oh yes, yes. But she talks such rubbish now. I
    worry she might really be ill.

I return with Nancy and with a tray of tea and biscuits. Tea
and biscuits are consoling for Morris and work also as a sort of
Nancy-sedative. Then I resume the gardening. I start at one of
the borders that frame the pond, digging out deep-rooted mats
of trespassing lawn. Jack comes in his Wellies and shorts to
help, and gets into the water, a foot or so deep in its concrete
mold, pulling out great green ropes of smelly weed and shrieking. The dogs rush about chasing birds into bushes.

But I'm aware that an argument is brewing over in the corner.

"All I'm asking you for . . ." His voice.

Then hers, shrill with irritation. "Well, I'm not doing it. I
don't know where it is or what it is and I can't do it."

"Of course you can do it. I told you, it's on the chair in our sitting room. Our sitting room where the telly is."

"I am not going anywhere and you have no right! No right at all! To ask me anything at all!"

Out of confusion, anger springs.

I lay down my tools. "What is it, Morris? Something I can do?"

MORRIS: I'm feeling a bit cold and Nancy won't go and get my cardigan.

ME: Why didn't you say so? I can go.

When I get back, Nancy is over in the far corner, pulling hollyhocks out by the roots, and Morris is chiding her.

"I was told to do it," Nancy says, "by that man there."

"Here is Morris's cardigan, Nancy," I say to her. "Why don't you take it to him?"

Morris clears his throat. "Actually, do you think we could go in now, dear? My legs are bothering me."

Morris is supposed to be in charge of the kitchen garden, and the seed catalogs sit on the coffee table. The newspaper gets put on top, and the mail, and a packet of biscuits. I give him a notebook and pen and ask for ideas about how to lay the vegetables out, but these are put aside and forgotten about. There's a run of warm days, moist and fuggy. Deep white fogs roll in from the sea and engulf us. Chris gets the acres of grass cut, tractoring up and down on the ride-on mower in the fog, audible from the windows but invisible. The waves crash onto the beach with rhythmic suddenness, sounding bizarrely close, the distance distorted by the bowl of the sea fret, the bay licked by humid and milky mist. Directly overhead it thins a little like a balding head and the sky beyond is a rich and brilliant blue.

Morris and Nancy are invited to go to the Thursday Club

in the village. Morris doesn't want to go, but neither is he able to withstand the entreaties of the two women from the club who storm the house to persuade him otherwise. Other than for this weekly outing, Morris sits in front of the television almost all of the time. I've given him a little silver bell to ring if he needs tea, or the fire fed, or a sweater, or help with Nancy, and he uses it with enthusiasm. I have spiritless phone conversations with my mother about the *invalid role*. On sunnier days, I have been encouraging the children to ask him if he'd like a walk in the garden, to be pushed in the chair. He hates the chair and doesn't appear much to enjoy his excursions. In any case, the program comes to an abrupt halt one afternoon when Jack is taking him across the lawn to show him the greenhouse and the chair trips on a tussocky bit of grass, sending Morris flying out forward. Luckily the grass is soft and thick and only masculine pride is dented.

"Do something about it! Do something!" Nancy shouts as I rush to Morris's aid. "I can't do it. I can't do anything. It's only my first day here!"

As summer cools and the days shorten, the true nature of the life we have landed in begins to sharpen and clarify. Caregiving permeates everything and nothing is spared. If Chris and I leave Nancy and Morris alone, something occurs, some small but pertinent crisis. Teapots are dropped and people near scalded. Nancy is found with black hands, black handprints on her trousers and chair, having put coal in the fire without using the hearth tools. Outer doors have been opened and dogs let out. While we are gone retrieving them, there are other crises at home. Nancy has wandered off, leaving Morris panicky, unable to keep up with her. Nancy trips and injures herself. She puts herself to bed and promptly falls out, bashing her head on the bedside table and giving herself an impressive black eye. She is sent by Morris into the kitchen to get him a drink or a snack, and returns with the wrong thing, prompting an argument and

Nancy leaving home (again). Morris answers the phone and is stern with B and B guests, demanding to know what they want.

It has, in short, reached a point, *a point,* of constant supervision. If we go out we have to take Nancy and Morris with us, levering Morris into the high front seat of the Land Rover, belting Nancy into the back, taking them into town, round the stores with us, sitting in tea shops, dealing with Nancy's carsickness on the way home. Anything that is done without Morris and Nancy in attendance is done at risk, and risk assessment becomes a part of life. We don't go for walks anymore. We don't go out as a family anymore—just the five of us—unless we can go as seven. We go as seven to the cinema, out to dinner, to visit new friends. We're not often invited back.

I begin waking in the night in a panic, heart thumping, clammy. What is this future I appear to have solicited? I never imagined that the in-laws would become so immediately passive, and it didn't occur to me that it'd become so particularly my job to look after them, but that's how it falls, when men have proper jobs and women don't. The conscience is sated, plump and shiny, but the appetite for the day is shrunken, alarms going off all over the internal city. What kind of person is it that can give of herself this much, I think, jadedly, lying awake and waiting for dawn. People who feel guilty about happiness and freedom, I think (shamingly cynical). People who crave dependents, perhaps. People who never really had a life of their own and relish the absolute vocation of this role. This isn't me. This really isn't. I came looking for the Sublime. The hunt for the Sublime, however, has become a grimly private joke. It isn't out there, is stubbornly absent. And actually it's worse. Something else is out there, when I go off running toward the beach, sit on the dunes chewing on the pale inner bits of grass, wander entirely aimlessly along the neck of the headland toward the sandstone plunge of the cliffs. The anti-Sublime. The wilderness will only give me back what I yield up to it and all I have to offer is disheartedness. It lends me its own, magnified and in multiple. I'm not just uninspired, but positively oppressed by outdoors.

> *Uncontradicting solitude*
> *Supports me on its giant palm*
> *And like a sea-anemone*
> *or simple snail, there cautiously*
> *Unfolds, emerges, what I am.*

Philip Larkin has the idea of the Sublime in his sights. I want to unfold and emerge. But I'm having the opposite experience. It occurs to me, during one of these walks, that Nancy and I are engaged on parallel journeys, hers into death and mine into depression, though this is grandiose and probably also offensive. My problems are contingent, after all. Life will shift, the sun will come out (the plain fact that her death may be the engine of this improvement is something I prefer not to think about). I'd never claim her metaphorically, poor Nancy, who's twice my age and terminal, when all I can complain of is that I'm demoralized and low. But the beginnings of unhappiness are here, poised at the end of summer, for Nancy and also for me. And unhappiness distorts perspective. Thus it is that when I read on in my Larkin edition and come across one of his many poems about death, I see Nancy there and then myself.

> *This is what we fear—no sight, no sound*
> *No touch or taste or smell, nothing to think with*
> *Nothing to love or link with*
> *The anaesthetic from which none come round.*

Caring produces a kind of anesthetic in this narrow sense, in its full immersion into near-intolerable practicality. Ludwig Wittgenstein wrote that "philosophy is a battle against the bewitchment of our intelligence by means of language," and I'm aware that my feelings are being distorted by the anti-Sublime, the terrible useless self-pity I find down on the beach and transpose onto the pitying sea, the pitying sky, the pitying cliffs. Latching onto poetic sentiment has become a sort of literary defeatism. I am falling for the Romantic idea of myself as a victim. Caring is taking me somewhere new, somewhere poetry can't follow without hindering my settling into it. This is a life-and-death struggle I'm engaged in now, someone else's life-and-death struggle. It seems to blot the point of fiction out. I find I can't read novels anymore and turn to biography. Biography and nonfiction. Read Wittgenstein, not Keats, I tell myself. "Beauty is truth, truth beauty"—phooey. Read Wittgenstein. "The world is everything that is the case." That's all. Get used to it.

Chapter 6

Life does not consist mainly, or even largely, of facts and happenings. It consists mainly of the storm of thought that is forever flowing through one's head.

—MARK TWAIN

ALZHEIMER'S DISEASE CAUSES ONLY AROUND 65 PERcent of the dementia cases recorded, but people tend to use the terms *Alzheimer's* and *dementia* interchangeably. A friend of mine does this, referring to her mother's Alzheimer's, when it's fairly clear, meeting the mother in question, that some other kind of dementia is to blame for her illness.

Senile dementia as a term was coined in 1838 by one Jean-Étienne Esquirol, a doctor who noted a progressive loss of memory and initiative and creeping emotional instability in people over the age of sixty-five. The phrase may have been new, but the syndrome was already as old as the hills. Plato was involved in a discussion about dementia in the fifth century B.C. Lucullus, a Roman general, died of dementia, and his decline, as written about by Plutarch, is persuasively of the Alzheimer's kind. Marcus Aurelius, the Roman philosopher-emperor, writes in the second century A.D. that "even if a man lives a long time, it's doubtful his mind will survive him." He goes on to say that "the coming of senility may not be accompanied by respiratory or digestive disorders, no loss of the sensory life or of one's desires, but even so, the power of the faculties, of knowing and doing your duty, dealing with crises, sensing that the time has come to die—all of the decisions, in short, that demand proper thinking about, all of these will nonetheless already be fading away.

"We must get on and live life," he says, "not just because life is brief, but because our understanding may be briefer." It's an issue that has taxed individuals, their families, and the workings of society in all the years since. They worried about it in the fourteenth century: A test was discovered in the 1970s, an equivalent to the question-and-answer diagnostic test (MMSE) used today, that dated from 1383 and had been used to assess the competence of a woman in Cambridgeshire to run her own affairs. The 1970s were an important decade for dementia. It wasn't until the end of the 1960s that it was realized just how prevalent Alzheimer's is. Before that it was thought to be a rare disease, one small exotic branch of senility. Most cases were assumed to be of the vascular type, a furring up of brain arteries, which was still considered a normal part of aging. Alzheimer's was listed in the textbooks as uncommon. It was only when autopsies began to be done on brains in huge numbers, and retrospective microscopic examination of stored brains was undertaken, that it became startlingly clear that Alzheimer's was the main cause of dementia.

Dementia has been important in our history, then, and perhaps more important than is generally recognized. The tradition, or at least tendency, to elect men and women of mature years into power, and to allow people of over seventy to hang on to power, increases the risk that we will have leading statesmen and stateswomen—governors, presidents, and prime ministers—suffering from some form of dementia. It's only fairly recently been discovered that Harold Wilson stepped down as prime minister in 1976 because he'd become aware of his own mild cognitive impairment (MCI), and foresaw accurately that dementia was on its way. Not all politicians have the insight to abdicate so early in the disease. It's alleged that Woodrow Wilson had dementia in office, and that the resulting capriciousness of his decision making culminated in his failure to get Congress to approve the Versailles Treaty that ended World War I. It is also suggested that Stalin was a dementia sufferer, his failing intellect combining suggestively with increasing levels of aggression and paranoia. Roosevelt was evidently quite ill and possibly suffering symptoms of dementia when he had to negotiate with Stalin at Yalta in 1945 (he died two months later of a cerebral hemorrhage). The Labour prime minister Ramsay MacDonald is said to have struggled with dementia in office. Lenin died of dementia, which, as in the case of Stalin, was most likely brought on by syphilis. There seems little doubt that Urho Kekkonen, the president of Finland from 1956 to 1981, had Alzheimer's while in office, a fact actively covered up from about 1978 onward. Ronald Reagan showed early signs of the disease during his presidency.

Dementia is fast becoming the condition that's cited by the young and healthy as the disease that is most feared. It's not curable, unlike cancer. It's not able to be tackled with drastic measures, unlike heart disease and its bypasses and transplants. It's more fundamental than that. We don't *have* brains; we *are* our brains. You can lose a leg or an arm, or accept the gift of another person's heart and lungs, and still be yourself. The brain is where the self lives. Lose the use of your brain by degrees and the self is stripped away, layer by layer. In the early stages, the middle stages, even in the early part of the late stage this may well be something you are conscious of, the lights going out one by one.

The dementia numbers are ascribed to our soaring life expectancy rates. It's only an epidemic, so the orthodoxy goes, because we are living long enough to develop it. In 1910, when very little dementia was recorded, only 15 percent of people lived longer than the age of fifty. Life expectancy then was around forty-eight for men and fifty-two for women. We live, on average, around thirty years longer than we did a hundred years ago. Add to this another salient statistic: namely, the number of people over sixty-five worldwide is expected to double in the next twenty years. There's the engine of the epidemic on a plate.

Vascular dementia, the artery-furring sort, is the second biggest dementia disease group by numbers of sufferers. Around 20 percent of dementia victims have this one, and another 20 percent may have a vascular/Alzheimer's combination. It's the dementia that's most equivalent to heart disease. Vein damage prevents blood from getting to parts of the brain; neurons are starved and die. Vascular dementia can be caused by stroke: single-infarct dementia, if it's a single serious stroke; multi-infarct dementia, if it's lots of little strokes, some so tiny as barely to register symptoms, and this is the most common sort. A rare variant called Binswanger's disease begins in blood vessels deep in the brain and may start to show itself with walking problems.

King Lear has been diagnosed, from the verbal evidence of the play, to have suffered from vascular dementia. There's no doubt he suffered from one kind or another of dementing illness. "Methinks I should know you, and know this man," he says in act 4. "Yet I am doubtful; for I am mainly ignorant / What place this is; and all the skill I have / Remembers not these garments; nor I know not / Where I did lodge last night. Do not laugh at me."

The third most common sort is dementia with Lewy bodies (DLB); in fact, some studies claim it's the second most common. Notoriously difficult to diagnose, it overlaps with other dementias. At least 20 percent of Americans with dementia are thought to have DLB, and among the elderly demented the percentage is much higher. Dr. Frederich Lewy identified this variant in 1912, having spotted tiny foreign bodies (proteins again) in the neurons in the brain. Parkinson's disease also has these bodies, though in the case of Parkinson's they're confined to one brain area, the substantia nigra. Symptoms can mimic Alzheimer's, though DLB victims may have more specific problems, with near-normal memory and language skills but trouble with abstract thinking. Hallucinations are so common as to be diagnostic, much more so than in Alzheimer's. Sufferers may also have Parkinson's-like symptoms, trouble with movement and tremors. It's a very up-and-down disease with good days and bad days, good hours and bad hours.

The best known of the frontotemporal dementias is Pick's disease, named after a Czech neurologist, Arnold Pick (1851–1924). Pick's was isolated and named in 1892. Specks known as Pick's bodies are found in the frontal and temporal lobes, to which this variant is confined. Pick's can be nasty: It comes on early, can instigate massive personality change, and sufferers exhibit an unfortunate tendency toward lechery.

Frontotemporal dementia (FTD) also includes particular niche dementias, like aphasia dementia (loss of language) and semantic dementia, in which the connections between words and meanings are lost. Frontotemporal dementia sufferers have specific problems with language, behavior, and emotional response. In research results, FTD has been more strongly linked with tau proteins than with plaques. No drugs are available: Alzheimer's medications seem only to make things worse.

Other conditions can lead to dementia. Parkinson's has already been mentioned. Variant CJD is another. AIDS can lead to dementia. People with Down syndrome or Huntington's disease are at risk. Damage caused by long-term alcoholism can mimic dementia (Korsakoff's syndrome), as can B vitamin deficiency, diabetes, kidney failure, thyroid problems, liver dysfunction, anemia, or electrolyte imbalance, though these are only apparent dementias from which people can recover.

Chapter 7

Our business in this world is not to succeed, but to continue to fail in good spirits.

—ROBERT LOUIS STEVENSON

IT'S AUTUMN ON THE PENINSULA, AND MORRIS IS RUSHED into hospital. He gets up out of his chair to go to bed, puts his foot forward awkwardly, and goes down hard, breaking his leg at the top by the hip. Nancy doesn't know this, although she was with him when he fell, and held his hand until the ambulance came, and has visited him every afternoon. We keep it from her—or so she accuses, when it occurs to her to ask where he has gone, two or three dozen times a day. She doesn't take the news very well. Her face puckers up pinkly.

"Why didn't anyone tell me he was in hospital? That's just ridiculous." She sweeps out of the room in a huff, or tries to, her shuffling waddle a little faster than usual, her hands outstretched to grasp the door handle, like a great outsize wrinkled toddler.

There are days when the toddler similarity is persuasive and bizarre. Days when I feel like a babysitter, a new and inexperienced one, given care of a reluctant and stroppy child, having to make it up as I go along, trying more and more desperately to mollify and distract, and feeling that dark needle of fear when nothing I do makes any difference. She shakes her head and stamps her foot and has tantrums. She asks for her father and gets agitated when he can't be produced, looks horrified when I confess that he and her mother are dead. Then, shocked by my own bluntness, I add, "But that's because you are an old lady now." She looks baffled. "You see, you're almost eighty. You don't have parents any longer, but you have children, and grandchildren. Six grandchildren. Three of them are in Canada, and three of them live here with you."

Nancy's face acquires a stony set look. "My. Parents. Are. Coming for me."

When the forest fire of Alzheimer's causes havoc in the frontal lobe, it attacks the site that most approximates our adult selves. Frontal lobe damage can return dementia sufferers to childlikeness, and also childishness. Childishness is the worst because it's coated in a veneer of adult power, assumed authority, and physical strength. Sufferers can become unpredictably emotional, and this is likely to worsen until—probably late in stage 6—it burns itself out, the sufferer too ill to feel anything much. This is a fact I take comfort in, and the idea, leading on from this, that consciousness itself is eroded, so that by stage 7 there's too little left of the self to experience anything much of what's happening. In dementia, emotions can become dislocated from feelings. Emotions are bodily reactions, and feelings intellectual ones. The emotions are produced but the feelings—emotional impulses translated by the thinking mind—are lost or locked off. Nancy is emotional, now that Morris is in hospital, but she doesn't understand it. She cries and is grumpy and cries again and apologizes to us all. "I don't know what's the matter with me," she tells us, and that's literally true. It takes a facility for remembering in order to know what it is you are feeling and why.

Poor Morris is likely to be in hospital for a while. He's been to the county hospital for an operation to reset the bone, and is now back in the town, in the cottage hospital there, in his own room, with a television and a lifetime supply of toffee. The toffee is a way of dealing with the forcible giving up of nicotine. He's become a chain toffee eater. We speak to the doctors about Nancy's urgent need to have him home, in his usual chair. No dice; Morris won't be released until he's a bit more mobile. Nancy sits holding his hand and looks utterly blank. Having no memory of the accident, and unable to remember the hospital from one day to the next, she's having trouble with the context of his being there sufficient to undermine her ideas about who Morris is, exactly. She's no longer entirely sure.

We have horses now, two cobs: a chestnut one and a gray. Mine, the gray, is huge, like a medieval war horse with a long wavy mane. In the evenings, when the children are in place and happy to Nancy-sit, Chris and I ride out onto the headland. Curious bullocks come to the fences and snort, or dash across the pasture kicking their muddy heels, fizzing our horses into a froth. Sheep take off in a sinuous swarm, sticking together but running scared. Blown shreds of feed and fertilizer bags flap against barbed wire. I'm reminded that there's another way of being out in wild places, something that supersedes introspection. Staying on board, the physical harmony of it, negotiating hazards and the intermittent thrill of speed: I may be beginning to see the point of sport.

October stretches out mild and sunny, and the horses sit together, legs tucked sweetly under their tummies, in the long meadow grasses of the lower paddock, fed to satiation and drugged on sunshine. I take Nancy with me, under the white tape of the electric fence, presenting unexpected carrots from coat pockets, scratching under chins and into furry ears.

"Nice doggies," she says. And then, "Listen to me, saying nice doggies! What a fool I am sometimes. They're not doggies, of course. I can't think precisely of the word, though."

"Horses. They're horses."

"Course they are!"

She puts a tentative hand out to a velvety nose. "Nice doggies."

* * *

NOW THAT WE have her to ourselves, Nancy comes everywhere with us. She sits with us to have breakfast, belching and apologizing, a faraway look in her eyes. (Something's wrong, something's missing, but what?) She's becoming vague, losing track of where she is and what for. It was Morris who anchored her days. We need to prompt her to go to the bathroom now, and prompt her to come out again, or she'd sit there most of the morning. Hands are washed with transfixing care, each finger done scrupulously, like a surgeon scrubbing up, and then a lengthy towel-drying ritual begins. I have to remove the towel after a few minutes, when this threatens to go on and on and fingers are beginning to be rubbed red and raw.

After breakfast, if we're not going to town for shopping, we go to the village. Nancy likes to go into the shop and look at all the packets, the piles and rows, the colors. She picks up biscuits and cake and bars of chocolate: things she knows she likes. It's another Alzheimer's way-marker, this childish craving for sugar. She likes to talk to the shop assistant. "Look at that, you're very clever the way you do that," she says as the assistant rings up the prices. "I'm sure I could never do anything remotely like that, to be quite truthful."

We drive home the two miles along the winding seaside road, Nancy holding onto the carrier bag in the backseat and keeping up a steady monologue.

"Look at those things there. Look how far apart they are."

"You mean the sheep?" I crane my neck to look round at her.

"Sheep, is that what it is? They're animals of some kind." She sounds as if she's reminding herself. In Alzheimer's, the learned subtleties of categories of objects become less and less refined over time: A butterfly becomes an insect, and then an animal, and then a thing.

"Look, Nancy, there are cows, on the right; no, the right."

"They're amazing, aren't they? They're so big. You don't think they're going to be so big but they are. They probably always have been. Just me being daft again."

"You're not daft, you've just lost your memory," I tell her.

"That looks like the sea," she says, sounding surprised.

"It is the sea. You live by the sea."

"I didn't used to. I never saw it from one year to the next, to be quite truthful."

WE TAKE THE shopping into the kitchen. "Can I help you with all of this?" she asks, eager to be useful.

"Okay, then. You pass me the milk and I'll put it in the fridge."

"Is this the right thing?" She hands me the newspaper. The matching up of word and object is seriously adrift.

"No, the milk. Big tall carton, white. Cold. There. In the bag."

She hesitates. The old hands, mauve and white and heavy with their burden of rings, hover over the bags. "I can't see it."

It's not happening for her now. It's disquieting. The words *milk, big, tall, carton, white*: They don't add up anymore to the object right in front of her.

"That's fine, just pass me anything."

She hands me the newspaper again. I put it aside. "Thank you. Now, something else?" She's holding the new jar of coffee.

"Can you put that in the coffee cupboard for me?"

"Yes, I'd be delighted, if you tell me where it is."

"Go toward your room a bit. No. The other way. That's right. Along there and . . . that's it, stop. You're there. Right there. The cupboard."

She bends to the floor and runs her hand along it.

Why does she do this? Are words and objects jumbling

themselves, so that *cupboard* mismatches itself with *floor*? Or is it just that she sees I expect something of her, and the floor's the first thing that comes to mind?

"No, not down there. The cupboard. The door. Open the door."

She pulls one of the kitchen chairs out from the table.

I go to rescue her. "Look, here it is. Turn around a bit. There you go. See the cupboard?" She goes to pick up the kettle off its stand. I put my hand over hers and lift it slightly to the handle of the wall unit. "There you go. Cupboard. Remember? Where we keep the coffee and tea. Open it and look inside."

"You're quite right. All the things are in there."

I give her the coffee jar. "Can you put this in for me?"

She holds the jar up and pushes it a little further until it hits a can of chocolate powder. Then she brings it down again. "It won't do it for me."

She has enough latent knowledge to understand what's needed to put something somewhere, lifting the jar into place, but doesn't seem to recognize any longer that there needs to be a gap, a coffee-jar-shaped vacancy on the shelf. Nor can she coordinate the movements to place an object down and let go of it.

Nancy enjoys going into town. It's an ideal size and shape for her, our little town. There's just one main road, snaking from the harbor round into the high street, where for a brief stretch it's been pedestrianized before opening out again by the church. There are side streets leading off, but most of the shopping is here, along the high street, which is crowded with eighteenth- and nineteenth-century buildings and twentieth-century shop fronts, some of them early twentieth century by the look of them, with prewar sign writing. There's a stationer, a music shop, a delicatessen, a ladies' wear shop with just the kind of skirts and shirts and cardigans that appeal to Nancy (but not to teenage girls), two small boutiques (that do appeal to teenage girls, but sell £80-a-pop jeans, so not to their mothers), old-fashioned drapers, Boots the chemist and Woolworths, plus jewelry and gift shops that rely on the tourists. Socially Nancy's become entirely liberated from convention. Meeting people for the first time, she'll likely as not embrace them and, tears welling, say how glad she is to see them again. "I knew you once when I was very small," she'll say emotionally when introduced. Random strangers are hailed in the street.

Nancy likes to go round the ladies' wear shop commenting on things. If I want to make her laugh I suggest something for her in green. She can't abide green: It's one of the few things I can count on for her to remember.

One of the assistants might approach. "Need any help?"

"These were very popular, I was just saying to this lady here"—Nancy gestures toward me—"and everybody wore them when I was young."

The assistant looks at the cardigans dubiously.

"They're everywhere the ones like this in the place, all around us," Nancy says. "And it's really nice to see them again, you know, all together again because they like that. What am I saying? Listen to me blathering on. 'They like that,' she says. Honest to god, I'm losing my mind, I think. But, you know, they're nice, these things, aren't they?"

"Oh yes."

"It's awfully pretty! I was just saying to this lady here when you came in"—she gestures toward me again—"but she thought it wasn't. So. We all have different tastes and it would be a dull world if we didn't."

"That's very true," the assistant says, giving me a special look and retreating. Nancy grins after her and her teeth are appalling, yellow and coated and every crevice jammed with food. She no longer wants to take her false teeth out and clean them and won't countenance their cleaning in situ. Attempts have been made and abandoned. There were tears, fisticuffs, and biting. We're used to the state of them but strangers recoil.

Nancy looks lingeringly after the assistant.

"What a lovely person she is," Nancy says.

Babies in strollers are followed round the drugstore, waved at, sung to, engaged in one-sided conversations, which their mothers consent to warily.

"Look at you, you're gorgeous, and you know it, don't you? You're much more beautiful than the others." She leans forward, tries to pinch a rosy cheek. "The others are nasty about you, but don't you listen."

She's transfixed by the sight of so many racks of nail polish.

"You used to wear this all the time when you were younger, when you were working, do you remember?" I say to her. She'd spend part of every evening laboriously doing her nails, taking off the day's keyboard-chipped varnish, filing into soft points, applying various unguents and then color and topcoat from a vast collection on her dressing table. Morris filled her Christmas stocking with polishes.

She smiles delightedly. "How do you know that?" she asks. "You've been talking to someone, haven't you? But it wasn't this sort. It was the other kind, not in the same one, I mean. Jings crivens, I'm having trouble expressing myself today."

I take her to the shampoos. These now take up a whole aisle. Every time I come in here there are more brands, more daring claims.

"Which one shall we get?" I ask Nancy.

"Oh, don't ask me. I wouldn't know where to start."

"Between you and me I think they're all the same, except that some of the expensive ones are terrible, too busy trying to do other stuff to your hair to clean it."

"That's very true," Nancy says.

"So why don't you just pick the prettiest?" I say to her.

She starts to laugh. "No, no, I couldn't."

"Go on. The prettiest bottle."

She stands with her hand raised, looking embarrassed. She

seems to find it impossible to make a choice, or understand what choosing is. Perhaps memory is essential for selecting. How else do we know what we like?

"Just choose one. Anything. Whatever appeals."

She begins to mutter to herself. Her blush deepens.

"What about this pale blue one?" I say. "You like blue."

"Oh yes! That's wonderful."

We pay for our toiletries and Nancy tells the checkout girl that she has lovely hair. She reaches out to touch it but I intercept her arm and hold on to it.

In Woolworths, while I'm buying magazines and having a look at the latest films on offer, Nancy wants to talk to small children. Preschool children, little girls in pink anoraks, small square-jawed boys with buzz cuts and suspicious eyes, hang on tighter to their mothers as Nancy stalks the aisles looking for somebody of three or four to talk to.

"Look at you, you totey wee thing," she says, bending to smile her toxic-toothed smile. A little girl with fair curls smiles back, twisting her Barbie in her hands. Nancy reaches out. "Can I see your dolly?" The Barbie is handed over. "Oh, look at this, she's absolutely beautiful, look at her gorgeous dress." Nancy beams.

"I'm buying her a new dress," the poppet squeaks.

"Kelly! Kelly!" The mother approaches, looking alarmed. "Come on, I said." Poppet is dragged off unwillingly and we hear her mother saying, "I told you not to talk to strangers. How many times have I told you?"

I leave Nancy choosing a chocolate bar and go to get a magazine for Jack, and when I come back, I find her standing by the pick-and-mix with a fistful of truffles, mouth working furiously, three gold sweet papers at her feet.

Obviously, this is a very minor kind of criminal behavior (though I'm glad that the staff here know us, nonetheless), but the principle that makes Nancy feel entitled to the chocolates is one that's dangerous to apply to life in general. The loss of frontal lobe wisdom, moral sense, any kind of brakes on her impulses: It might just as easily apply to a soft-top car, a diamond bracelet, somebody's baby in a buggy. For Nancy, everything is available. It's fair game. If she wants something she takes it. And she believes that everybody in the world operates that way. The idea of ownership is gone, which isn't to say that she doesn't assert that things are hers and hers only; what's gone, specifically, is the idea of other people's ownership of things she might want for herself. This is becoming a problem in the United States, where the huge number of Alzheimer's sufferers means that the legal system is having to grapple with issues of culpability surrounding dementia-sufferer crime. It's a thorny problem. If repeatedly you steal things because you no longer understand what stealing is, what is the state to do with you? What can the mechanics of civilian control do with otherwise fully functioning and peaceable adults who can no longer be reasoned with?

Nancy's hesitant, out on the street. She doesn't like the paving stones, carefully avoiding the cracks, looking down and adjusting her feet as she goes, first with small steps and then at a stride—an inconsistency that is tricky when your arms are linked together. She no longer deals well with changes of level, either, hesitating before going up or down from road to curb. At home, she has developed a thing about the black-painted slate floor in the back corridor, pausing as she comes off the carpet and dipping a toe in the "water" first. She thinks it's going to be wet. Sometimes she thinks it's a hole and I have to go first.

If it's blowy on the high street she hangs on to her hat, laughing near hysterically. We go into the council-run coffee shop, the Victorian Gothic ex–council headquarters, and eat a subsidized bit of apple pie with scalding weak coffee. Nancy likes it in here. She eats her pie with relish and licks the plastic container.

She's happy in town. It's when we get back that the trouble starts. She has no memory of being here, but emotional associations with things remain, subconscious associations, and Nancy's begun to associate the house with incarceration. Her spirits wilt visibly as she trundles back into the kitchen, and is steered toward her sitting room. She doesn't want to take her coat off or her shoes. She retreats to her bedroom, putting her bathrobe on over her coat. I go and crouch at her knee and take her hands and look up at her. She looks angry.

"Don't speak to me. Don't say a word," she growls.

"What's the matter?"

"Nobody talks to me. Nobody wants anything to do with me. They invite me here but then they ignore me. I'm going to take my things and go."

"But Nancy. We're your family. We look after you."

"You DO NOT."

"But Nancy. You don't know where you are."

She laughs mirthlessly. "That's what you say."

"Okay, then." My dander is up. The apple pie will go unrewarded. No kindness will go unpunished.

"Tell me where we are, then. Go on. Tell me."

She looks out the window. "We're here, of course."

"But where are we?"

"Edinburgh."

"We're not in Edinburgh."

"Well, you aren't." She puts great emphasis on the *you*. Is this a metaphysical point? I wonder. "I'm going home," she adds.

"How are you going to get home?"

"I'll be fine."

"It's a two-mile walk to the village bus, and even then . . ."

"Well, that's me, then. I'll say good-bye to you."

I follow her out. She's standing in the yard, looking in astonishment at the great open garden, the wall, the sea, the sky. What must it be like, to be as sure as you can be sure of any-

thing that you're awake and in your own city, and open the
door and find the ocean there?

"Come on, let's go in, it's starting to rain," I say. She follows me meekly indoors.

NANCY'S MOODS TAKE a decisive downturn. Daily she tells us
that none of us love her, that none of us like her, that none of
us want her here. We spend a lot of our weekends trying to
convince her that she's wrong. Trying to convince somebody
that you love them is exhausting work. Particularly when you
need to reiterate it all, almost word for word, twenty minutes
later. Chris takes on the job of trying to distract her at the
weekends so that I can have a break. But, of course, I feel terrible, sitting by the fire with the Saturday papers and hearing it
all going on. I go into the kitchen to make coffee and find the
two of them, Chris and Nancy, sitting at the table making
soup. Nancy has her own chopping board, her own knife, and
is busy mangling a potato. Chris is saying, "The thing is,
Mother, that we don't ignore you on purpose. The thing is that
we all have busy lives, and things we want to do. We both have
to work, we're working people who have to make a living in
order to pay the mortgage on this big house and look after you.
And when we're not working, we have other things we want
to do sometimes. We want to go out, and spend time with our
children, and paint pictures, and read books. We can't be sitting with you talking every minute of the day and you have to
understand that."

Nancy says nothing, her knife jabbing at the potato.

Later on, when everybody is called for supper, Nancy refuses to get out of her armchair.

"I'm not coming."

"Supper time. Soup and lovely homemade bread and apple
pie. You helped make it, remember?"

"I'm. Not. Coming."

"Aren't you hungry?"

She looks at me, takes a breath. Thinks better of it. Then takes another.

"I know very well what you're trying to do. You're trying to get me out of here."

"That's right. It's supper time. It's just through there. That door. The kitchen. Your food is waiting for you."

"I know very well what you're doing. I'm not allowed out of here. I'm to stay here. I've been told that I'm to stay here and not move. I'm not to move a muscle. I'm not allowed in there, oh no, that's what she said, she said I was to stay put and not move. The people who own this place told me that I'm to stay right here and *I'm* not allowed anything to eat at all."

Scraps of information in Nancy's paranoia are traceable. I do tell her to "stay there" when I go off to get her supper. I do tell her she can't have a whole tin of shortbread to herself, that she's not allowed it (especially not five minutes before supper). These oddments get mangled, garbled, by the disease. Jigsaw pieces that don't fit are forced together to make a whole new picture.

I take her supper to her on a tray. The rest of us eat our dinner in silence, subdued by the outburst, hearing Nancy telling her soupspoon her troubles.

When I take her coffee in, she is crying. I crouch by her.

"What is it? What on earth's the matter?"

"It's nothing," she sobs. "Nothing at all. Just people being nasty to me. It's always happened so I shouldn't be surprised."

"What people?"

"Not you. I'm not talking about you. You're very nice. You're the only one that's nice. The rest of them are nasty to me. And they laugh at me, those nasty children. They laugh at me behind my back."

I can feel my hackles rising. "Don't you dare talk about my

children that way," I say hotly. "Those are your grandchildren, and one of them, your grandson, tried to help you today and you called him an arsehole."

The idea of Nancy calling anybody anything remotely this rude is pretty funny, in retrospect, but it isn't amusing at the time.

"Granny's gone to the dark side," Jack warns his friends when they come to tea. Jack and his friends can handle it, raising their eyebrows at each other and making themselves scarce, but I am a lot less sanguine.

I've wondered, since this period, whether Nancy was bullied as a child. Whether long-term memory is creating long shadows in her dealing with children, now that she's ill. Her grandchildren are indescribably sweet and tolerant, rushing to her aid whenever she's troubled, trying to anticipate her needs. So either the brain is inventing maliciously—can misfiring neurons be said to be malicious?—or there's something from the past that's got mixed in, released by the subconscious and bobbing to the surface.

Nancy's wandering at night, presumably looking for Morris. I am dimly aware of this, surfacing from sleep half a dozen times, aware of noises below. Doors opening and closing. Someone talking. But I can't wake myself up enough to go and do anything about it. When we come down in the mornings we find all the doors open, things rearranged, piles of Nancy's clothes on the pool table.

Chapter 8

Trust the instinct to the end, though you can render no reason.

—RALPH WALDO EMERSON

NANCY AND MORRIS HAVE HAD FIVE PROPERTY STAGES of life, which have mirrored what you might call the Five Ages of Nancy. These have been, in brief, apartment–house–apartment–bungalow–us. Property number one, the original apartment, was part of a period-house conversion in the city. They bought it before they were married and worked on it on weekends leading up to the big day. They graduated to property two, a stone-built row house at the end of a row, with its family bedrooms, little garden, handiness for the park and the primary school, as a prelude to the adoption of two children, first Chris and then his sister, who lives in Canada with her own young family and is rarely in touch. Downsizing to number three, a ground-floor retirement apartment, came at the point at which there were young granddaughters, and Morris could walk only with sticks. They were intending to stay at property three for the rest of their lives, but there were two other unexpected moves to come, as a response to encroaching dementia. Three, if you count the nursing home.

Alzheimer's crept up slowly, like Granny's footsteps in the game "What Time Is It, Mr. Wolf?" (Mr. Wolf isn't sure. Mr. Wolf has forgotten how to read a clock.) The first obvious clue was the classic one: forgetting things, being *absentminded*. "Where are the keys? Where? *What* clay pot on the dresser?"

But then, over three, four years a bad memory became something else. Nancy needed reminding about money and its rudimentary mathematics, how the door opened and was locked, and about things we'd just talked about. Eventually, under pressure, she saw her doctor and ended up at the memory clinic at the hospital. We'd had no encounters with dementia before, and stupidly we failed to realize that *memory clinic* is a euphemism. We'd ask, on the phone and on our visits, how things were, what the clinic had to say, but Nancy was vague and Morris studiedly vaguer. "I think she's getting on fine, though her memory's terrible. They've put her on some pills."

The pill, it turns out, was galantamine. Alzheimer's wasn't mentioned. It was on her file, though. A later doctor would mention it almost casually, would see our faces, would be shocked by our not knowing. "It helps with memory loss" was all that was said at the time, about the prescription; a fudge enacted by the clinic for an anxious spouse's sake, perhaps, or, more disingenuously, by Morris for ours. There's no cure for dementia. There's no partial cure. All that's available is a slowing down of the symptoms of fire damage. Sufferers' experience of the drugs available is patchy and inconsistent. They don't work for everyone. They're hit and miss, and usually only of short- to medium-term use.

The current drugs work by targeting the synapses, the gaps between neurons through which all information must pass if a brain is to function. To cross the synapse the electrical impulse becomes briefly a chemical entity, a neurotransmitter. It's as if lorries bring goods to the port and unload them briefly onto ships to cross a river to the other side, where other lorries wait to be loaded for the next road journey.

Of the four Alzheimer drugs currently prescribed, three of them—Aricept (donepezil hydrochloride); Reminyl, known as Razadyne in the United States (galantamine); and Exelon (rivastigmine)—work as acetylcholinesterase (AChE) inhibitors.

(The first of this class of drug to be launched in the United States, Cognex [tacrine], is now used only rarely because of the severity of side effects.) AChE is the enzyme that breaks down the neurotransmitter acetylcholine, getting rid of it once it's been used so that fresh neurotransmitter can be produced. In Alzheimer's fresh neurotransmitter isn't being produced as much, so the drugs work by keeping the old stuff going for longer and preventing it from breaking down. A fourth drug, a newer one called Ebixa, also known as Namenda (memantine), which may herald a new generation of drugs called NMDA receptor antagonists, blocks the overproduction of another neurotransmitter called glutamate, a glut of which causes cell damage. U.S. studies have found that Ebixa can be taken with one of the other sort of drugs to beneficial effect, but this, of course, is an expensive approach, and the UK National Health Service is unlikely to go for it. (More important, I'm told that its early promise has come to naught and it isn't much good anyway.) Additionally, it seems that these Alzheimer's drugs are proving in clinical practice to be quite good with other forms of dementia, specifically with suppression of bizarre behaviors, and are beginning to be used in place of antipsychotics. Antipsychotics are widely overprescribed. There's no doubt that in many cases dementia patients in homes are given them in order to make the staff's lives easier. It's estimated that around 100,000 people in nursing homes in the United Kingdom are misdosed or overdosed in this way, and many more in the United States, despite regular outcries in media such as the *New York Times:* people rendered doped-up and compliant. There must be a great many more on the drugs cared for at home, thanks to doctors' prescriptions. The legitimate use of antipsychotics may be helpful in moderate doses for particular problems in dementia, but there's no doubt they impair thinking and speaking abilities. In addition, it's estimated that

25 percent of those taking them will die prematurely as a direct result. Stroke is a particular risk.

By 2012 there should be another name on the market, to add to the Big Four. The benefits of Rember (methylene blue) have been the cause of excitement among those involved in the trials. Methylene blue isn't, it seems, a new drug at all, but one new to the treatment of Alzheimer's. It appears to be effective as a tau protein inhibitor, attacking the tangles. Unfortunately, it's likely that political questions, having to do with who will get it and how much it will cost, will shadow its UK launch publicity. Plus, it remains to be seen how effective the wonder drug will be in real time and on actual humans. As someone working in the field told me, "Brains are so blooming complicated that the potential benefits from drug effects are often not really well understood for years after the drug hits the general market and doctors in ordinary places on earth (as opposed to research clinics) get to use them routinely."

Until then, only the usual pharmaceutical suspects are available. It's no wonder that people look for alternative approaches, ginkgo biloba, fish oil, folic acid, turmeric (curcumin), and HRT (hormone replacement therapy) among them. The medical establishment is trying to think laterally. Blood pressure medications and cholesterol-reducing statins have shown promise. Great things are claimed for vitamin E, which in vast doses has been shown to slow the disease, though other studies pinpoint vast doses of vitamin E as a killer. Anti-inflammatories like ibuprofen may slow or even prevent Alzheimer's; inflammation in the brain is a busy area of research. More cheeringly, it seems that one generous alcoholic drink a day may be protective. Some little-publicized research has shown that smoking might, also. Of course, at this level of selection, it's what you die of that becomes the issue.

I wonder now how many years Nancy was having problems

before memory loss became obvious. Was there an even longer, slower fade than we thought? She'd not wanted to deal
with meals and cooking for years, had been strongly averse to
supermarket shopping for many years before that. Nancy's
known for hating supermarkets. Is that where it started, that
first tickle of dementia—in not being able to deal with the
navigational demands of Safeway? Recently researchers have
pinpointed the entorhinal cortex, which feeds into the hippocampus, as the more exact starting point of Alzheimer's in the
brain. There isn't merely memory consolidation at stake in the
entorhinal zone, but also mapping, mapping the location of
objects in relation to the self. Alzheimer's may announce itself
with navigational problems rather than memory loss as such.

It has the subtlest of beginnings, fuzzy and subjective.
There's no absolute starting point. It doesn't start with pain, a
suspicious lump, blue spots, an *attack*. It's easy for dementia to
be self-diagnosed, or even medically diagnosed, as something
else entirely. Natural aging. Middle-aged confusion. *Senior moments*. The doctor confesses he forgets just as easily and is just as
erratic—him, at only fifty-six—and not to worry, and it's hard
to argue. It's a creeping illness. It creeps up on people. People
get used to their own very slow changes and make allowances
for themselves. It's possible to muddle through life with conviction and survive perfectly well as a muddler, and among the
elderly it's considered reasonably normal. We use words like
dotty, and smile about it; being in a muddle is often endearing.
MCI, mild cognitive impairment, is after all only *mild,* and only
an *impairment*: It doesn't sound too threatening.

In his account of the seven stages of Alzheimer's, the
behavior-based guide to severity devised by Dr. Barry Reisberg in the United States twenty-five years ago and still widely
consulted, other people notice the changes only when they've
reached stage 3. Stage 1 has no impairment evident. That's the
slow burn. Stage 2 is the dotty stage, with intermittent memory

lapses (and intermittent *anything* can be explained away), forgetting where you put things, forgetting words and names. Described like that, most of us post-forty-five could, with the aid of hypochondria, believe ourselves at stage 2. Stage 3 has taken us only as far as MCI, when others begin to notice something amiss, and less endearing kinds of muddle arise—trouble retaining information, with short-term memory, with reading and organizing. We're still on the fringes of what we'd consider normal for the elderly in stage 4: trouble talking about world issues, trouble with mental arithmetic, trouble with trivial activities like making supper—these in themselves may not ring alarm bells. And yet it could have been ten years, the road from stages 1 to 4. Someone's had Alzheimer's for ten years and nobody's yet recognized it.

Stage 5 is considered the first of the three obvious dementia stages. At stage 5 help is needed. The sufferer might forget his own address, phone number, the names of family members, and be hazy on major autobiographical events. He begins to lose his grip on what day, month, year it is. He may need help with dressing. At stage 6, there are noticeable personality changes in play. The sufferer loses a coherent sense of his environment, is cut off from his own history, may not recognize his spouse. All of this brings fear, and in its wake, aggression. The person needs help with all domestic tasks, including toileting. There may be some incontinence. Wandering becomes an issue. Delusions and hallucinations may begin or worsen. He may talk to himself in the mirror and adopt compulsive behaviors.

Stage 7 casts the darkest shadow. The sufferer loses the ability to talk, walk, eat. Gradually he becomes bedridden, immobile, and helpless. The horrific thing, should we dwell on it too long, is that stage 7 has been known to last for six or more years. But not everybody gets to stage 7. These markers are, remember, just averaged out, just the rule from which exceptions spring.

Ralph Waldo Emerson (1803–1882) was an example of the long, slow fade. The American poet and essayist died of dementia (probably Alzheimer's, which is the only backdated diagnosis possible), a fate he'd already recognized by 1866, the date his son gives to "Terminus," which begins:

> It is time to be old,
> To take in sail:——
> The god of bounds,
> Who sets to seas a shore,
> Came to me in his fatal rounds,
> And said: "No more!
> No farther shoot
> Thy broad ambitious branches, and thy root.
> Fancy departs: no more invent;
> Contract thy firmament
> To compass of a tent.

Emerson would live for another sixteen years after writing this. The epigrammatic and quirky nature of his transcendentalism helped disguise his affliction until very late. Mark Twain famously made fun of him in a speech at a dinner five years before Emerson's death, parodying one of his poems, not realizing he was ill (though, in fact, Emerson was by then far too ill to take offense, as his daughter explained in a letter). Robert Graves (1895–1985), poet and author of *I, Claudius,* had an even slower fade. It's said by his friends and biographers that his dementia was apparent even in the 1960s, though he masked it well with outrageous eccentricity. Among elderly artists and writers, there is sometimes a difficulty in knowing where art stops and Alzheimer's starts. Graves became passionate about astrology and bowed to the moon. He became convinced that he was the mortal mouthpiece for the White Goddess. He was ill for a long time and spent the last decade of his life virtually in silence. Dementia took its time.

It's an oddity of the disease that the first phase can present itself quasi-positively. Sufferers may not be seen to be suffering. They might seem to be happier. Among the great ocean of Alzheimer's writing online and all its many miseries, there's the occasional early-diagnosed commentator, reporting on experiences in a way that seems near euphoric. People with early Alzheimer's have reported a heightened sensory experience of life: Perhaps the senses sharpen as the thinking and remembering self begins to dwindle.

THIS GIVES ME an understanding of how it seemed with Nancy in the mildly muddled early years. Nancy seemed a happier person and more relaxed. She made more of a fuss over her grandchildren, especially her toddler grandson, apple of her eye. The children were greeted with outstretched arms and Jack was invited onto her knee shortly after. The granddaughters were allowed to take Granny off to the bedroom and give her a full makeover. She'd return merrily in odd combinations of evening clothes, her hair stiff with gel, wearing stripes of blue eye shadow and heavily rouged.

The truth of things came out piecemeal. Things had reached a stage beyond forgetfulness. Morris and Nancy were beginning to fight: him accusing her of not listening; her defending herself energetically. Things had taken a downturn domestically—though even in her prime Nancy was never much of a cook. They both worked long hours and Nancy became a dab hand at short-cut cuisine; macaroni made with Campbell's tomato soup sauce stands out in the memory. But everybody worshipped Nancy's raspberry jam. There were never jokes or winks about the jam. A jar had such currency that my father hid his from the rest of us at home, on a high shelf in the kitchen. One of my earliest memories of Nancy sees her presiding over great bucket-sized preserving pans, sterilized jars set out ready. Ironically, one of my first conversations with her—while helping with the raspberries, and I can't remember how the subject came up—was about euthanasia. It would turn out to be a pet subject. "There's no point keeping people alive who are useless," she'd say, in addition to the usual line about "dogs in that state not left to suffer by the vet." I was afraid to inquire what "useless" meant. Looking back on it, I'm certain that elderly dementia sufferers would have been counted among the condemned.

After she and Morris moved from their house to their apartment, Nancy began sifting. It's typical Alzheimer's behavior to embark on pointless projects like turning out all the old linens, or books from the bookcase, and abandoning them half sorted on the floor. The power to organize simple tasks, like the few sequential steps that make up emptying out a drawer and restoring it to tidiness (life is all about sequential steps), is hindered and then obliterated by the advance of Alzheimer's into the frontal lobe. The impact of frontal lobe damage is enormous. When lobotomies were commonplace, its victims became passive and easy to handle. Unfortunately, they also lost the ability to make a sandwich or tie their shoes.

Then, on one visit to Edinburgh, we found the kitchen cupboards bare. Eventually the truth was admitted to. Morris couldn't any longer walk as far as the shop. Nancy could, but she couldn't find it. She'd go out to get milk and bread, a tin of luncheon meat, and come back without them. Some days it took her a long while to come back empty-handed, as if she'd been lost. Nancy, it transpired, hadn't been to the corner grocer for six months.

"Six months! But why didn't you tell us?"

"It's all right, though, because our neighbor does it for us, when we ask her," Morris said.

A home help was appointed for three mornings and things were stable for a while. I took charge of their food shopping. Morris dictated his list on the phone and I organized the supermarket to deliver.

They began to be prey to unscrupulous salesmen. Morris amassed a suitcase full of jewelry and watches, bought from a "friend" nearby who *knew somebody* and appeared regularly at the door with bargains. Four televisions were purchased, two hi-fi systems. Boxes of wine began appearing, stacked behind armchairs: Morris spent thousands ordering a massage chair, then canceled it and was only partially reimbursed. Brochures for new kitchens, double glazing, time shares, and computer systems littered the house, with local agents' names attached stapled on business cards. Rug hawkers called in unmarked vans.

Nancy continued to be busy. The bath and bed sheets were gray with grime, but the kitchen surfaces were cleaned over and over. The sink was scrubbed silver, and the dishes, greasy or not, were washed under cold running water.

Visiting with the children was becoming difficult. In the old days, Chris and I would have been able to take up the offer of an evening's babysitting and go to the cinema. Now that had to be abandoned. We'd get back and find wakeful children crying in the sofa bed the three of them shared in the study.

"What on earth did you do?" I'd ask.

"Nothing, really. We might have been a bit noisy. We were just excited. But Granny got annoyed and Granddad completely lost his temper." In the old days, there'd be a child-grandparental conspiracy to get us out of the apartment. It was a game we played and that we all enjoyed. Chris and I would lay down the rules—an early night, no adult TV, no sweets or fizzy drinks—knowing that flouting them was entirely the point. Sure enough, we'd get home at midnight to see children scurrying to bed, chocolate round their mouths, and hear happy giggling. But those days seemed to be over.

Nancy and Morris became isolated, cut off from old friendships. Did they jump or were they pushed? It's hard to say. In all likelihood there was both jumping and pushing. Nancy had become a social liability and Morris, perhaps, thought himself protective of her in cutting the ropes that had so long linked them to their Edinburgh circle. For whatever reason, the Saturday night out with the gang came to a dead stop. Nancy's oldest friend, Carol, was deterred from visiting. People were fended off and kept at a distance. Morris dug the moat and took up the drawbridge. And gradually, his relationship with Nancy changed from husband to keeper.

Chapter 9

There seems something more speakingly incomprehensible in the powers, the failures, the inequalities of memory, than in any other of our intelligences.

—JANE AUSTEN

THE MOVE UP FROM EDINBURGH WAS PROMPTED BY health incidents. Morris had fallen several times, and on one of these occasions broken his shoulder. Nancy had been admitted to hospital twice with a blockage in the bowel, thanks to poor nutrition and dehydration. Chris found his life punctuated by panicked phone calls. The rest of us found our lives punctuated by long absences, the Land Rover roaring off late at night on another rescue mission.

There were high expectations of the bungalow. Theoretically the bungalow was perfect: two miles from us in a small development just off the center of a charming village. We were confident that this, a supervised life, would work, so the fact of its being so spectacularly disastrous was doubly surprising.

Health professionals have said to us since that it was a mistake to move Nancy to the peninsula, but they are missing the point. Moving her from the city apartment was the error. She'd moved into the apartment ten years earlier healthy, mildly impaired at worst. When she left she was ill with Alzheimer's, but she had a residual identity there, residual mapping of her location, and this provided her with some bearings. It doesn't really matter how many times you move an Alzheimer's patient once functionally the hippocampus is gone. Everything is new, every day, and, living in the present tense, the best that can be hoped for is present happiness.

By the time she moved north, Nancy had lost the ability to lay down new memories, literally lost it. The hippocampus was wiped, deleted, shot through with holes. It wasn't that she *had trouble remembering things,* a phrase easy to use but that hints at a patchy up-and-down kind of unreliability, books misfiled in the personal mental library. This wasn't about memory retrieval, but about memory formation. It wasn't a Romantic matter, of locked-off bookshelves and mental caverns without sunshine, but physiological and technical. No new memories could be made. Nancy couldn't learn her new surroundings. She couldn't map the village, nor learn the layout of the bungalow. She'd ask Morris, twenty times a day, how to get to the bathroom and where the kettle was. She patrolled the house, wearing a groove in the new carpets, wringing her hands and weeping. Every day she asked if they could go home. Morris wasn't sympathetic.

"When will you get it into your head? We live here. This is home now."

But that was exactly and entirely the problem. She couldn't get it into her head. Morris spent long periods sitting in the courtyard at our house smoking, Nancy dancing attendance, asking what she should do for him and failing to carry out his instructions.

"I said my stick! My stick! I need my stick to get back into the house, not the newspaper!"

"Ashtray, Nancy, ashtray. You know what an ashtray is. Go and find Andrea. What do you mean, 'who?' Look, that's her there, in the kitchen. Kitchen! Through the door. Where are you going now? The door, door! For Christ's sake!"

"Why are Granny and Granddad always arguing?" Jack asked. "And why doesn't Granny know what a fork is?"

When Nancy had a minor stroke and spent three days in hospital, Morris moved in with us. He sat crumpled by the fire, lamenting. "Nancy, my Nancy! I can't lose her. She's all I have. What will I do? What will become of me? I don't think she's going to make it. She's going to die and leave me all alone." Nancy, meanwhile, was fast becoming the ward's most challenging resident. She heckled the nursing staff. All the doors had to be locked and windows secured because she was determined to escape. She did a remarkable impression of somebody not remotely at death's door.

ZOOM FORWARD A year. It's the end of October, our first autumn in the north, and we have friends to stay for Halloween. Nancy is a lamb. Nancy is a trouper. Nancy is conversational and light of heart. Then the health visitor drops in to see us and chats to Nancy, and Nancy handles this magnificently— seems actively, intently to be *handling* it.

"How are you, Nancy?" the health visitor asks.

"Can't complain," Nancy says. "Well, I could complain, of course, but I won't." (Laughter.) Wit will always win the argument. "And how are you, yourself?" she goes on, all frowning and earnest solicitude. "Are you keeping well? You're obviously very busy. But keeping well, I hope." The health visitor is charmed. The health visitor, on her departure, is heard to use the word *sweet*. Instinctively, provoked by the institutional air and antiseptic smell of the visitor, Nancy knew she had to perform well and Nancy dug deep. The health visitor was managed. She was wrangled. This seemingly contrived approach to social situations is a new feature in Nancy's decline but also, it turns out, classic Alzheimer's. The American dementia blogs, particularly, are full of astounded remarks about severely ill and abusive relatives being winning, engaging, almost like their old selves when doctors come to call.

Dramatic news from the hospital: Morris needs a second operation, having dislocated his hip while recuperating, probably through inadvisable crossing of legs. He's sent back to the city, the rest of us into despondency.

November 5 is the windiest Guy Fawkes Night we've ever seen. We abandon the idea of the traditional bonfire (though we've never made and burned a puppet Guy Fawkes to go on the top, so it wasn't ever that traditional), and then even the packet of sparklers is judged too dangerous to use. The gale blows and howls round the eaves and the heating's snuffed out. It's 7:00 P.M. Up the back stairs, in the guest apartment, the last B and B guests of the year have retreated to bed and are watching a DVD from under the duvet. The wind roars down the chimneys and the drawing room is full of smoke. It appears to be windy *inside* the house. The next morning, our visitors attempt to walk the beach in a sandstorm, though summer's lovely strand is kelp and refuse scattered. They attempt (inadvisably) a walk on the cliffs. They go out in the car for lunch and come back soaked to the bone. They are relieved to go home.

The north of Scotland needs a broader vocabulary for weather, such as the Inuit are said to have. We need thirty words for wind in all its variations. Its principal variant is aggressive. It slams. It blows dog ears flat, knocks children over, gets into a coat and sends it soaring. It's best not to open an umbrella unless the full Mary Poppins experience is desired. It forces entry into the esophagus, making breathing feel like work. Hats become offerings. They're whisked away, dropped into far fields, into the sea, off cliffs, deposited muddily on roads awaiting their next victim. An old scarf, very long and broad in a brown check, has become my constant companion. The scarf is applied to the head, wrapped securely and tied at the neck. Scarf, long waxed coat, Wellies: I don't leave the house without these three items. It's my new silhouette. A Barbour bag lady.

In late November, we wake after a stormy night to find that an enormous chunk of the flower garden wall is missing, some twenty feet across and eight feet high. Sheep were sheltering behind the wall and two of them were killed, crushed under falling stone. The farmer comes round to see us. His reputation has preceded him so we expect to be presented with a bill, or with some cunning and unusual revenge. Instead he's philosophical. These things happen. He won't hear of payment. He helps stack a delivery of hay bales into the barn, and goes off whistling.

I start writing in bed, late at night and very early in the morning, the rest of the household asleep. In daylight hours it's proving impossible, that is, until 4:00 P.M. when the cavalry arrives, disheveled and hungry with schoolbags on shoulders. I leave toast-eating granny-sitters in charge and sneak off to get on with things. It doesn't work. Nancy comes shuffling in after me.

"Excuse me, lady. I'm sorry to bother you, but I need to ask you something. Have you seen my husband?"

I close the laptop lid and we have the conversation, the full-length one that reprises her life so far, her marriage, her children, her retirement from work, her move here, and Morris's accident.

"Oh," she says. "I wasn't told any of that. Would be nice if people told me things."

She shuffles out. Then she shuffles back. "Excuse me, lady, I need to ask you something. . . ." It all begins again, an almost word-perfect repetition. The only way out is to hide, and we take turns spending prolonged periods secreted upstairs, where Nancy doesn't go; she has developed a fear of stairways.

My transformation into her mother is complete. She wants to be where I am. If we're apart for more than a few minutes, she begins to fret. When she finds me in the drawing room her voice is full of relief.

"Ahh, there you are, I was worried."

I explain that I'm trying to get a few minutes' peace, reading a book by the fire. Would she like to sit with me and look at a book?

"Yes, I'd love it. I've been all on my own, nobody speaking to me at all." She then proceeds to free-associate. I put the book down.

"Okay, but as I say, I'm trying to read just now, so . . . Listen, do you think you could mind the children for me for a while?"

"Oh yes, I'd be happy to. Where are they?"

I take her back to her sitting room and introduce her to her grandchildren, whom she greets as if for the first time, introducing herself conscientiously. Then I rush back to the fireside and the novel, knowing I have seven or eight minutes until she shuffles in again.

"Ahh, there you are, I was worried."

EMOTIONAL, SUBCONSCIOUS ASSOCIATIONS are in the ascendant. She can spend all day bearing a grudge and render the consolations of the afternoon film useless by monologuing over the top of it. And the delusions are beginning. Nancy's chief delusion is that she's in charge.

"Nobody ever talks to me here. Nobody pays any attention to me at all. I may as well be dead. People are always telling me what to do—*me*! And I own this house. They work for me. They all work for me." Jack comes into the room and then retreats again. "Those horrible children laugh at me and call me names behind my back. . . ."

They go on and on for hours, these monologues. Luckily a response isn't expected. It's more in the way of a performance. I am learning to tune her out. I do the ironing standing in her sitting room and train my mind elsewhere, while Nancy sits and narrates her way through a series of grisly daytime TV programs.

Eventually even television fails. Jack, trying to tell her not to go outside because it's raining, is called a bastard and then a bitch for good measure. It's difficult to convey just how sinister these verbal attacks are, so out of the blue and so quietly passionate, her expression so malevolent. They wrong-foot all of us emotionally, but the children especially, who are shocked by the suddenness with which the mood turns. I understand their tears and hurt. It's like having your face slapped, is very like it, by someone you thought was on your team—slapped hard and unexpectedly.

There's an upset almost every afternoon, and because it's the children under attack and nothing else is as provoking as a bully, I find myself yelling at her, Nancy yelling back. I contrive to do this when there are other people in the house, friends of the children or plumbers or electricians, the tradesmen pausing to listen, shocked rigid by the shouting. "Listen to that! She's screaming at her poor mother-in-law, that sweet, gray-haired old lady!" They're rooted to the spot. Visiting children turn wide-eyed and silent as I rip out of the kitchen and tear a strip off Granny. Nancy denies everything, always. "I did not. Did not. Did not. That boy is a liar. A liar, always a liar, a nasty little liar, telling lies. It's all lies and rubbish."

I can't help myself from insisting that she is wrong and that she's behaved badly. I can't seem to stop myself from insisting she change her ways. Why do I waste my breath? Morality, misplaced and useless, is at the heart of it. Families are constructed from a shared sense of justice, and sail out on its complicated hidden currents. The children have been indoctrinated in the ways of fairness. Granny's dementia smashes right through their early training and leaves a trail of moral wreckage that constantly needs to be accounted for.

Help is close at hand. The Charity. The Charity employs people to provide short home-based bursts of respite care. The dictionary defines *respite* as an interval of rest and relief, but we define it as time to act, to move and act unhindered, to resume life, if only for the short period in which someone else is in charge. If it wasn't for The Charity, many families would have no home-visit respite at all. We are offered two sessions a week, on Monday and Wednesday mornings. The Monday caregiver, Sian, a Rubenesque Essex blonde, deals with Angry-Nancy by imposing routine on her. The routine is a brisk itinerary encompassing hot shower, hairstyling, car trip, shopping, coffeehouse, and home. The Wednesday caregiver, Harriet, on the point of retirement herself, is a lithe, warmhearted northerner with kind blue eyes. If Sian's approach is dogged, unemotive, unflappable persistence, then Harriet's is more in the way of love-bombing. "Come on now, lovey, you can put your shoes on yourself, a big girl like you. . . . Yes! That's right! That's brilliant. Clever girl." The only thing Nancy really doesn't like is the packet of felt tips Harriet brings with her, and the bumper book of coloring, featuring girls with lambs and flower baskets, and elephants in lederhosen driving cars. Nancy can't color inside the fat black lines and doesn't see why she should try. Once Harriet is waved off on Wednesday lunchtimes, the pages left behind for Nancy to finish are verbally abused, ripped into pieces, and thrown in the fire.

THE CHARITY MANAGER is on the phone, asking how things are going with the caregivers, and I am properly grateful but frank about Nancy's bitter mood swings. "You'll need to think about residential care at some point," she says.

"At some point," I agree, "but we're hoping that Morris's return will restore the equilibrium. We should have a few years in the arrangement yet, I hope."

"You should talk to the social work department," she says brightly. "You could get some more help. You could get a care manager to coordinate everything."

"I'm sure," I say, "but we'd really rather not institutionalize things or get too many experts wading in. We manage fine. We struggle along."

The following week, we admit our first expert to the house. He talks briefly to Nancy and at length to the two of us and convinces us that joining in is possible as a nonjoiner, in situations like this. Chris and I are reluctant. We don't want to be part of the care machinery and enter the social work filing system. We don't think Morris would want it, either. How will he react, in any case, on his return, to the new Nancy that Sian and Harriet have created, the one that's talked to as if she is five and behaves accordingly? How will he deal with their taking charge of Nancy and redefining her, leaving him a helpless witness?

"We'll leave things as they are for now," the expert says. "But what I can do for you is organize a program of nursing home respite for next year. You're entitled to six weeks. I'll book Nancy in for six separate weeks, and I'll be in touch with dates."

Chapter 10

ALZHEIMER'S DISEASE IS NAMED AFTER A GERMAN psychiatrist and neuropathologist. In a lecture in 1906, Alois Alzheimer reported seeing the characteristic plaques and tangles in the brain of fifty-five-year-old Auguste Deter, a sufferer of early-onset disease who'd died earlier that year. "*Ich hab mich verloren* [I have lost myself]," she had said to Alzheimer, when first she was admitted to the Frankfurt asylum at age fifty-one.

Alzheimer didn't discover the disease as such. It had been observed and written about before, notably by an early brain researcher named Beljahow, who reported brain plaques in dementia in 1887. Likewise, the presence of tangles had been announced by other neuroscientists before Alzheimer gave his lecture, but nothing formal had got into the textbooks. What was remarkable and newsworthy about Auguste Deter's case was her disease's very early onset. This helped make a splash. It was a sensation. Publicity was the key. Alzheimer's boss, friend, and coresearcher, Emil Kraepelin, happened also to be a powerful figure in neurology and in science publishing. Today regarded as the father of mental disorder classification, Kraepelin named the disease Alzheimer's in 1910, in the course of a description in his new textbook. He did so almost casually, in a paragraph of notorious vagueness, referring to "this

Alzheimer's Disease," a reference that surprised his readers and colleagues. To quibble, the label *Alzheimer's* ought in all justice to have been confined to the early-onset variant only, since that's what the Auguste Deter research was concerned with. It's also interesting to note that Alzheimer himself didn't think the late-onset condition ought to be classified as a disease as such. It was his contention that Alzheimer's happens to all brains in the end—they wear out, like hips and knees—it's just the speed and volume of plaque growth, he argued, that marks the syndrome out. The speed is remarkable. Neuron loss in Alzheimer's has been calculated as ten times the speed of that entailed in normal aging.

A sense of theater, a gift for PR, the pressing financial need to impress funding bodies: It's suggested that all these led Krae-pelin to make Alzheimer the eponym. Kraepelin's battle with his great rival Sigmund Freud, as to whether such disorders were organic or psychiatric in origin, was another factor; Alzheimer had been supportive in putting Freud in his place. It helped that Alzheimer's time was one of diagnostic breakthrough. Modern Zeiss microscopes (the original slides have been discovered and preserved) and the advent of silver nitrate tissue-staining process (the innovation of Alzheimer's colleague Franz Nissl), which illuminated slices of the brain as never before, meant Alzheimer's work had the benefit of technological advance over that of his rivals.

Alzheimer had left Frankfurt and was working for Kraepe-lin in Munich by the time Auguste Deter died in 1906. Her brain and spinal cord were sent to him by train in a box.

Her case was unusual and even today would be regarded so, not only because she was so young—fifty-one is very early onset and fifty-five a very early dementia death—but also be-cause it came on so aggressively and fast. The polite confu-sion she showed on admission very quickly declined into raving and wailing and wordless wounded animal misery. A stark black-and-white photograph of her while in the asylum shows a woman who appears to be in her seventies, her brow furrowed into deep ridges, her face ravaged and baggy, a bewildered look in her eyes.

ALZHEIMER'S OWN RECORD of their first conversation survives. He writes that she looks helpless. He asks her name.

"Auguste," she tells him.

"And what is your husband's name?"

"Auguste."

"Your husband?"

"Ah, my husband."

She doesn't appear to understand that it's a question.

"Are you married?" he persists.

"To Auguste," she says.

"How long have you been here?" he asks her.

"Three weeks," she says with confidence (though in fact she was admitted the day before).

She can still identify a pen, bag, key, diary, and cigar.

She is given pork and cauliflower for lunch, but when asked what she's having, answers "Spinach." When asked again she says, "Potatoes and horseradish."

He notes that objects shown to her are forgotten about almost immediately. In between she seems to have an obsessive interest in twins.

He asks her to write her name. She starts to write "Frau" and then gives up. Several attempts are made to write Auguste. First Augh. Then Auguse D, leaving out the *t*. That evening, Alzheimer writes, her conversation is full of non sequiturs and obsessive elements like perseverations, in which sufferers return to a subject, an idea, a phrase, again and again without making their meaning clear. (It's not so much that they persevere with a subject, but that the subject perseveres with them.)

★ ★ ★

THERE'S AN IRONIC footnote to the story. Auguste Deter's cause of death appears principally to have been arteriosclerosis of the brain: what's now classified as vascular dementia, rather than Alzheimer's disease. There's also a poignant footnote. Auguste's husband, on delivering her to the Frankfurt asylum, complained about her unreasonable jealousy. She was convinced, he said, that he was having an affair with a neighbor and had become irrational about it. Apparently he married this neighbor the year after Auguste died. Just because you're paranoid, it doesn't mean they're not out to get you.

On his way to a new job in Breslau in 1912, Alzheimer became ill on the train with a sore throat, which led in turn to rheumatic fever. He died in 1915 of heart failure, in effect from complications of tonsillitis. He was fifty-one.

Chapter 11

The real voyage of discovery consists not in seeking new landscapes but in having new eyes.

—MARCEL PROUST

DECEMBER, AND WE ARE PLUNGED INTO DARKNESS. IT'S dark when the children go off to school, dark long before they come home. The daylight window shrinks to seven hours of pearly gray, the morning half opening its eye; the nights are profoundly black and long. But into this darkness comes a great light. A twinkle light. Christmas. Thank God for Christmas.

Morris is still in the city hospital but, as a result of Chris's ongoing appeals, is returned to the local hospital a week before the day. He's been put on Prozac for his depression. The hospital consultant wonders aloud if Morris is succumbing to dementia. Depression, particularly in the elderly, is often misdiagnosed as Alzheimer's, and vice versa.

I sit upstairs in the bay window of the upper sitting room and try to work. It's difficult to concentrate. I'm becoming a connoisseur of weather systems, watching fronts invade and recede, break, roll, gather, disperse. There are weird lighting effects, lurid green clouds, and the winter sea is mercury silver, thick and lazy, lapping viscous onto the beach. Harriet's singsong voice echoes up from downstairs. Harriet's adopted approach is Not to Stop Talking. She blocks Nancy's monologues by providing her own.

"Now, dear, shall we get a nice cup of tea? A cup of tea

would be lovely, wouldn't it? A lovely cup of tea. Right then, here we go, into the kitchen. Oopsadaisy and along to the kettle. Here's the kettle and we lift it. Now what do we do with it? Fill it with water, that's right. Here we go then, darling, here we go, along to the tap. Can you turn the tap on? That's right, what a girl you are, what a clever girl. And off again. Good. That's very good. Now we need cups. . . ." She must be exhausted to the point of annihilation when she leaves here. She doesn't stop narrating for three hours straight.

Nancy's become fixated on the kitchen. Perhaps it's to do with Christmas busyness, the spice fruit pie making, the aromas, or perhaps it's to do with her own definition of womanliness, this not being able to stay away, haunting the stove and the sink. I can tell it's her who's coming into the kitchen, even if the children are home, because of the struggle with the handle, and the way the door opens ever so slowly. Then she's there, saying the same thing every time. "Oh. Sorry. Sorry, didn't know anybody else was here. Sorry."

"Come in, Nancy," I say. "It's fine. It's just me."

"Oh, it's yourself. Well, that's fine." She walks the length of the room, turns, and goes back, wringing her hands and muttering. Goes along the length of the hall, wringing her hands. "I'm so useless, I'm not any good for anything, I'm no use to anybody, I may as well be dead."

She's become compulsive about going through doors. Later, I come across a paper about frontal lobe damage and visual prompts, in connection with wandering, which advises covering doorknobs with handkerchiefs or something similar. Alzheimer's can damage the decision-making process so badly that a prompt like a door handle becomes, in the sufferer's mind, an instruction. There's no particular content to the trying of door handles, the neurologist author says. It isn't necessarily anything to do with escape. Just a recognition that handles need turning, translating itself into the burden of having to turn them. It might actually be a relief, he says, to have the stimulus removed.

The busier the household gets, cooking and decorating and preparing for Christmas, the meaner Nancy's mood. There's protracted complaining about The Woman, the one who makes her do everything and does none of the work herself. I find myself wondering if it would be better for female Alzheimer's sufferers to have male caregivers. Nancy would be happier with a man in my place. She'd get to flirt with him. She'd probably be more respectful—women of her generation have a natural deference, the kind that feeds men first and takes the leavings. She'd not be preoccupied with this jostling for matriarchal precedence. Though sexual confusion might become an issue. Dementia patients can suffer an embarrassing loss of inhibition. Lately, Nancy has made suggestions that make Chris squirm. "Come to bed with me, come on," she says to him. "I'll warm you up all right. Come and cuddle up," patting the mattress suggestively.

Among the confusion and rage are flashes of good humor. I can make her good humor flash. If I worked harder to make her happy, it would flash oftener and longer. I'm aware of this. It's a fertile source of self-reproach. I can take her by the hands and cheer her up, with smiles and tone of voice and suggestions of things we might do together. They have to be things we do together. Things she could do alone don't work. But if I begin a sentence with "Why don't you and I . . ." her face lights up.

"Will you come and look at the drawing room with me?"

"Yes, of course. What will we do there?"

"Come and tell me what you think about the decor." I lead her into the room. We hold hands now when we're together. "Look. Green walls. Horrible. Pond green. A pond-that's-gone-off-and-smells kind of green."

Nancy's giggling. "You're right, you're right! It's horrible. I've always hated green."

I know that, Nancy.

"I'm going to get a repro wallpaper," I say. "I'm thinking of one of the chinoiserie style ones with birds and trees. What do you think?"

"Oh, but look at that," she says, pointing in admiration at one of the twin sofas by the fire. "That's gorgeous. That's gorgeous, isn't it?"

"Do you like it?"

"I love it."

"Even though it's green?"

"It isn't green, is it?"

"It's a sort of greeny-blue. Turquoise."

"Oh no. It's green. I hate green. It's the only color I really hate, to be quite truthful. I don't like it at all."

I persuade her to sit on one of the green sofas, and go and fetch a pot of tea.

"Ooh, cake. I like cake."

I know that, Nancy.

She eats and drinks and rubs her hands together, looking into the fire, logs crackling and spitting.

"Did they say when they'd be coming back?" she asks suddenly.

"Who?"

"The boys."

"Do you mean . . ."

"I mean the boys. My brothers."

"You only have one brother, don't you? I thought you only had one. Angus. In Australia."

"He's in Australia? Why didn't anybody say so?"

"He's been there over forty years, Nancy. Have some more cake."

She eats it, looking thoughtful. Then she says, "When are my brothers coming?"

HER FAMILY IS on her mind, it seems. Later, in the early evening, as I sit with her watching a nature documentary, she says, "When did he say he was coming back?"

"Who?" I'm reading the paper, not really listening. That's the kind of bad mother I am.

"My father."

The newspaper dips. Our eyes meet.

"Your father died a long time ago, Nancy, when your children were small."

(As you can see, I'm inconsistent with the validation habit. Often it's simply forgetfulness. I'm too used to telling the truth, bad at remembering to play along with the delusions.)

"I don't have children," Nancy says, mildly outraged. "I never married."

Don't bite. Don't. I obey, raising the paper again.

"When did he say he'd be back?"

"Who, Nancy?"

"My father. He isn't usually this late."

Nancy often refers to her childhood, but always in this same impersonal way. It's on her mind, but floats free of content. I've never heard her refer to the far past, to the 1930s, for instance, when she was a child, in any other way than this. I'd expected that the loss of short-term memory in Alzheimer's would bring the long-term memory sharply into focus. I've been reading Patrick Leigh Fermor's books about his epic walk across Europe just prior to the Second World War, which he wrote largely from memory decades later, the earliest of his notebooks having been lost during the trek. He said that writing the account was like trying to reconstruct a dinosaur from a miscellaneous bag of bones. I didn't expect the whole dinosaur skeleton from Nancy, but I expected to be shown the bag of bones at least, and nothing remotely like that has happened. She has vague persistent cravings for her parents—her father especially—and talks a lot about the "brothers," but that's as far as it goes. No telling details emerge, have ever emerged, and didn't, not even when I first knew her. I don't know anything about her. Chris doesn't know much more. Morris isn't expansive on the question.

I sit with Nancy in front of the television and escape down my own wormhole, the one provided by the Internet, laptop balanced on lap. Somebody out in the odd, dislocated world of anonymous, typed-and-not-spoken conversation makes a lighthearted remark about the spiritual advantages of Alzheimer's. I don't bother shouting him down, as I know from previous experience that hundreds will be racing to do just that. Dementia caregivers are everywhere and fatuity isn't tolerated. The person (no gender ascribed, even) makes the point that living in the moment, only in The Now, is surely the target state of Buddhist teachings; that Nirvana is a state of perfection attained by being cut off from past and future and their attendant states of wanting and anxiety. I can see what they're driving at and it's an interesting starting point for a discussion, but it's a debate that will never take place, as the self-appointed moral guardians who cluster at all such sites zoom in for the kill, hungry for the acclaim that will follow. Unfortunately, a state of bliss isn't the end point of Alzheimer's. Quite the reverse. The reality of having no past or future is that it isn't a state of perfection but of absence. The brain can't handle the absence and a chaotic, scrabbling sort of panic for order and meaning ensues. The Buddhist idea of living in The Now is, surely, something achieved through dealing with past and future, and not their absence—of quenching their demands and silencing their voices. These are sleeping dogs, not missing dogs. In a state of Nirvana we'd have total control over them, reconciled, having triumphed. An end to wanting and anxiety isn't ever going to be achieved through amnesia.

WILD WEATHER. IT'S too cold to do anything much, other than huddle by the stove and drink tea and eat muffins. I could do this with Nancy, of course, and do. But doing it alone seems like a treat. It amuses visitors that all of us in the family have adopted a great thick blanket each and wear these like cloaks in the house. I sit by the stove with my blanket tightly wrapped, just a hand and a paperback sticking out. Bitter, scouring north winds blow, gale force 8 or 9, not the strongest we've had but impressively gusty, and sufficient, earlier, to blow my new striped hat off my head, right over the top of the coach house and into the sheep field next door. It's my own fault. I know about hats. In any case, it's irretrievable: There's a foot of mud at least to navigate and the damn thing has disappeared under a stampede of ewes, charging toward me, hungry and hoping for food. The chickens huddle together under the laburnum tree. I take hay to the horse paddock and am almost blown over. The poor horses chase wispy escaped sections around the field as it blows along like tumbleweed.

We have a Christmas party at home and invite everybody we know or have come across since we arrived. Neighbors, other school parents, villagers, people we've met through gallery visits, the organic farmers from over the hill. Over a hundred people turn up and I worry that I'll have to introduce everybody but, of course, it's only us who are strangers. Everyone else is connected in the firm, elastic web of rural relationships and they greet each other like the old friends that they are. We have hired musicians for the evening, a fiddle player and a guitarist. I place them in a corner of the drawing room, they start to play, and immediately, as if given the nod, the fire begins billowing smoke. Nancy circulates, asking everybody if this is

their house, thanking bemused guests for inviting her, repri-
manding six-year-olds for running, and getting sloshed on
whisky. She retreats to her armchair and half a dozen kind
souls gather round her to chat. I am visited by a surge of well-
being, rightness, and good fortune. This is a good community,
and it's Christmas. The hall table is piled with presents. The
night is crisp and snowy. Cars are parked all along the drive, half
on the lawns and paddocks, all along the verges of the road.
People arrive with cold feet and go home tipsy, squeaking along,
leaving trails in the white, shouting "Happy Christmas" into the
dark.

I've been reading about Marcel Proust. His hero in *In Search
of Lost Time* (*À la recherche du temps perdu,* also known as *Re-
membrance of Things Past*) has an epiphany, a moment of physical and psychic joy, synthesizing childhood recall and a sense
of the unity of life, while dipping a madeleine into a cup of
lime blossom tea. This much is well known. Proust's experience of memory was multisensory, engaging taste and smell,
and was auditory. Other people have told me they hear music
in their dreams and in recollecting, though I never hear music
in mine, which tend to be faded celluloid moments with the
sound turned down low. Proust insists that it isn't necessary to
go out in search of a connection with the Sublime. He finds
meaning in small domestic details. He says that the ordinary
world of eating and drinking and being alive is full of wonder
and beauty and charm, and ours is the ordinary collective failure of failing to look at and relish it properly. (I do sometimes
wonder what else was in the lime blossom tea.) In any case,
Proust's life can hardly be described as dreary, or burdened by
necessary altruism. He was blessed by untroubled self-absorption.
Ill, fragile, hypochondriac, he still managed a lively Parisian
social life, had servants, lived at home, and was fussed over
throughout by his mother until she died when he was thirty-
four. He inherited the equivalent of £3 million, and spent as

much of his life as he wished in writing absurdly long novels in bed. "Proust on the Peninsula" is a book that will never be written.

We have neighbors for Christmas lunch, neighbors whose old kitchen's been ripped asunder, but whose new kitchen didn't quite arrive in time, and who were contemplating microwaved turkey for five. We go into town to see Morris late on Christmas afternoon. The starkly cube-based bungalow interior of the hospital smells mildly of figgy pudding, a new aroma to add to its usual bleach-and-plastics, sweat-and-gravy smell. The nurses are giddy, teasing, prompting jollity like summer-camp counselors. Sad swaths of thin green and red tinsel droop from ceilings. A little plastic tree is gaudy with baubles. Despite all this, Morris is not going to play the Christmas game. Presents don't cheer him up. He opens them all with an air of great monotony, says little, doesn't wish the children a happy Christmas. Nancy sits by him with her eyes fixed on me, the question in them unmistakable: What on earth am I doing here? The difference is that she means it literally.

Chapter 12

When a lot of remedies are suggested for a disease, that means it can't be cured.

—ANTON CHEKHOV

BECAUSE THERE'S NO SINGLE, UNIFIED THEORY OF ALZheimer's, teams across the world are working on different bits of it, hoping that their approach will prove to be the key that unlocks the disease. Rather like the Indian fable about the six blind men trying to identify an elephant, some research programs deal with the trunk, some with the tail, some with the leg and others with the ears, some with the torso and others with the tusks, and all have different ideas about what it is they're identifying. It's a race, not just because cracking Alzheimer's this year could save hundreds of millions of people in years to come (it's a prestigious race) but also because the saving of hundreds of millions of people will involve billions of packets of drugs (it's also a profitable race). There are fortunes to be made here, beyond the dreams of avarice. The latest estimate online put the dementia drugs market at $37 billion, and that was several years out of date, and is, of course, the pre-breakthrough figure, should the breakthrough ever come. Though it's possible—some scientists say probable—that Alzheimer's will never be cured as such, but will be managed with better drugs that keep it at bay, rather like HIV is managed today.

As far as causes of Alzheimer's go, there are two main camps.

One of them, what you might call the plaque orthodoxy, is much bigger and better funded than the other. The plaque orthodoxy says that the formation of plaques is the key process. The other camp, the tau heresy, begs to differ. It suggests that plaque is a red herring and that the answer lies in the tangles, the crumpling and snagging of the ladder rungs in the microtubules, the neuron's internal communication lines. Work by the tau camp has focused on the adherence of surplus phosphorous molecules onto the tau protein, arguing this is the key process of Alzheimer's, most probably caused by a genetic switch that could be turned off.

The plaque orthodoxy looks for ways to defuse the beta-amyloid crisis that seems to take place in the brain of sufferers, creating characteristic aggregations between neurons, clogging the neural glue with what look like suspect moles, crusty rounded lumps of something unevenly brownish. Bits of the cells that produce the neurotransmitter acetylcholine break down and become part of the plaque blobs. The plaque orthodoxy, which has been in place now for over twenty years, sees tangles as mysteriously secondary. Some tau heretics have a stiff rebuttal to this: Plaques, they say, are not only a red herring, but might be heroes rather than villains. Plaque, they say, is a sign of the brain trying to protect itself from something (the something that causes the tau to mangle). Plaque, they point out, has been seen in quantity in other instances of brain damage. Alzheimer himself was a tau man.

Don't go away with the impression that this is a gentlemanly dispute (though it's true that gentlemanly disputes have been taken into the woods at dawn with pistols). Pistols at dawn is more like it. Pro-tau scientists have had enormous trouble getting research grants or getting their results published in medical journals. The plaque orthodoxy has become quite medieval in its tolerance of heretics. So it's heartening to see that the latest wonder drug, Rember, is a tau-directed one. Perhaps the orthodoxy is being challenged now. I hope so. I hope the tau-research-blocking drug companies have the good grace to look a little sheepish.

The question is, what's really behind the mechanism, whether beta-amyloid or tau? What's making beta-amyloid run wildly out of hand; what's going on with the tau-tangling phosphorous? Presently, there are two answers: (a) genetic and (b) environmental. It's conventional to ascribe the root causes of Alzheimer's to a combination of both. A genetic predisposition and an environmental trigger: that's mainstream science's current best guess.

There are those inclined to lay the blame entirely on environment. Those who insist that Alzheimer's, though not a new condition, is essentially a modern condition, a zeitgeist condition, the defining twenty-first-century disease, also tend to point the finger at multiple pollution. And once pollution is mentioned, a whole underworld of subgroups comes to light. In the United States, there's been a widespread scare about amalgam fillings in teeth, and the resultant potential for mercury poisoning. Another points the finger at aluminum and other metals in the drinking water; yet another claims it can show evidence that pesticide poisoning in food is to blame. Manganese is spoken of suspiciously. These lines of inquiry may get somewhere or nowhere.

Two other theories doing the rounds:

1. That Alzheimer's is a prion disease. Prions are peculiar things, infectious proteins whose molecules nudge up to healthy cells and corrupt them. The best known prion disease is called variant CJD, or the human form of mad cow disease. In research, transgenic (genetically modified) mice were given Alzheimer's by being injected

with autopsied brain material. Thus Alzheimer's was shown to be infectious, though only in this rather specialized and perverse manner.

2. That Alzheimer's is caused by a virus. Hepatitis C has been mentioned. There has been more convincing talk of herpes simplex, which infects a good many of the world's population in a dormant state and can be activated by illness, stress, or inflammation.

IN TERMS OF treatment, immunization may be the way forward, certainly in the plaque camp. This idea was scorned when first suggested, but has been piloted with some success. The idea is that it works rather like the polio vaccine: The body attacks the injected beta-amyloid and with any luck also sweeps up the plaques in the brain (though whether this is fundamentally a good idea remains moot). Tiny amounts of vaccine get past the fine mesh of the blood-brain barrier, which protects the narrow blood vessels in the head from clogging. Early results claimed a 50 percent plaque clearance rate in some brain areas in transgenic mice. Unfortunately, when it was trialed on humans, the immune reaction was so pronounced that brains swelled dangerously. The latest research in Tokyo, going on as I write this, is focusing on injecting DNA that "codes for" beta-amyloid, provoking a gentler immune response. There are also trials going on for a pill that binds the amyloid and stops it from accumulating.

If Alzheimer's proves to be a genetic condition, then genetic work is the way forward, and in terms of gene therapy we live in an age of wonders, with new diseases being identified and marked with a highlighter pen in the DNA all the time. There's a rare inheritable form of Alzheimer's, familial Alzheimer's disease, that strikes people young—perhaps even in their thirties—and will go on to affect 50 percent of their children on average. It's one very small subset of early-onset Alzheimer's, which is classified as beginning at under the age of sixty-five. Familial Alzheimer's has been found lurking at chromosomes 14 and 21 (and also at chromosome 1 in the American population). Regular Alzheimer's—for want of a better description— the noninheritable kind, is thought to be indicated genetically by the gene *Apolipoprotein E* (*APOE*). *APOE4,* one of its four variants, is associated with high risk. If both parents carry *APOE4,* their children will have ten times the average risk of developing Alzheimer's. It's not all bad news. *APOE2* appears to indicate a much lower risk than is average of developing the disease.

Genetic diagnosis and manipulation is at a stage roughly similar to that of the New World three hundred years ago. It's still in the maps, marvels, and flag-planting era, but once domination of the genome begins in earnest, and the railroad is built to traverse it, capitulation will surely follow in a rush. For now, it's at an early, exploratory stage, a Wild West full of frontier towns and gunslingers. The encouraging thing is that it's begun.

Chapter 13

*I have said nothing. I leave nothing. I have not said what
I wanted to say. I have so much more to say.*

—MAURICE RAVEL

WINTER ARRIVES WITH A VENGEANCE AND THE PENinsula feels intensely vulnerable, low-lying in an
angry sea. It's as if, were we to go up another notch
in the storm conditions, it might all be swept away, scouring
the place of buildings, washing the cattle barns and cottages
into the ocean. I imagine us all, humankind and livestock together, found floating in the bay, distended, by a passing ship. It's
a sailing ship and it seems to be the early eighteenth century.
What disaster hath happened here? I'm having peculiar daydreams.
I sit at the drawing room window watching the hedges and
shrubs blown flat and gray in mouse-colored rain, the sky low
and woolly, looking at the distant dark peak of the mountain
across the bay. A cloud sits over this hilltop, raining on it.

Morris is still in hospital. Progress, officially, is "slow." The
idea of mobility has been abandoned, though nobody's explicit. Instead, the *W* word begins to be mentioned: *wheelchair.*
Nancy sits in her chair for long periods, rubbing her hands. It's
too cold in the hallway for wandering, even with all the bottle-
gas heating chugging away, the old electric storage heaters
pumping out on max, every coal fire in action. No one hangs
about between internal destinations. Washing and dressing are
done at a gallop. Nancy is feeling the cold acutely, despite the
customary five cardigans. She has taken to wearing a hat indoors,

a dark blue felt number with a jaunty feather. Her hands are cold and so I retrieve a cashmere blanket from her cupboard, one in fine-woven gray that we gave her for Christmas once, tucking it around her lap and legs. Thus immobilized, Nancy's a picture of a woman lost in a dream. Her hand rubbing has become systematic, ritualized. First, palms are placed together at right angles making a cross shape, rubbed as if rolling dough into a sausage. Then the back of each hand is rubbed briskly by the other palm in turn. After this, she interlocks her fingers, jamming them tight together and releasing, jamming and releasing, before the sequence begins again. Later, I read an identical account online of somebody's mother's behavior, and begin to see Nancy as pulled helplessly along bizarre, well-trodden tracks of disease, along Dr. Reisberg's railway.

At intervals in the hand rituals, she twiddles her hair. Her gaze is averted from the television pictures flashing in front of her, off toward the window, toward the fire, or dipped carpet-ward, as she captures and twirls sections in turn. Her hair begins to develop twiddled kinks. These, the hand rubbing and hair twiddling, must be signs of distress. But what's to be done about them?

We realize that Morris is a skilled Alzheimer's companion, in his way. His way consists of the sharing of all-day television. He watches everything, anything, is a habitual channel flicker, and keeps up a steady dialogue with the programming that is really a way of talking to his wife. The sharing is crucial.

"Just look at that suit! What does she look like?"

"Three hundred fifty pounds? I wouldn't give him ten bob for that vase, would you?"

"Look at the colors in the trees! I'd no idea Bulgaria was hilly, did you, dear?"

He uses television as an intermediary. He talks, and then from time to time, when it's clear a response is required, Nancy joins in. "Oh yes, you're quite right. . . ." She might almost pull it off, the illusion that she understands the question, but then likely as not will blow it: "And I have always thought so, but not many people, not many other people I should say, can see it that way, you know, and it's been like that my whole life."

Morris, in Alzheimer's denial, can't let such wittering pass uncontested.

"What are you talking about, you silly woman? It's bloody Bulgaria!"

But Morris is still in hospital, and Nancy finds me lacking as a television companion. I'm not given to being surprised by television, or to arguing with it, or to commenting on people's appearance. I don't really watch it. I sit with her in front of it but my mind is elsewhere. Her mind is elsewhere, too. Or nowhere. It's hard to know what or where her mind is now or whether she has, in any meaningful sense, a mind at all. Her brain functions well in instructing her body as to movement, forward propulsion, the signals required to bend and pick up a crumb from the carpet and eat it. If you ask a question, she'll answer it, in a fashion: *Are you hungry?* I could eat something nice. *Do you like this color?* I think it's very nice. *Do you want to go to bed?* Bed might be nice. But I'm not sure this is evidence of a mind. Are these her answers, the answers she gives me, or are they any old answers found in a box, retrieved from those that have survived the fire? Alzheimer's robs the brain of time travel, of its customary and constant roaming forward and back, the past stretching behind and the future ahead. That's how people operate. We put everything into context. But Nancy's marooned in the present. I'm only just beginning to see how fundamental this is. As Milton writes in *Paradise Lost,* "that must end us; that must be our cure— / To be no more. Sad cure! For who would lose / Though full of pain, this intellectual being / Those thoughts that wander through eternity." That's what I want from my experience of outdoors, from my walks along the cliffs: thoughts that wander through eternity, escaping the tyrannies of the lists, and the intimate tedium of the caregiver's day.

I'm not entertaining enough a television companion, though I try. If Nancy's especially restless or upset, I'll try to talk her through what's happening on-screen. But it isn't the same as having Morris here. He's belligerent, and that amuses her. He's a fund of trivia about various actors and their lives, who they married and divorced, their war service, other things they've been in. He makes cynical remarks about the soap plotlines, predicts what's going to happen, whoops with pleasure when he's right. Nancy loves all this and whoops along. Not much whooping is going on now. None. My heart isn't in it. I remember, guiltily, that I had much the same trouble once with children's television, and it occurs to me, not for the first time, that it might be me that has the problem.

"Do you like that dress, Nancy?" I'll ask, rather desperately, as Nancy gets up to leave (leave home). "What do you think of that pink sari?"

"It's very nice," she says, but she isn't engaged. It may be that my voice isn't the right trigger. There's nothing left that's equipped to recognize me anymore. I'm a stranger, a pleasant enough stranger staying at the same hotel. Those are today's assigned roles, it seems, to judge from the things Nancy tells me. She complains about the service, the temperature of the tea, the quality of the lunch. "They're really not very good here at all," she confides, leaning in toward my ear. "It's gone downhill, this establishment, since the old days." I sit with her after lunch and find "a nice film," but eleven minutes later she's up and out of the room. Eleven minutes has become her attention span for television pictures.

"I'm just going for a wee walk."

Shortly after, I find her in Chris's office, interrupting a business call.

"Perhaps this gentleman can help me," she says, gesturing toward her son, her voice full of emotion. "Can you tell me where I am?" Tears course down her cheeks.

A NEW CAMPAIGN of making Nancy happy commences. We do housework together after breakfast—five times more housework than I would normally do—Nancy poignantly grateful at being allowed to share in the tasks. We clean windows, Nancy rubbing away at one pane of glass with a piece of kitchen towel and singing. "When all my eyes are finished, and the world is bright and free, then I will be there and I know I can come, and that's the one for me." She can still rhyme. Though she's unhappy about having to do a different pane.

"There's nothing wrong with this one and it said it liked it."

"Yes, but look, the other ones are dirty."

"Nonsense."

"Its friends, you see them, look, here and here. Its friends are dirty and they will be embarrassed."

"Oh dear. Oh deary, deary me, that will never do." She changes panes. I'm aware that a lot of what I do with Nancy plays on the subject of shame. For this generation it's powerfully embedded in, the worry about what people will think, and I exploit it thoroughly.

We vacuum rooms, Nancy going over the same piece of carpet back and forth. I leave her vacuuming and go to put some washing in the machine, and as I bend to slam the porthole door, I hear shrieking of a familiar kind. I go back to her sitting room at a run and find Nancy standing with her hands in her mouth and the Dyson lying on its back roaring. "It doesn't work! It's falling down!"

I get her into a rhythm again, but when I leave the room she begins to howl. My head comes round the door. "What is it now?"

"Could you do it? Could you take it? I can't do it." She withdraws to the safety of the wall but can't take her eyes off the thing. It's as if she's forgotten how vacuum cleaners behave. This one might do something spontaneous and dangerous.

I vacuum the room and Nancy watches. "You're so clever," she says. "You make it look like nothing at all." She begins to sing her "Irish Eyes" variant.

I'VE BEEN READING about music and dementia. The composer Maurice Ravel (1875–1937) had (probable) early-onset disease from about the age of fifty-two and died ten years later following unsuccessful exploratory neurosurgery. His most famous work, *Boléro,* whose sweeping repetitions are now firmly associated with ice-skating, has been cited as an example of dementia composing. He wrote *Boléro* in the year after becoming ill. The question that's unanswerable is: Would a healthy Ravel have written the same score, or is it one of the best-known examples of perseveration in art? His own judgment seems clear; he referred to *Boléro* as "orchestral fabric without music." Ravel's dementia first presented itself as confusion about his touring schedule. He lost luggage, lost his tickets, and traveled with hoarded letters in his pockets. He forgot how to swim—the procedural memory having failed him—and almost drowned. In 1933, four years before his death, he told friends that he wouldn't after all be able to write his planned opera *Jeanne d'Arc,* saying he could hear the music in his head but couldn't access it. "It's over," he said.

We deal with laundry, Nancy and I. Laundry is a big part of the day. But now, it's too cold to hang it outside and make laundry into a journey. The truth is, there aren't many days when washing dries outside hereabouts: The growing season is short and the drying season shorter. It's too windy much of the time, the clothes disappearing over the wall, or cast into bushes, muddy and torn. Laundry goes out warm and wet and comes back in cold and wet so there's little point. Today it would return stiff and white with frost. Nancy stands at one end of the old-fashioned pulley in the utility room and I stand at the other. I pass her clothes from the basket and she pauses to pass comment on them.

"Those are underpants. They are not my underpants. They are horrible, actually."

"They are your underpants."

"Are they? Are they? Who said that was a very bad person because it's entirely the other way."

"Hang them over the pole. Like this, look."

She has the elastic waist of a pair of pink underpants clutched tight in her fingers. She moves her whole hand forward but it doesn't connect with the pole. Watching her, it occurs to me that the trouble she's having is like using a mirror to try and fasten an earring or snip at a stray bit of hair. Fingers and scissors don't move in quite the expected way. The mind plays spatial tricks of distance and direction.

"It doesn't want to go," she says. She jerks her hand forward further and overshoots. The underpants disappear over the other side and flutter to the ground. "There," she says. "Give me another one."

I give her a pair of socks. I put my hands over hers and guide them to the pole. She puts one on top of the other and fusses with them, trying to get them straight. I get on with the rest of the hanging up. "It's quite something watching you do that," she says admiringly. "You know just how it works. I think I used to know but I don't know now, that's for sure."

I stop and look at her, a child's school sweatshirt in my hand. "Do you remember being young and having washing to do?" I ask.

"It's all somewhere else. My father was there."

"You're always talking about your father but you never mention your mother," I say.

"Well, she was there, I expect. But I didn't know her, really."

"Why's that? Didn't you get along well?"

Nancy's eyes are watering. It's hard to know if this is weeping or whether the smell of detergent has triggered her allergic rhinitis. The rhinitis distracts her.

"I used to go along the street, you know, and I'd be crying. I have these terrible watery eyes and people would stop me and say, 'What on earth's the matter?' and I'd say it's just my watery eyes but you could see they didn't believe it."

"That's a shame, poor you."

"They'd stop me in the street and say, 'What's the matter with you?' and I'd tell them straight, I have this condition but you could see they didn't believe a word of it."

"Didn't they? That must have been annoying."

"I'd be walking along the road, and people would see me crying and it was amazing really—"

"Shall we stop now and have some coffee?" I interject.

What would we do without coffee breaks? They stitch the caregiver's day together.

We sit at the table and eat cake. Nancy is buzzing with energy but I am exhausted. The only real benefit is to the state of the house. I am that most conflicted of creatures, a house-proud sloth, so all this effort pays off in terms of the secret pleasure I take in order. Like nature, I can't abide a vacuum (cleaner), but on the other hand I can't settle to writing if the carpets are filthy, a curse that may be peculiar to womankind. So this is how I live now. I make an effort to be Mrs. Tiggy-Winkle in the mornings, and to include the elderly, confused hedgehog of my acquaintance in housewifely activities. Then, after lunch, counting on the aftereffects of physical effort and the sedating power of a cheese toastie, I chum my mother-in-law in her TV room. Nancy mutters and twiddles and hand-rubs away, and then dozes in front of the television and I—though sitting with her, in Morris's electric armchair—disappear into my preferred world of words.

THERE IS CHANGE afoot and changes come as steps and not as slopes. There are sudden downward movements and this is the latest one. It seems quite suddenly true that Nancy doesn't know her grandchildren. This seems to be another instance of parietal lobe damage. Alzheimer's patients rarely have trouble with vision as such: The occipital lobe isn't usually affected, but family-member recognition is a subtler, deeper-buried form of word-object connection. The truth is that she hasn't known the children for quite a while. If you asked her about them, in the abstract, while cleaning windows, she'd deny having any or say they were all grown up and worked at Kmart, or some such random answer. She hasn't known their names for two or three years. But now she doesn't respond to them visually, either. The visual prompt of a little boy face appearing and grinning at her might elicit a happy response, but only because it's a little boy and (usually) she loves small children.

"Hello," she'll greet him with exaggerated surprise. "Look, a wee boy. Come in, come in, I won't bite. Let me look at you. You're a fine fellow. What's your name?"

Jack falls for this sometimes, despite knowing that Granny will turn on him in the end. "You're a little bastard, aren't you? Get out of here."

The granddaughters, being self-possessed young women, are ignored or dealt with in tones of wilting sarcasm. She mutters into her hand when they talk to her, as if her palm is an improvised gossiping friend.

Children following her into her bedroom—"You all right, Gran? You looking for something?"—are rounded on.

"Why do you keep following me everywhere? Why can't you just leave me alone?"

Then she'll come and find me, complaining bitterly. "I have to say I'm absolutely pig sick of all these young people that seem to live here."

ONE AFTERNOON THERE'S an unseemly and pointless row, utterly counterproductive. It starts when Jack is called a series of unfortunate names: Alzheimer's dished up with a side order of Tourette's. Jack's so upset that Chris is drawn into the row. Nancy's told the blunt facts: that we can only put up with so much. The *H* word is mentioned: the *home*. The one she'll be shipped off to if she doesn't mind her mouth. Net result: two days of hand-wringing.

"I didn't do it! I didn't do anything bad!" Over and over and over. It's difficult to distract her from these ongoing, all-day denials.

"Would you like a cup of tea?"

"But I didn't do it! I didn't! I didn't do anything bad!"

"No. Listen. Tea. Do you want some? A biscuit?"

"But I didn't do anything! It's all a load of rubbish!"

And then, on the third day, calmer but no less angrily: "I'm afraid I have to tell you that unfortunately your children are liars. They're all bitches."

All of which begs the question: How did she remember the incident so long? Or did she? Perhaps it was another example of a contentless verbal loop—something that bypasses memory— and rage is just very sustaining. Emotional events have their own kind of longevity. I look up swearing and Alzheimer's, and it seems that it's to do with damage deep in the limbic system, in the amygdala. Amygdala damage has been linked to bad language, undressing in public, lechery, unprovoked hostility. Amygdala atrophy has been seen in Alzheimer's autopsy.

Morris comes home for a day visit, with an occupational therapist and various mobility aids. Nancy stays out of the way.

"Come on, Nancy," I chivy, putting my arm round her shoulders. "Morris is here. He's home for the day."

"Oh. Is he. Is he. Right," she says, pretending to watch the television.

"Morris! Your husband! He's here. Come on. Let's go and say hello."

"Oh, all right, then. If you say so."

We make our way with exaggerated slowness through the kitchen.

"You do know who Morris is," I venture.

"No."

"Your husband."

"Oh."

"Come on, then." I open the bedroom door and there's Morris, looking absolutely spent.

"Hello, dear," Morris says.

Nancy is blushing. "Hello," she says timidly.

"Amn't I going to get a kiss?"

She goes over and kisses him and then returns to my side.

"I'm just home for the day," Morris tells her. "But I should be back soon."

"Oh," Nancy says.

HARRIET DECLARES HERSELF available for granny-sitting, and we're invited to eat with neighbors who have a tree-growing business. Jane has a mother with Alzheimer's in a nursing home in England. Whenever Jane and I begin to talk, we fall down the same conversational black hole. I hate it that I seem able to

talk only about Nancy these days. I have become very boring—
not least to myself—a judgment confirmed by another supper
party, where I fall into the black hole again, monologuing on
the Nancy subject, even though nobody else present has caregiving problems. I must do something. I must do something about
this. I must restrain myself from downloading. I see the tedium
cross people's faces, the light go out of their eyes. I am beginning to repel people. Dementia caregiving is isolating in more
subtle ways than I'd imagined. Though the community here is
a friendly one, real friendships are slow to take shape. I don't
go out of the walled kingdom of the house often on my own,
and when I do I'm very dull company, and people don't visit
much. Who can blame them? Nancy's likely to want to join in,
seating herself close by and chuntering. And when she doesn't,
she and Morris are all I seem able to discuss.

Chapter 14

It is useless to attempt to reason a man out of a thing he was never reasoned into.

—Jonathan Swift

My birthday falls in February and is a blizzardy day, with snow brought by a north wind that puts the heating out and makes the chimneys unusable, so I spend most of the occasion wrapped in a duvet in the drawing room, alone and reading, Chris having taken on the Nancy-minding in my honor. In the evening, determined not to stay at home with pizza and a movie, we go into town with Nancy and end up at the American diner, eating pizza, and going to see a movie. The pizza is disgusting. Then the movie's delayed. After a half-hour wait in the cinema, house lights up, joking that they can't find the right movie reels, the manager comes in to explain that the bulb has blown in the projector and they can't find a spare.

I am not feeling well. This not-feeling-well feeling is persistent and low-key. I am not going to the doctor. I don't want to have a conversation about stress and embarrass myself. *Stress* would be the word used at the consultation. It's an easy word, protectively imprecise, a useful box to tip your feelings into. But a better word would be *incompatibility*. It's the shock of daily, ongoing proximity to this "vegetable universe" of my in-laws: their lives pared back to the bone, to the medical, physiological, placed squarely in the raw, reduced to material struggle, an easy decline the most that can be hoped for. It's William Blake, the source of the phrase: "Imagination is the real and eternal world of which this vegetable universe is but a faint shadow." There are plenty of people who'd phrase it directly in reverse, insisting that the vegetable universe is what's real and the world of the mind the shadow, Morris and Nancy among them. There can be no communication. There never has been on any real level, but since moving here we've both of us, both camps, been pushed further to the extreme of our position and the gulf has been rendered unbridgeable. This, I have self-diagnosed as the root of the trouble.

I am having funny turns, two or three a week, in which I get attacks of something like vertigo. The room spins, my head swirls, and I am intensely nauseous. Sometimes it happens in the car and that's the worst. I have to hold on to my head because it feels too heavy to hold up. The scenery rushes past the window at odd angles and small hills feel like a fairground ride. It goes beyond nausea; it's more like my whole body seeking to turn itself inside out.

When I can I confine myself to bed, propped up with pillows, and read, and surf the Internet for celebrity dementia sufferers, a strange new hobby. Jonathan Swift (1667–1745), author of *Gulliver's Travels,* spent his healthy adult years fearing dementia in just the same preoccupied way that Philip Larkin brooded on death. In 1717, on a country walk, he remarked of a tree whose upper canopy was shriveled, "I shall be like that tree, I shall die at the top." His forebodings were spot-on, though ironically what he believed to be early signs of brain disease was probably Ménière's, a vertigo-causing disorder of the inner ear, a condition it's possible I'm also suffering from. Swift started losing his memory in 1735 and was declared incompetent to handle his own affairs in 1742. His obsession with senility, while still in his prime, led him to invent the Struldbruggs, immortals born randomly among a mortal race, in book 3 of the *Travels* (written in 1724). The Struldbruggs, far from satisfying Gulliver's excited anticipation of wisdom, have forgotten the common names for things, can no longer read, and are emotionally incontinent, nasty and feared. They are in rapid decline at about the age of eighty and are then demented for eternity, unable to die, "peevish, covetous, morose . . . uncapable of friendship, and dead to all natural affection." Swift's probable Alzheimer's was misunderstood as ill temper and as lunacy by contemporaries and by critics. Samuel Johnson, writing in 1779, blamed Swift's dementia on his refusal to wear glasses. "His ideas, therefore being neither renovated by discourse nor increased by reading, wore gradually away, and left his mind vacant to the vexations of the hour, till at last his anger was heightened into madness."

Morris is still in hospital.

Nancy doesn't mention him anymore. I ask her about her family sometimes (her family are elsewhere; her family, she suspects, are all dead), reminding her that she has a brother who lives in Australia.

"He's in Australia? Has he been there long?"

I mention Morris's name. Does she know who that is? I show her a photograph.

"He's my brother."

"No, he's your husband."

"Oh. Is he. Oh." Indifferently.

"He's in hospital."

"Is he? Oh dear, oh dear. Oh dear me. Well. I'd better just go a wee walk."

Some days, though, the story is different.

"I don't like to pry," one of the day center volunteers says to me, "but she's been saying that she hasn't been allowed to see her husband. . . ."

That'll be the husband that she sits with in the afternoons, then. She sits at his bedside and holds his hand and becomes tearful, as does he. We leave them to it and go off to do errands and when we get back find Morris looking perplexed.

"She's been talking absolute gibberish."

"Morris. You do understand what Alzheimer's disease is, don't you?"

"Of course, but even so, absolute gibberish."

Nancy begins going to the day center in the town. A minibus comes and picks her up at the conservatory door on Tuesday mornings. This means that all her weekdays now have something going on in them other than Friday. Friday becomes a black day. We dread Fridays.

Her old love of housework has quite abruptly evaporated.

"I wasn't brought here to do this!" she cries, throwing the duster down.

"Would you like to vacuum your sitting room for me? Look at all the dog hair."

"I don't think that's my job."

"Help me hang the washing, then. You like that. We'll get the pulley down."

"I'm not at all interested." Eyelids nervously fluttering. "And you should know that I'm going home in a minute."

I put the television on for her, provide magazines to look at, cake and tea, her favorite soft toys, and put her beloved blue handbag onto her lap, the one with the assortment of things in it that she likes to take out and put in again. But none of this interests her on Fridays.

She turns the television off—or rather gets me to—and sits looking forlorn. This is niggling. It isn't possible to work. I crouch at her knee looking up into her face, taking her cold hands in mine, trying to coax her into wanting something out of the day.

"Just leave her to it," Chris says. His patience is worn very thin.

"I can't just leave her sitting there."

"That's what she wants. If she wants to brood, then let her."

"But . . ."

"You've spent most of the last five months with her. It's all right. Look. Just go. Go and do something somewhere else. I'll sit with her for a bit."

Chris installs himself with his work project in Morris's chair, and makes business calls there from his mobile. His mother sits a few feet away staring straight ahead and not saying anything. But the expression on her face is pretty noisy and her hands are in continual motion.

I sit in the drawing room at the window, wrapped in my blanket, watching foul weather hurtle itself toward us from the Atlantic, great low barrels of cloud rolling in, gray rain turning sleety. The wind is oddly comforting, a soothing white noise, baffing at the windows like a heartbeat. *There there. There. There. There there now.* But despite this I find it difficult to work. My concentration skims the surface of the job at hand. I need to write about the people in the novel that I'm supposed to be writing as if they were real. I need to build walls around them, conjure up the house that they live in, which is as important a character in the book as anyone; feel their breath, read their minds, give their situation depth. The vividness of the impression needs to come off the page at you. I know all this. But it isn't happening. The problem is that I'm not really present in the story. I read and reread paragraphs of the draft hoping and failing to catch the tide. But I'm half listening for trouble, and for the door to open, which it does, Nancy shuffling in and saying, "Ah, there you are, I thought I'd lost you," and Chris coming in after her, "No, Mother, she's working just now; come on, come back with me."

I go back through to make coffee a half hour later and find Chris watching a western and Nancy fast asleep.

Next, Nancy turns against her galantamine. She secretes

her pills up her sleeve and is cunning about it. She takes them apparently happily, and pretends to glug them down with water, but when I check later, they're tucked up her cardigan arm, saliva-softened and encased in tissue paper.

"They're not mine!"

"Yes, they are. It's important you take them."

"What's it got to do with you?"

"I'm the one that looks after you."

"Oh, are you. Are you indeed."

"Here's one, look, take it from my hand."

She clamps her jaw shut and looks like she can't hear me, and only intense negotiation gets the pills properly swallowed.

SHE BEGINS TO suffer quite dramatically from *sundowning.* There's a noticeable deterioration of mood, shortening of temper, worsening of speech, a sharp downturn in reasoning capacity, at around four to five o'clock in the afternoons. There are sundowning incidents. She begins hitting. Caitlin's slapped hard, and Nancy is completely and utterly unrepentant. This is worrying. I look it up and it seems to be connected with frontal lobe damage, again. The "prefrontal" lobe (the very front, behind the forehead) appears to be the site of our moral selves, and is crucial in triggering appropriate emotional responses. It bestows on us the very human qualities of guilt, embarrassment, and self-reproach, things Nancy no longer feels. Everything I read at this time seems to have some link into dementia. Even, unexpectedly, *Middlemarch,* in which George Eliot writes: "With memory set smarting like a reopened wound, a man's past is not simply a dead history, an outworn preparation of the present . . . it is a still quivering part of himself, bringing shudders and bitter flavors and the tinglings of a merited shame." Nancy's tingling days seem to be over.

She gets a wild look in her eye when anyone asks anything of her.

"I'm going to report you to the manager," she says to me one day as I'm handing her a glass of her favorite lemon squash.

"What?"

"I think it's only fair to forewarn you."

"Nancy. Who do you think I am?"

"I know very well who you are."

"Who? Who am I?"

"What insolence," she says.

Chris comes into the room. "Trouble?"

"You have no idea who I am. To whom I am," Nancy says in a more formal voice than is usual.

"Oh? Who are you, then?" Chris asks her.

"I. Am. The. King of Scotland," she says.

"You're what?"

"Yes. Nobody knows yet. The king of Scotland and this is all mine."

One evening, when Chris is in London, Nancy is mislaid for a while. Eventually I find her in the tractor shed in the yard. She's closed the door behind her and is standing expressionless by the ride-on mower.

"Nancy. Thank god. What are you doing in here?" It's dark in there and oily smelling.

"I'm looking for my father."

"Come inside, it's cold, you'll catch your death out here."

"No! I won't! I'm going home!"

She looks meaningfully at the mower.

"Nancy, you're in the yard in February wearing a cotton nightdress and a bath towel. You need to come inside."

I take her by the arm and she snaps it away violently. I take it again more firmly. She resists and a tussle develops, Nancy shouting at the top of her voice.

"Go away! Leave [shrug] me [yank] alone [push]."

I manhandle her back into the boot room. She's icy to the touch and bluish. She stands in front of the open glass door into the house, barring the way, hands spanning the width, holding on tight to the door frame, bracing herself and white-knuckled.

"You're not going in," she says in a low voice.

"What do you mean? Those are my children in there."

"No. I was born here. And you are not welcome."

"Nancy. Let me in."

"You are not welcome." It's said with genuine menace and I feel a shiver of fear. I'm reminded of something Nancy's friend Carol said, the last time she phoned. Carol's late mother had Alzheimer's and thought Carol an intruder. She'd stalk the house with a carving knife, intending to do poor Carol harm. What if Nancy had a knife right now? By the look of her, she'd not be shy in brandishing it.

I try to pry her fingers but she's supernaturally strong. She lets go all of a sudden, lurches forward, and pushes me backward. I fall on some shoes in an undignified heap. It must be hilarious from her viewpoint: my surprised face as I land legs akimbo in a muddy pile of Wellies. I'd be laughing if it were me. But Nancy has a very serious look on her face, and glinting malice in her eye. She returns to the barricade.

"Nancy. Listen. You are my mother-in-law. I am married to your son."

She snorts. "That's ridiculous."

"Nancy. Just let me into the house, please."

"No."

"I need to go in now. It's cold. And I need to get your supper ready."

She relaxes her grip. "I'm hungry right enough."

"Let me make you something tasty to eat. And we'll have a pot of milky coffee, shall we?"

Now she's all smiles, clutching her hands under her chin like a Victorian heroine.

"Oh, that would be lovely! You're very kind to me."

She's already had some pasta with us, but I make her scrambled eggs on toast and she wolfs it down.

Then it starts again.

"My house. They say it's not but it is and they'll be sorry. They'll find out forever. They say what they like but they don't know anything." She sees a pound coin sitting on the carpet and picks it up. For the next half hour she turns it over in her hands, examining it closely.

Eventually she speaks.

"This is all there is," she says to me, holding the coin in front of her face.

"There was only one," I admit.

"What have you done with the rest of it?" she demands.

"Sorry?"

"My money. This is all I have left. This is all I have now. The rest has been stolen. You took it. You took it, you stole my money."

Distraction is the only way out.

"Would you like some more toast?" I ask her brightly. "Because I'm jolly well going to have some. Toast with cherry jam and tea. What do you say?"

"Oooh, lovely. I like jam."

She follows me into the kitchen. "How nice you are and how beautiful you are," she says, running her hand over my neck.

When I put her to bed she stands with her arms outstretched, consenting to be undressed, accepts the flannel nightdress, gets into bed with her blue teddy, then bursts into tears.

"What on earth's the matter now?"

"It's just that you're all, all so k-kind t-to m-me," she blubbers, nose and eyes streaming. "You're all so very kind and I don't know what to d-do about it."

"You don't need to do anything. I hope you have a good night's sleep."

I put a gathered-up tissue over her nose and instruct, "Blow, please." She blows.

"I have to reward you somehow," she gushes. "I need to give you something. Some money. Would you like some money?" She reaches for the pound coin on the bedside table.

"No, thank you. Just go to sleep." She's sleeping within ten minutes.

Half an hour later she's up again. I hear her coming, the slamming of doors, the raised old-lady inflection. A voice declaring, "I never heard anything so stupid in my life!"

I go out into the corridor. "Nancy?"

She's holding a toilet roll. I take her to the bathroom. When I try to get her back into bed she takes a swing at me with her arm, her fist balled up. "Don't you touch me. Don't ever touch me again!" she screams.

That's Saturday. Sunday is worse. Caitlin is slapped again, and Jack's yelled at, and then I'm denounced for interfering. There is trouble from breakfast to bedtime, one thing after another. Caitlin spends most of the afternoon sobbing and Jack joins in. "W-why is G-granny so m-m-mean to us?" We have another (one in a series) of our conversations about Alzheimer's.

"That's not really your granny any longer," I find myself saying. "Your granny is gone." Harsh words, but they pour oil on the waters.

On Monday we make a telephone call to the health visitor. She turns up that same afternoon, with a colleague and a file full of paperwork, to talk about The Future. The great steam engine of the National Health Service is seen lurching from standstill to a creaking, groaning forward crawl. There are things nobody tells you unless you know the right questions to ask. I stare at the paperwork, the forms, the pen poised over them. At least drugs are free here, doctors and hospitals are free, day centers are free—aside from a small charge for tea and cake. I feel sorry for friends in the United States in a similar position, caught up in long tangles of red tape: the details of Medicare benefits, rights to Medicaid, drug bureaucracy, health insurance companies and their cunning opt-outs, and almost everything coming back to money, money, money. At least the health visitor (another free service in the United Kingdom) isn't advising us to see a lawyer specializing in dementia in order to have our rights and our options explained at the outset. We will need to see the doctor, see the memory team, be assessed. We shrink from institutionalizing. Just three months ago we'd been dismissive about getting help, but now we're greedy for information. We say that we've read somewhere that it was a good idea to get names down as soon as possible for residential care, a long way in advance. The health visitor doesn't laugh, but her eyes register our naïveté. That's not going to be available until things are much, much worse. And it isn't going to be free. Instead, it's going to become clear that care of the elderly is a business, and a highly profitable one at that.

Millie's had good exam news, so we decide at the last minute to go to the Indian restaurant in the town to celebrate. There isn't time to get Nancy in the bath and we're aware, in the restaurant, that she's rather grimy, her cardigan food spattered and the smell unmistakable. She doesn't say anything all evening, just rubs her hands in her usual three-stage way, twiddles her hair, sings a bit. But then, for the first time ever, she has trouble with the cutlery. We put her fork in her hand but she can't seem to coordinate it from plate to mouth, and abandons it for her knife. We cut her food up and take her knife away and give her the fork again. She puts it down and refuses to use it and eats curry with her fingers. We've ordered her a chicken korma, and it's difficult to eat with the hands. We give her plenty of bread but she doesn't seem able to scoop. She picks up rice a few grains at a time in her fingertips and stuffs it in; then pieces of saucy chicken, licking her fingers with pleasure. People stare.

THE GLOOM OF February is eased by decorating, every room de-greened, and the weather is briefly in harmony, giving us a week of crisp and sunny weather, windless and almost balmy, days that end in stupendous sunsets, orange and red over a lilac-colored sea. Thousands and thousands of bulbs are sprouting in the wood, bouquets of white and purple crocuses under the trees, a carpet of snowdrops stretching between; the taller, stouter foliage surrounding them promising a field of daffodils preparing to show itself, and bluebells for later on.

Nancy has her first respite week at the nursing home, and the rest of us go to London. It's our final weekend before Morris's return, and we need to gird our loins. We are all in frisky, happy form, cavorting like horses let out of winter stabling onto spring grass. We can't stop chattering. Morose tourists with heavy cameras look at us thoughtfully on the train.

Morris is brought home in an ambulance on the last day of the month. Preceding his arrival, the home care manager visits. She's heard already that Morris is severely disabled and will need home support. He is weak and can't walk at all, has trouble even taking a step, we confirm, and is unlikely to improve, though it's hard to say the words. The home care manager takes us in hand. Over the few days before Morris returns, a steady stream of assessors, builders, physical therapists, and equipment specialists tramp in and out measuring, advising, talking gadgets. We're advised that he'll need a wet room and given consultation on where and how to construct it. Morris is equipped with an inflating and lifting bed, humming along on its electrical supply, a ramp for wheelchair access from bedroom to sitting room, toilet frames and urine bottles. I'm reminded of his and Nancy's old family home, the row house, which had a handrail fixed onto the wall of the downstairs toilet, a relic of Nancy's mother's long-term stay in what had been their dining room. A Zimmer frame sits by his electric chair, for getting in and out, which I'm learning to call "transferring." He can't transfer alone.

There are gales, and heavy rain. But at least there are snow-drops in the wood. Our decorator, an ex–creel fisherman, goes diving in the sound and finds a treasure trove, the seabed lit-tered with scallops. He brings me a fertilizer bag full, a gift. Chris spends a whole day shucking. We eat some of them cooked in garlic butter with pasta. We have some for breakfast. Then we freeze the rest for another day, a day when we'll have visitors and can share our good fortune.

Chapter 15

Alas, must it ever be so?
Do we stand in our own light, wherever we go,
And fight our own shadows forever?
— EDWARD BULWER-LYTTON

I T'S DOUBTFUL THAT MORRIS WILL EVER WALK ANY BETTER than this. He comes home with exercises the physical therapist gave him, a cardboard tube he's supposed to manipulate with his legs, but he isn't doing it and has no intention of bothering. Reminding him that he's supposed to exercise constitutes nagging. "Don't nag me," he says. "I have a wife for that." I look at Nancy, sitting looking blank in her chair, and raise an eyebrow.

"It's not nagging," I tell him. "It's what you need to do to improve. Don't you want to improve?"

"All right! All right, all right!" he snaps. I withdraw. But I can't leave it at that. Somebody has to chivy him. So every day after breakfast I place the cardboard tube and the instruction sheet on his side table and pat it. "Here's the thing for your exercises," I say. "Yes, boss," he says, not looking away from the television.

Boss is my new name. Nancy likes it. It makes her giggle when Morris calls me boss. It's plain to her, you see, that I have a junior position in the household and that Morris is in charge. Men are always in charge. I get called boss every day. I only get called boss when I exceed my authority. Thus is it made clear that I exceed my authority a lot. I do it when I suggest that he eat more fruit and fewer biscuits. I do it when I suggest that he try to walk a few steps, or recommend that he call me before the fire has gone out or the tea's soaked into the chair, or before his need for the bathroom is urgent. It seems that our relationship, mine and Morris's, has entered a new phase. Perhaps it's to do with having been nursed and unhappy in hospital for so many months. He has begun to see my role as caregiver as an attempt at power over the two of them, and has begun to resist.

We'd been looking forward to him coming home. We'd been counting on it stabilizing Nancy. But with Alzheimer's there's rarely any hope of going back a step. And actually it's worse. Morris's return has the opposite effect. She finds his sudden appearance in the chair next to hers, the bed next to hers, alarming. An enormous downward step is in the process of taking place. Something momentous. Not recognizing Morris.

"Who is that man?" she'll ask me in a low and confidential tone, as we clear the breakfast things away.

"Man?"

"That one in there. The one sitting in there." And then, as I go to look in the direction that she's gesturing in, "Don't look! He'll see you."

"That's your husband."

"Is it?"

"Yes."

"Oh."

It's "oh" for now because she trusts me. She won't trust me much longer and then her reaction will be different.

We have reached the apotheosis of forgetting. Morris the man, Morris the husband, and all the years and memories that Morris encapsulates. In 2004, the anterior cingulate was identified as the missing link in memory production, controlling the storage and retrieval of long-term memory. The area lights up in brain scans once memories the subject is engaging with are several months old. When the anterior cingulate, which is part of the wrap of functions around the limbic system, is damaged by dementia, its malfunction means that only parts of the long-term memory are accessible, and these bits can't come together in a meaningful way. Perhaps, in terms of emotional impact, it's worse to have parts than none at all. If the anterior cingulate is disabled entirely, the access to the past is completely blocked off.

It isn't in Nancy's case. Not yet. Instead it fluctuates like bad radio reception, going on and off station. It's worse for Morris to have her memory of him come and go so seemingly arbitrarily. From minute to minute, he doesn't know whether she knows him or not. He's exhausted by the inconsistency. When she does know him, she's loving, fussing over him, and getting onto his lap (getting onto his lap and crying). It's as if she has missed him. When she doesn't know him, the manner of her rejection chills the blood, and it's Morris's turn to weep.

Now that Morris is home, the television is on all day. He's getting a bit deaf and the volume's turned up high. Thus we all get to share in his televisual life, which kicks off with the confessional shows first thing in the morning, the accusations flying, and follows an itinerary that soaks up as many soaps and police and hospital dramas as can be managed. Their sitting room becomes a little self-contained universe of televisual strife: assault, adultery, divorce, neglect, crime, rip-roaring arguments: all these keep Nancy smiling and the rest of us depressed. (I'm with Groucho Marx when he said, or is said to have said, "I find television very educational—every time someone switches it on, I go into another room and read a book.") A constant melodramatic state of crisis thrums under the door, seeping out and spreading its antilove around. Nancy likes it in there when the soaps are blaring. She sits and twiddles away at her hair with one finger and smiles. The rest of the house is too quiet, too harmonious for her. We bore her. She wants talking, talking, all the time talking; can no longer tolerate anyone reading, has to interrupt; comes and looms over people until they pay attention to her. I'm reminded of a particularly needy cat we had once that attacked opened newspapers. Though he didn't go in much for existential angst.

Nancy's care plan arrives in the post from the Tuesday day center. Two copies. We're to read it, sign it, add any comments, send a copy back. "Nancy may try to put used toilet tissue paper up her sleeve," it says. "In the interests of her dignity she has begun eating lunch with a caregiver in a separate room." Nothing is said specifically about mood swings, nor about pinning the lunchtime helper's hand to the table with a fork, so we are quietly encouraged.

Morris decides against resuming at the Thursday club and no longer leaves the house, but the trappings of a sort of a social life are the unpredicted benefit of having the home care team in. A lady comes in at 9:30 A.M. to get him up, another at 8:30 P.M. to get him to bed. The lead home care aide, the one usually on duty, is between generations, Morris's and ours, and in the early days proves a useful bridge between Chris and his father. She shares Morris's cynicism, his knee-jerk conservatism, enjoys his anecdotes, laughs at his jokes. And slowly, she becomes his confidante. This is the point at which things change. She and Morris have long and private conversations, while she's getting him up and getting him to bed again. Getting him up and getting him to bed begin to take longer. She stops telling us what Morris thinks, though useful snippets are cast our way. We hear that he despairs of Nancy getting better. We hear that he doesn't ever want to go to a day center again. We hear whether or not he's enjoying the meals we cook for him. It's the things we don't hear about that intrigue us. And in time, this new relationship in the house becomes both a bridge and a wedge.

The phone starts ringing, now that Morris is home. Professionals on the line. We're one of the plates the care profession has to keep spinning. People checking up on Morris, and also on me, who's been flagged, perhaps, as most likely to crack. Something I have said in a low moment has been talked about, has been the subject of an e-mail, or has become a sentence in a file. There may be a blue Biro question mark by a note about my own mental health. The only outcome of this intuition, however, is a renewed determination on my part to clam up. I feel bad about this, about my concerted noncompliance. It's their job, their jobs collectively, after all, to follow up on Morris and Nancy, to make sure they're okay and that their caregivers are caring and coping. I feel bad about resenting their concern. I ought to be grateful. It's churlish to be otherwise. But it's difficult to convey just how little I like to talk about my problems with concerned professionals on the phone. I hate the phone, anyway, always have. I hate it ringing when I'm doing something else and people blithely expecting me to be ready to give considered answers to their questions. I'm not, in any case, a talker. The words in my head go from brain to fingertip, not from brain to tongue. I can't do justice to myself, and especially not in these circumstances, when it's *off the cuff* but also *on the record,* which is how these phone calls seem. Being caught on the hop makes it infinitely worse. I say the first thing that comes into my head, and this might very easily be untrue, unfair, something true or fair today but not tomorrow (caregiving is a mood-swinging business), irrelevant, repetitive, self-pitying. Quite often, increasingly often, it's all of these things crammed triumphantly into one conversation. People ask me how things are. That's generally the first sentence spoken. "It's X here; how are things?" I can't tell them I have no idea. I have to produce something. What I produce is entirely random. Quite often it's blacker than is accurate, because I'm irritated by being interrupted and by being expected continually to give an account of the state of things. I don't know how I am, how things are. I'm just doing this. I do it, over and over, every day. There isn't any alternative, is there? Other than a nursing home. "So, have you talked to Morris about residential care lately?" the professionals ask. As if it's like ordering coal.

There's no room in the nursing homes, anyway. There are waiting lists. And it will cost a fortune, eroding their life savings away until the money's all gone. How can we be responsible for the loss of their life savings? It's not something anybody could enter into lightly. There's only one private home in our county and it doesn't have an Alzheimer's unit. Nancy isn't severe enough a case, nothing like severe enough, to be taken into council-sponsored care. That has been made very plain. She'll have to be completely doolally, physically frail, incontinent, not eating, and have sawn off one of Jack's limbs with a bread knife, before urgent action will be taken of that kind. The state of things is that I am lumbered, and am resentful about it, but resigned. That is how I am. But I don't say that.

I say, "How am I? I'm okay. Functioning. But it's hard work and getting harder." That's on a good day. On a good day, I'll follow this up with the latest Nancy anecdotes and will tell them in such a way that we both end up laughing, my interlocutor and I. On a bad day, I'm impatient with the phone person and incapable of being funny about the anecdotes. I sound terrible. I'm aware of this, and I mind. I wish they'd stop phoning to sympathize because in this situation, pity isn't any use, and an emotional phone conversation throws long shadows on the day. The worst of it is that nobody ever phones to sympathize in brief. The conversations go on for twenty, thirty minutes, forty. We go through it all again. Her behavior. Her condition. Her decline. Morris's state of health and prognosis. His behavior. His condition. His decline. His interaction with Nancy, his desperate unhappy bullying. The effect that all the above are having on the family.

I become markedly less grateful for official concern as time goes on. I hit the ball back over the net with topspin. "Hello there, bad timing, unfortunately, just going out." They ask if they can ring back. "Tell me what it is you want, if you like, but can you make it quick? I'm really busy."

I interrupt them midstream. "Thanks for this, for phoning, but now I need to get on." I invent things. "Can't talk now, Nancy is in the bath." "Nancy and I were just about to play badminton." "Sorry to interrupt, but I see Nancy making off down the drive." I start making my answers short, pointedly so. Eventually it's open rebellion. "Look, can we not have any more meetings? Can you not call quite so often? I already have very little time to myself and having meetings isn't what I need. Sympathy isn't what I need. If you can suggest anything we can do to make Nancy less angry and Morris less depressed and me less tired, that'd be great. Otherwise, perhaps you could e-mail? E-mail's better for me."

PEOPLE ARE OFFENDED left, right, and center. They're not accustomed to being headed off at the pass. Perhaps they categorize my unwillingness as indicative of neglect? Perhaps, in their training, their trained way of seeing the world, my being flippant is considered a marker of something. I don't know. They must be accustomed to other sorts of people being caregivers, I decide. Perhaps they're used to people who like this endless going over things. It must be seen as therapeutic, cathartic. It's supposed to be bad to bottle things up, isn't it, unhealthy? I, however, am of the opposite view. I don't relate to the lanced-boil metaphor. I tend to think that a problem shared is a problem doubled. Or quadrupled. A problem shared, hereabouts, is generally a problem that's gossiped about.

March brings its usual last blast of winter to blow away the spring. We find ourselves snowed in for almost a fortnight, transport canceled, schools closed, the world quiet in that uniquely quiet, snow-muffled way. We don't get that much snow, but the little that falls is blown impressively into drifts sufficient to immobilize a bus, and subzero temperatures freeze the slush on the roads, and that brings the whole region to a halt. We can get no farther than the village shop. Potatoes, cabbage, frozen fish, bacon: these become, temporarily, a big part of the diet.

In late March I have a new project. I organize myself a whole other life. A house in Turkey. We've sold our ruin in Normandy that we bought to renovate and never will, and want spring and autumn sun. The project starts as a house in Bulgaria, as I have seen houses on eBay going for £8,000, though Bulgarian trawling ends in a cul-de-sac. It's Greece we want but we can't afford Greece. I go online across the water into Turkey, and find that a tiny cement house by the sea is possible at the £25,000 level. And so I spend two weeks doing nothing but chasing leads, drawing up a short list, pestering agents. The in-laws, Chris, and the children are kept at arm's length. Dealing with the inevitable, inescapable day-to-day slog, unpaid and thankless—running the household, dealing with Morris's mild but needling hostility, coping with Nancy's bizarre and darkening world—all of that, I can deal with because round the corner, in laptop-land, life-changing things are afoot.

Chapter 16

One need not be a chamber to be haunted;
One need not be a house;
The brain has corridors surpassing
Material place.

—EMILY DICKINSON

WHAT HAPPENS WHEN THE ABYSS OF AMNESIA IS opening constantly at your feet, as it appears to be with Nancy? Some days it appears that her brain is compensating by creating and supplying its own answers, its own improvisations: fictions that keep her afloat. It isn't that nothing is going on in there, in her brain. She improvises her reality from minute to minute. This is on my mind today, a stormy April morning, and as it happens, the first anniversary of our agreeing to buy the house, because I dreamed last night that Nancy was a sales representative, working in a postapocalyptic landscape. There was a war-blackened ruinous backdrop of burnt-out skyscrapers; it didn't much resemble Edinburgh. The company she worked for had gone, as had all the other personnel, leaving her alone in the city, but she kept going, working out of her car and flying by the seat of her pants. My dreams lately have tended to the metaphorical.

It isn't possible to have identity without a history. Pascal was wrong when he wrote, "If somebody loves me for my judgment, or my memory, do they love me? Me myself? No, because I could lose these qualities without losing my self." The more I think about this statement of his, the odder it seems. It's normal for selves continually to be evolving, and in that sense Nancy's improvisations are reassuring. Something is happening. It hasn't all come to a halt. I am writing this in bed, early in the morning, the rest of the family asleep. Since waking I have thought, apparently randomly, fleetingly, about a whole array of insignificant things and in making decisions, reflecting on them, I have become a new person, albeit in a trivial sense. As Heraclitus had it, you can never step into the same river twice.

Which rivers does Nancy put a toe in? Which river is she wading in, thigh deep, in those periods of sitting in her chair hand rubbing and looking deep in thought? It's clear from her eye movements, her mouthings, her shifting expressions that something is happening. Are they words, pictures? Is she thinking in the first person, or does her voice come at her like dictation? Where is her mind taking her right now, lying awake in her twin bed, the light vivid at the edges of the curtains, Morris snoring lightly and curled in a fetal circle? She's lying facing the door, facing her upright wood-framed chair, the clothes laid on it from yesterday; she can see Morris and the entrance to the bathroom. What occurs to her about these things that she's looking at? What content and format do the improvisations take? The little output that does reach us—*this is my house; you work for me; I was born here; my father is in the garden; I must get to the office; the friends are on their way*—doesn't hint at much in the way of a coherent alter ego, nor the creation of whole new identities, if you discount one-offs like the king of Scotland episode. She doesn't claim to be anybody else, other than, on occasion, her younger self, unmarried, unburdened, childless, her whole life ahead of her (and don't we all imagine our immortal souls, our essential selves, to be fixed at around the age of twenty-eight?). Nancy's fictions are more to do with her brain coming up with scenarios that explain her life now. For half-hour periods, she is the owner of a big house in Edinburgh with staff (the rest of us), and/or somebody who has lived here her whole life, confusing it with the estate where she was born, and/or must get the house ready for a party because the friends (everybody from her past that she can remember, I assume) are on their way. They're called the friends, collectively. She no longer has a handle on any particular name or face, is just hopeful that they're out there and on their way to rescue her.

Waking this morning at six and listening to the wind rattling at the windows, I tried to fake being a person without a memory but it was impossible. Everything we are is the sum of our history, augmented by every new experience, each stone added to the cairn and modified by our thoughts about that stone, and about the shape the cairn is taking. Our selves are fed by our narrative, the story of our past and our imagined futures. Ask me who I am and I turn immediately to memory. It isn't possible to answer the question "Could you tell me something about yourself?" without recourse to biography. Even aside from replies that start, "Well, I was born in . . ." (which are the most obviously memory driven), other kinds of responses, ones that try to avoid the straight biographical—"I am intelligent, curious, anxious, and usually hungry"—also rely entirely on memory. You only know yourself because of your memory. If you ask Nancy who she is, she can quote her name, but that's all that's likely to arise from her unprompted. If you ask her, "What are you like?" or "What kind of person are you?" she isn't able to answer. She'll appear to think about it. The eyes dart from side to side. But then she says, "I don't know, really," or "I couldn't exactly say" or laughs defensively. At a fundamental level there has been a disconnection and Nancy's self is locked in a room with no windows.

Who I am is what I've done and experienced, and what I think about it all; how other people make me feel about it all, how the books I've read and films I've seen have made me think and feel about it all, creating a unique and labyrinthine web of connections that is my self. I have a library of self at

hand. I can wander the halls of this library and choose which-
ever bit I like, and read from it and enjoy the indulgence of
having new ideas about the past. I find in the last few years that
I am dipping into it more and more and finding surprising
new connections between things. This, I suppose, is what people mean when they talk about personal growth and one of the
few compensations of being post-forty.

The only (inadequate) way I can relate to what Nancy experiences when she wakes is in recalling moments when I haven't
been sure where I was. Waking from an anesthetic. Or waking
up in a strange hotel room, with the wrong furniture, the
wrong shadows, the wrong smell, the door in the wrong place,
and that first mildly alarming recognition that this isn't home.
The alarm is barely formulated before it's redundant. The brain
steps in hurriedly with information, clears its throat: the effi-
cient personal secretary. *Ahem. I think you'll find you're in the
Travelodge. Half-term trip.* Ah. Yes. An instantaneous connection
is made between this room—the Travelodge, the half term, the
life I have—and the library of the past, which is always with
me, wherever I am. The Travelodge becomes another pebble
on the cairn.

This morning when I opened my eyes the room I put together was there, the anticipated objects, Chris sleeping, everything familiar and as it should be. I'm looking around it
now. It's cold and I'm wearing a sweater in bed. The clean
laundry is piled on the chair awaiting sorting. My new handbag
is hanging from the wardrobe door. I recognize the handbag. I
remember buying it. I don't bother to have the memory, in full,
of the shopping and acquisition; it's more like, in computer
terms, a shortcut on the desktop that I am confident leads to
the memory. I don't open the file, though I did, the morning
after buying it, reviewing the choice that was available and reassuring myself that I didn't want the red one with the too-short

handles that I was drawn to initially. That's all I needed to do. Now when I see the handbag all I see—and I don't even see it, I don't need to—is the shortcut on the mental desktop that connects me to the object. It's so brief as to be a shortcut to the shortcut. Recognition. It fits into my narrative and that's all that's needed. If I wake and see something that doesn't fit—a book I haven't seen before that's appeared on the bedside table, say—then my first instinct is to try and make it fit. There's a book there I don't recognize. How has it appeared on the bedside? I didn't put it there, did I? I do a brief file search. Oh yes, it was purchased in a rush in the city—I see the bookstore, I see the face of the assistant—bought for a birthday, and last night Chris was emptying the bags. He must have put it there when he came to bed, thinking it was for me. It's good to *see* the bookstore and the face of the assistant again. It reassures me that my narrative is intact.

But Nancy doesn't have any of this anymore. I don't know what she does have. Her mind, unable to deal with not being able to make sense of things, makes its own sense, delivering explanations up from fragments, inventing new scenarios that make things seem coherent. Whatever the case, it's clear that her self has been pared back to the minimal. She is operating on the level of the *core self,* which Antonio Damasio, a neurologist-neuroscientist at the University of Southern California, describes as "a transient entity, re-created for each and every object with which the brain interacts."

Nancy says to me almost every morning, "I'm sorry, I don't know where I am," and in the circumstances that seems a remarkably gracious response. It's her face that betrays her fear. The reason I'm not afraid on waking is that, stirring and stretching in bed, everything I see around me is explicable; it was *put.* Personal history isn't just about the CV, executive or social. We have history with everything surrounding us. The house is one we bought having sold the previous one. Our possessions carry with them their own stories, of how they were acquired and where, and their thing biographies, things that have happened since we got them. A chair used for reading is a highly evocative thing, or a sofa owned since the children were small. Look hard at that sofa and you'll see them, little pink and white people, fresh out the bath in clean pajamas, waiting for a story. An old pair of jeans carries history with it, that's why they're hard to part with. This isn't just sentimentality, but context. Imagine waking in the morning and finding everything around you is new: the building, the garden outside the windows, the people who talk to you as if you know each other, the shirt the stranger hands you, the chair they take you to, the man sitting in the other chair. If your brain were still intact enough to want to make a history out of things, it might get around the novelty of all this by explaining your real life as somewhere else. You are somewhere new and your life is somewhere else. All you're going to want to do is get back there.

I'm getting up now to make breakfast. The house layout is known to me. Rooms are subsequent in the expected way. The kitchen cupboards hold the things I put in them. I know where the frying pan is, the olive oil, the glazed bowl, and the whisk. There are leftover potatoes, garlic, some tomatoes for the omelet. As I rise and dress and go down to make the breakfast, I'm running through visual anticipations of how it will be, barely consciously if at all; each next step conjured and satisfied in turn. In a way, I'm remembering things before they happen.

Six months ago, Nancy may have appeared in the kitchen, hearing me up and about, and once I'd reassured her by appearing to know her and offering her tea, she'd ask if she could help. I miss helpful Nancy, wanting to do things. Although, asked to put eggs in a bowl, she couldn't even then have grasped what was being asked. She might, with encouragement, have put the eggs in the bowl, entire, shell on, and stared at them as if expecting them to act. She remembered "egg" then, though "bowl" was trickier. Always, with the progress of Alzheimer's, life is bound up with lists and ranks of objects, and tiny gradations of loss.

Chapter 17

*Time changes everything except something within us which
is always surprised by change.*

—THOMAS HARDY

SPRING BRINGS SUICIDE TALK. WE NO LONGER LEAVE
Nancy alone with Jack, since she started seeking counseling
from him about her urge to go and jump in the canal. She
means the canal that passed by their Edinburgh apartment, I
presume; a canal she's known twelve years, hanging grimly on
in episodic memory. Heaven knows why she picks on Jack, but
she does, singling him out and pinning him to the wall with
conversational monologuing, from which there is no easy escape; Jack signaling for help wild-eyed, like a desperate guest
at a cocktail party cornered by a bore. I look up dementia and
suicide and find there's no consensus on their interplay. The
orthodoxy is that suicidal feelings are burnt out early because
of the self-awareness that's required, though there are heretics
who say otherwise. Giving up eating and drinking, voluntarily
and abruptly, in a way that seems to have been considered and
decided upon, is known in nursing homes as Alzheimer's suicide. It's a not-uncommon way to go. Whether it is suicide is
debatable. If people live long enough, the disease will reach
the brain area that sponsors sensations of hunger and thirst.

Alzheimer's is set to become a hot potato when, eventually,
assisted suicide is legalized. Dignitas, the Swiss suicide organization, which offers a legal framework to the suicidal—providing
a house and a lethal dose of barbiturate, and leaving it to the

client's discretion whether they take the drug or not—was questioned a few years ago about the death of an Alzheimer's patient, and whether he could be guaranteed to have been of sound enough mind to make the contract between them legal. Dignitas responded that even someone with advanced dementia may have moments of sufficient lucidity to want to die. This idea has been shouted down as ludicrous but I'm not so sure. Nancy keeps talking about the canal.

She talks to her address book about it. She's carrying her address book everywhere with her now, and won't put it down. Not on the toilet. Not in the bath. Not in bed. She tells me she's heard "the people" plotting to take it. She sits in her armchair and talks to it. Sometimes to herself, about it, flicking the pages and narrating; sometimes to the book directly, asking it questions. She seems to recognize that it has something to do with her past. An address book is, after all, as personal as a photograph album. She's had this one for thirty years or more. Addresses in it are written in various inks, the handwriting varying according to mood and circumstances, health or tiredness, and whether the writing was done on lap or table or against the wall, the telephone receiver held tight under her chin. Numbers and names have been scratched out and replaced. Old friends, some of them long dead. People she worked with once. Relatives, former neighbors, and fellow school parents. The addresses Chris and I have lived at in our many nomadic wanderings, and those that track the life path of her daughter. It's a fairly small address book, small enough to fit in an ordinary business envelope, cream bound, tatty, its cover dotted with seventies-looking flowers and butterflies. The hinge of the binding is beginning to wear through, and pages are coming loose from the stitching.

Every time I go into the in-laws' sitting room, there's Nancy with the address book, head bent in concentration, flicking through and talking to herself in a low and urgent tone.

"And that's the one I want. That was always the one. Yes." She taps her finger on the page decisively. Her nails have grown long again and mysteriously they appear well shaped, with smooth semicircular ends. She must be using an emery board at night; there's one in her underwear drawer. Nail care, so much a part of her life once, must be embedded deep in long-term memory, one of those automatic activities that don't need thinking about. (Thank god for the cerebellum. Imagine having to learn to walk afresh every morning.) "And there it is," she says, confidentially to an entry in the address book, a pointed finger hovering. "There's the one. That's the one." Flick flick. "Ah, now look. That's the one I was meaning. I meant that one. That one there. That's it."

"You're not having it!" she shrieks at me when I try to put it on the coffee table.

"I'm not taking it, just putting it down. Right there. So you can eat your supper."

"It's not any of your business!"

"Here's your knife and fork, look. You're going to need two hands to eat this piece of chicken."

"I will do it as I do it and I thank you to keep your nose out."

"Okay, then."

She holds on, her grip white-fingered, to the book, and uses the fork a little. Then she puts the fork down and eats with her hand. The book is not relinquished.

She starts taking her teeth out in bed. This is a new development. It's been impossible to get her to take her false teeth out for years. But now she wakes with a jaw-caved-in look and speaks in a different way and it's obvious that they are out. We play hunt the falsies. They get put away in unpredictable places in the night: in drawers, under things, on windowsills. One morning we find them in the toilet, sitting unflushable under the water. On another, the Tuesday bus is kept waiting, engine running, at the conservatory door while we do a last frantic search.

"She'll just have to go without them," Chris says.

I pick up her wallet, her latest pet, which unaccountably she's left sitting by the bed, and find it is strangely lumpy. Sure enough the dentures are within, stuffed in tight and straining at the leather.

Next, the invasion begins. The in-laws are getting lots of visitors. Since I said to one of the health team that they should come straight in and not bother to knock, everybody now does this. Which is fine. We might not hear the doorbell, we might be on the phone. We don't, in any case, want to have to go to the door repeatedly and make stilted conversation with health visitors. Far better if they just come straight in. They know where to find Morris. Morris no longer moves. He keeps the urine bottle by his armchair and uses it in situ.

The house no longer feels the same. It no longer feels entirely like a house. The emphasis, once firmly on the children and on child raising, has shifted. We seem to have reached a tipping point, and tipped. Now it's all about Morris and Nancy. They sit at the center of it, two fat spiders in a web (not fat as it happens but you get the gist). I can't help thinking of *Charlie and the Chocolate Factory* and the four bedridden grandparents, living in the giant bed in the sitting room being fed cabbage soup. That is how home is becoming. The rest of us are satellite creatures with satellite lives.

An ancillary to this is the feeling that we are constantly on show. The house has to be kept tidy, approvably clean and swept of personality. Overdue bills can't be left sitting on tables, nor open books, letters, sales catalogs that might provoke comment, any signs of extravagance, unusual foodstuffs, alcohol of any kind, drawings half drawn and half-done crosswords nor anything to do with business. Sometimes when visitors come looking for me, wanting consultation about some Morris-and-Nancy matter, they find me on the sofa reading. Apparently doing nothing.

"How do you get the time to read so much?" one of the care ladies asks me, blushing pink, "because I *never* get the time," her eyes flickering toward the ironing pile. Our home aides aren't the kind of people who sit down much, and nor were Morris and Nancy in their prime. Working hours were long, for them, at home as well as the office. None of them associate sitting down with earning a living. Sitting down is something that's available when all possible chores have been done, late at night or not at all—and there's considerable kudos attached to never getting the chance. Nancy, when first we moved in, was heard to complain about the state of the housekeeping. "They're terrible here," she'd say, looking in horror at the dishes by the sink. "Look at this! It's terrible." Sitting down during the day might be construed as immorality. The owning of too many books, to some ways of thinking, is an admission that one misuses one's time.

Out here, far from everything, a village is a village and also a world. People talk. News and rumor are the lifeblood of isolation. Talking is a major activity and we're all too conscious of people's curiosity, their assumptions and misconceptions. Private conversations can't be had until late at night, phone calls can't be enjoyed: not in daylight hours when there are likely to be outsiders present. I can't be seen in the kitchen in my bathrobe (not after 8:00 A.M.! "Have you had a nice lie-in today? Lucky for some"), nor am I happy to have the children seen in theirs. Judgment, both real and imaginary, hangs heavy over us. Downstairs has become a public zone. Dogs must be locked away upstairs in case they escape. Chris and I start having daytime conversations by e-mail. Doing otherwise risks being overheard, at least before 9:00 P.M., when the back door closes the final time and the home care lady is gone. At nine o'clock we all relax. But that's also Jack's bedtime. The window of ordinary family interaction has shrunk alarmingly.

The phone calls continue and are on occasion deeply aggravating. The physical therapist rings to ask why we haven't had the wet room installed that she recommended. From health and social workers, recommendations are usually orders. Someone else rings to report that Morris, at the day hospital, has complained that Nancy's being unsettled at night is keeping him awake and that he worries we won't hear him if he calls for help. She is insistent that we install a baby monitor, so we can listen to Nancy and Morris, reassure ourselves that they are sleeping, and be alert to anything we ought to go and sort out. This phone call has a peculiarly depressing effect. The house has become an institution and we are its night staff. And we ought to be aware that a part of our duties is lying awake listening to Nancy monologuing away in the early hours, and Morris shrieking at her to shut the fuck up and go to sleep.

Then one of the nurses at the day hospital telephones to say that Morris is complaining of being lonely. She mentions the name of the day center, the Thursday day center he point-blank refuses to attend.

"But he doesn't like the day center!" I retort, perhaps too vociferously. "He used to go to it. He canceled it. He hated it."

"Well, I'm just ringing to let you know that I have booked him in to recommence. He'll start on Thursday. Okay?"

Morris makes a face when I pass the message on. "I didn't really have any choice," he grimaces, though when Thursday comes he goes off on the bus cheerfully enough. What does he really think about the day center? What does he really think about anything?

As if in punishment for our not agreeing to the baby monitor, we have a series of late-evening and early-morning crises. Nancy begins getting up and getting dressed at two or three in the morning, and trying to get to Somewhere Else. I no longer believe the "doorknob prompts" theory. These are breakouts. I find her downstairs rattling at the door that leads from the main hall into the porch. It's a half-glass-, half-wood-paneled door, a Victorian door, and heavy. When it's rattled it swings in its housing and echoes through the house like thunder.

"Nancy. It's you. Couldn't figure out what the noise was. You gave me a fright."

"I need to go now. I'm late."

"Come back to bed. It's the middle of the night."

"That's all right for you to say but I'm not supposed to be here!"

We meet Nancy almost every evening, on one of her moonlight sojourns. The drawing room door opens in spooky slow motion and she shuffles in, waddling from side to side, shoes on the wrong feet, holding some combination of possessions: her handbag, clothes, a pair of shoes, her address book, her teeth in a handkerchief. Quite often she's singing, to the usual tune.

"When I am young and busy, and the world will have to be, and the thing that comes down is the thing I brought here, and that's the same to me."

She will be in one of two moods, black and white. Either very glad to see us and intent on joining in our late-night whisky, or misanthropic and full of gloom. And she can still rhyme.

I feel bad about putting her to bed so early, but this is how it is. Morris has no choice but to be put to bed at eight-thirty; that's the only slot he could get in the home care schedule, and quite often he's glad of it, his legs bothering him, bed wanted. Nancy must go with Morris. There has to be some granny-free time and this is it. Nine P.M. to 11:00 P.M. is sacred. I've gone the other way on occasion: taken pity on her restlessness, sat with her in front of the television till after midnight, till she began at last to flag, remade the fire, made her toast and hot milk and been tolerant about the ranting. But I can't do it anymore. Besides which, if Nancy is absent, Morris can't sleep. He stays awake waiting for her return. He grows agitated, wondering what she's up to.

Late one weekend evening, while the rest of us are upstairs in the family room, there is a sudden hullabaloo from downstairs. A frantic impassioned yelling. It takes a few moments to register that it's somebody calling out Chris's name and sounding desperate about it. Chris and I jump up and go down, insisting the children stay put.

"Oh god, it's Granddad!" Millie cries out. Jack bursts into tears and Caitlin follows. Millie joins in and the three of them stand on the top landing, snuffling and clutching each other.

When we get to Morris's bedroom the door's open and he's by the threshold, on the chair at the end of Nancy's bed. He's managed to stagger to the door and open it in order to shout for help, but has not been able to get further.

He looks ghostly, yellow, terrified.

"Oh, son," he says, emotionally. "It's Nancy. My Nancy. I think she's dead." She's lying on her back, utterly still with her arms by her sides. Chris listens to her chest and puts his ear to her mouth. Then he listens to her chest again.

"Her pulse is regular," he says.

"Oh thank god, thank god. I've been trying to wake her up for a good half hour. Normally she's awake at this time and chatting to me. I couldn't get her to answer."

Chris helps his father back into bed. Meanwhile I sit with Nancy and talk to her. "Nancy. Na-an-cy. Nancy! Nancy! Wakey wakey. Hello-o. Are you there?" I squeeze her hands. She doesn't respond. Ten minutes pass like this: me tickling and squeezing and shouting and demanding that she wake up, get up, right now; Nancy unresponsive and apparently unconscious. I keep going. Finally, when I squeeze her big toe, she kicks out at me with a sleepy growl.

"Nancy," I say, very firmly, my head dipped close to hers. "You need to get up now. Come on. I need to speak to you. Open your eyes."

"No," a small voice says.

"Come on." I pull at her arms and she rises, eyes still closed, and puts her legs out of the side of the bed. I pull gently on her arms and she glides to a standing position. I take her, slowly, eyes still closed, to the bathroom, where she sits and has a pee. Then I put her, eyes still closed, back to bed. She's grumbling under her breath.

"I just need to speak to you for a moment," I say, knowing Morris is still in a panic. "I need to ask you a question. Would you like a drink of water?"

"Bugger off," the voice says, from between near-closed lips.

"Thank god," Morris says. "She's fine."

AT THE END of the month, as the school Easter holidays begin, Chris goes off with his good mate Michael for a week's sailing course. I've known about this booking for a long while and am in favor, despite dreading it. An annual week off from family life to do something independently is official marital policy; it's just that I never take mine. It isn't a happy week for the nonsailors. The weather is cold and rainy. The children and I have to be on hand, on duty, in case of upset or crisis, so we hang out in the drawing room most of the day, where we can keep an ear and eye on things. Nancy comes in at regular intervals to ask for help with *the chap through there*.

"I can't help you with that, Granny, sorry," the children say, as coached.

"No. No. You don't understand," Nancy tells them. "You have to come and talk to him. He seems to think we know each other and he's being annoying."

Eventually, weary of interceding, the four of us take to

hiding upstairs, reading by the fire, Jack playing his self-absorbed role-playing games with guns, coded messages, cloaks, and light sabers. We work through a stockpile of films, magazines, and chocolate. Chris and Michael have a freezing cold, challenging week on the water, with bad weather and plenty of chucking-up and have the time of their lives. It isn't such a vintage week at home: I'm up early, mucking out horses in a gale force 7 and horizontal hail showers.

Each of the seven days Chris is away there are tears. Sometimes mine. Almost daily Nancy's. "This man is NOT MY HUSBAND," she insists. "He's NOT, he's NOT, I've never seen him before in my LIFE." She means it. She's frantic, and she can't understand why I'm not equally exercised by the stranger in the sitting room. It's particularly bad timing, as poor Morris is beginning to have embarrassing "toileting issues," to use the social care argot. He is soiling himself in bed. As is the way of things, this begins in spectacular style while Chris is away. The morning home care lady arrives to find her charge awake and mortified. She deals with the worst of it (getting him up and clean is her remit) and then hands me the marigolds (getting the bed clean isn't). I text Chris, who is night sailing in the Cromarty Firth. *Yr parents hell. You owe me big time fr this chum.* It's decided that we'll look for a privately employed home help to work twenty hours a week.

The council announces a residential care crisis (another in a series), and all respite at the town nursing home is revoked for the year, all six weeks that were so painstakingly negotiated. It's a financial crisis, one being experienced simultaneously all over the United Kingdom. The council doesn't have enough in the budget to run their homes, to hire their staff (nor can they keep them: We hear constantly how low morale is among the workers at the town home), and so, in this situation, cancellation of the bookings of respite clients—who will only be there for a few days, or a fortnight at a time—is the immediate money-saving mechanism. They know, even so, at the council that there will have to be some negotiating and exceptions will have to be made. Several emotional phone calls later, Nancy's April week is rearranged. She's to go to the new home, the countryside home, a swish bungalow-based home with an Alzheimer's unit, half of which is locked off unused because there isn't the funding to run it. So Nancy goes there, and Morris goes to the seaside home: separate destinations because it's judged that he needs a break also. Respite requires a formal social work assessment on each occasion, which entails a pot of tea with our care manager in the conservatory, answering detailed questions about the in-laws' abilities or lack thereof, and the exactitude of need. Questions, I can't help thinking, that could have been asked on the phone. It can only be that they want to run an expert eye over the household, sniff the air, and gauge the mood.

It's a busy week, full of incident. My horse has become un-governable with the coming of spring, and first Chris and then I am bucked off, in his case flat on his back onto tarmac, and in mine upside down against a wall, denting a drainpipe and slamming into a water tank. I hobble round the house doing the holiday packing, limp in and out of care meetings, shuffle bruisedly onto the plane. We go to Turkey and buy a teeny house, not much bigger than a beach hut, but with drainage and a veranda, on a holiday site on the Aegean coast, spending the bulk of the French *ruine* money.

The plan to get extra paid help doesn't go quite to plan. The person I had in mind has taken a job at the town nursing home. I consider putting an advertisement postcard in the post office but am dissuaded by a friend. Mightn't that be awkward—interviewing people you know from the village and then not hiring them? She has a point. Still, there doesn't seem to be any alternative. I ask the lead home aide what she thinks, and she offers herself for two hours each weekday, to keep an eye on the in-laws and help with the housework. I accept with gratitude.

The B and B takes off with a whoosh, with a rush of inquiries by e-mail and others by phone. My irritation with the telephone means that e-mail queries are far more likely to be successful. I develop a highly unscientific method of weeding people out. I attempt to instigate an e-mail conversation. If people are irritable, blunt, or evasive, if they can't spell or want a discount, they're turned away. My approach is fearlessly partisan. But the days when there are guests departing and arriving are always, whether by coincidence or not, the days when Nancy's most troublesome.

Chapter 18

Nothing is at last sacred but the integrity of your own mind.

—RALPH WALDO EMERSON

THE RELATIONSHIP BETWEEN MIND AND BRAIN APpears, at first sight, to be a relatively easy one to grasp, even for the amateur neurologist. Brain is the machine, mind its creation. Brain is the cinema equipment, mind the feature film. Brain is the cluster of tiny lasers on the podium, and mind the holographic image of the Fabergé egg. Brain is the instrument, and mind the consciousness that arises out of it, orchestrated by millions of neurons working in concert. It's your brain, not your mind, that the surgeon sticks the scalpel into. It's your mind, not your brain, that feels nervous at the prospect. Simplistic, but so far so good. It's when you get into the relationship between brain, mind, self, and soul that things become more speculative and more prone to prejudice, not least of the religious kind.

Aristotle set the agenda in the fourth century B.C. as a materialist, arguing that the soul (mind) can't exist without the body, which sounds impressively modern until you take into account his insistence that the heart was the location of the thinking self, and the brain some kind of body-cooling device. In general the more modern the thinker, the more integrated brain and self are assumed to be. So it's mildly shocking to read something as recent as Carl Gustav Jung's *The Interpretation of Nature and the Psyche* (1955) and find him asserting that "we must completely give up the idea of the psyche being somehow connected to the brain." Mary Baker Eddy, founder of the Christian Science movement, agreed. "Give up the belief that mind is, even temporarily, compressed within the skull, and you will quickly become more manly or womanly," she wrote. "You will understand yourself and your Maker better than before."

In contradiction of this, the most recent crop of popular science writing is at pains to point out that in every way that really matters, we are our minds, and that our minds and our brains are wholly interdependent. In his idea that psyche is something separate, Jung isn't far from the mind-set of René Descartes (1596–1650) and his firm division of body and self, the self (soul) merely residing in the (mortal, transient) body until such time as immortality can be earned and achieved. It's assumed that this philosophy is biblical, but in fact you'll struggle to find supportive evidence there: the idea of dualism is essentially Greek, and man in the Bible is a holistic, whole creature, body and soul together, anticipating bodily resurrection. The Greek idea is that immortality is a fundamental human attribute; in Christianity it's a gift from God. Plato was Descartes's model, in his belief that an immortal self enters the body somehow, and departs it intact after death. (Descartes struggled with his faith. Having coined *cogito, ergo sum*—I think, therefore I am— he worried that perhaps his thinking self was all that he was, and no more.)

It looks like a two-horse race. Either the brain is all there is to us, personalized through genetic inheritance and through the individuality of experience into a mind, creating the illusion of soul through its clever holographic tricks, and we die with our neurons, *or* the brain is simply the machinery the self/ soul employs for its brief stay on earth and in time, and the self/soul, the *ghost in the machine,* survives us. Any mortal creature would wish Descartes fervently to be right. Added to which, the idea that there is some higher order of personal reality beyond the body, the state of the brain, the workings of the mind—this has a special resonance for dementia sufferers. It introduces the hope that their essential self survives the apparent disintegration dementia brings, locked away safe from the banality of disease.

Descartes thought the soul entered the body through the pineal gland, choosing this entry point because there wasn't then any other obvious use for it, and it was thought to be specifically a human piece of kit. He was, for obvious reasons, an established church favorite, despite his doubts. The establishment was less keen on Franz Joseph Gall (1758–1828), inventor of phrenology (head bump reading), who having surveyed the head shapes of the criminal class, placed subtleties of personality in specific brain regions, which seem to us now entirely random: self-esteem in the parietal lobe, for instance, secretiveness in the temporal lobes, and friendship in the occipital. Less eccentrically, this led him, and the population at large, to the conclusion that self is biology. This was enough to get him expelled from Austria by the emperor Francis I.

If brain is mind, and mind's thought equivalent to self, self equivalent to soul, theological problems are going to arise. There are neurologists writing now who are confident that consciousness itself will before long be "located" and explained as utterly physiological, a line of thought that Francis Crick, the DNA Nobel winner, popularized in his book *The Astonishing Hypothesis* (1994). In his last paper (2004), Crick suggested the claustrum, a "sheet" located beneath the inner surface of the neocortex, which receives information from all areas of the cortex and returns information back into it, might be the seat of consciousness. The truth is that science doesn't yet have the answer to the mystery: how it is that a subjective self comes about at all (known as the Easy Problem) and achieves self-awareness (the Hard Problem).

The phrase *ghost in the machine,* incidentally, was coined by a British philosopher, Gilbert Ryle, in 1949, in mockery of Descartes's dualism. Arthur Koestler's book of the same name (1967) was interested in a different kind of ghost, one associated with the amygdala, deep in the limbic system, creator of impulses concerned with gut instinct, fear, aggression. He suggested that our social evolution has far outstripped our brain evolution, and that we are held back by the primitive emotions and functions of obsolete but still-powerful remnants of our prehistoric selves, which can be held accountable for our being warlike, suspicious, and bigoted.

When the frontal lobe is damaged by Alzheimer's and the self is fractured by the forest fire of neuron death, maybe other parts of the brain rise up to compensate. When rationality is damaged or lost, it is perhaps more primitive parts of the brain and the great hidden sea of the unconscious that prompt facets to rise unexpectedly into view, redirecting the personality of the dementia sufferer into something the caregiver doesn't recognize, with new preoccupations, hostilities, and weirdness. As Freud wrote, though we are more sure of ourselves than of anything, confident that a self is something autonomous and self-contained, the truth is that "the ego extends inwards with no clear boundary into an unconscious psychical entity." As social philosophers of the seventeenth century might have put it, Nancy has lost her Natural Government, and is in danger of relapsing into a state of nature.

It isn't necessarily a two-horse race. The German philosopher Arthur Schopenhauer seems to have been an adherent of a third way, the idea that though there is no immortality of the individual earthly self, we are more than our brains, and return after death to the same state of existence we enjoyed before birth, giving up (with relief, he claimed) the painful and limited animal consciousness of being human and existing in time. "Consciousness is destroyed in death," he wrote, "but that which created it is by no means destroyed." He wasn't the first to see things this way. Anaxagoras, in the fifth century B.C., is thought to have introduced the idea of mind (*nous*) as something infinite and immortal, emanating from The One, the collective human entity that organizes matter and survives it.

Others take a more Platonic route. As the Scottish psychiatrist R. D. Laing wrote, "If my physical frame dissolves, I can't live in this world any more, because this world is a transform: the brain is the transformer and is itself a transform." (A *transform* is reality as delivered up by our perceptions.) It's perhaps Laing who puts the problem of brain and self most succinctly when he goes on to say, "[T]his collection of cells has the impression that it is I. This is a proposition I do not necessarily agree with."

Chapter 19

The trouble with troubleshooting is that trouble shoots back.

—ANONYMOUS

HERE'S SOMETHING NOT COVERED BY THE BOOK, other than in a veiled and decorous way. *Sufferers will need help using the bathroom.* Unfortunately, Nancy won't accept help using the bathroom. She won't *go* if anyone else is present, and is outraged by the suggestion that she use the paper hanging by the toilet. We change her underwear at least once a day. Bedding is also affected, and added to Morris's problems, this means that quite suddenly we have masses of washing to do. But that's not the worst of it. That's just laundry. The much worse thing that's new is that Nancy has started squatting on the floor. Sometimes she tries to hide it. Excreta are found behind the toilet, lurking behind curtains on windowsills, and on one memorable occasion, hidden behind paperbacks in the library—the kind of discovery that's unexpected late at night when you're looking for something to read. If she can be persuaded to use paper it is rare that it's flushed away. Unpleasant sections of toilet roll emerge from cardigan sleeves. She's taken to cleaning the toilet bowl with her hands, so we are careful about not letting her touch food. The long fingernails have to go.

Stuck at home a lot of the time, companion to a man she believes a stranger, Nancy becomes despondent. The fact of her no longer recognizing Morris has a huge emotional cost. She's alone in the world now, and unhappy, and it's as if her unhappiness is beginning to leach out. It fills the air. It coats the walls and furnishings. This isn't just metaphorical. Despite twice weekly baths, my mother-in-law has acquired a smell, a sweet and sweaty smell with a dark undercurrent: feces, armpit, old organs, fear.

Morris is ill and the doctor comes to visit. They have a long conversation together. Later she rings and tells me that Morris is convinced that Chris and I won't stay on the peninsula long, that we'll up and move to the south of France and leave the two of them here all alone.

"The south of France?" I echo. "What on earth gave him that idea?"

It's embarrassing. Is that what he's been telling his home care confidante, or perhaps, what she has been telling him, having misinterpreted something overheard—and is that why people in the village have been asking how long we'll be here?

Morris has grown dangerously unsteady on his feet. His aides have doubled in number so that twosomes can cooperate on the heavy lifting. The consequences of this prove far-reaching. He can't manage his bathroom visits alone any longer. He's too unstable to manage the pulling up and down of trousers. He has to keep his hands on the Zimmer frame or he will fall. This puts the poor man in a very tricky situation. What makes it especially tricky is that Nancy stops cooperating. The manner of his demanding that she help, and her refusing, becomes an explosive part of every day. Chris helps Morris when he can, but often Chris is on the phone at the crucial moment. Morris would, in any case, far prefer that Nancy help him. He certainly doesn't want me in there, a scruple for which I'm grateful.

"Nancy! Nancy!" we hear, urgently from the sitting room. "No! Not that! I need the Zimmer. The Zimmer frame, there. The silver thing with the . . . the frame, Nancy, the frame! The bars, the rack, the frame thing, there. *There!*" His conversations with her have become thesaurus-like. "The Zimmer. Right there, right in front of you. The thing right in front of you, the big silver thing, the Zimmer. No! Not the biscuit tin!" He takes a sharp breath inward and bellows, "THE ZIMMER!" Nothing I say to Morris can make him understand that *Zimmer* is part of the English that's become a foreign language to Nancy. She relies on cues now, cues and context, a "now you're hot, now you're cold again" kind of verbal directing, an impersonal in-car Sat Nav approach. He may as well use the word *zangle*.

Unfortunately, by the time I get Morris into the bathroom, Nancy has had enough of being yelled at, and is marching off in the other direction. I leave him standing, balancing precariously while I run after her, taking her hands in mine and imploring.

Her reaction is predictable.

"Why on earth should I help anybody? It's got nothing to do with me."

This is the crux of it. Nothing has anything to do with Nancy anymore. She floats free of connections to the world. Alzheimer's has invaded her empathy and placed its flag.

"That's your husband, though, Nancy," I tell her.

"No, it is not. It most certainly isn't."

"Yes, it is. Yes. Yes. You have to come and give him a hand."

"I never heard anything so ridiculous."

"He needs help with the bathroom. And you are his wife. You need to go and help."

I'm wasting my breath giving her the backstory. All she is listening to, responding to, is my authority over her, my determination that she should act. That alone will save the day. Her respect for my presumption of power is all that drives her acceptance of my orders.

Afterward she retreats to her bedroom, and that's where I

find her, sitting on the side of her single bed, hands in her lap, staring downward and utterly dejected. The conversation that we have now, the daily conversation about her living here with us, her family, and her forty-seven years of marriage, is becoming grindingly repetitive. As the saying (often attributed to Einstein) goes, the definition of madness is doing the same thing over and over again and expecting different results, and from that point of view my explaining things is a mad enterprise.

Except on one occasion. On that day, instead of staring at the floor, she turns to look at me as I come in.

"I'm so glad it's you," she says with feeling.

"What's up, Nancy? What's up, dear?" I ask, sitting by her. "It was only poor Morris having to go to the toilet. He has to go to the toilet every day in the afternoon and every day you help him. It isn't worth getting this upset about."

She fumbles with a paper handkerchief, twisting and untwisting it.

"I don't understand it," she says, looking into my face, her eyes wet with tears.

"What don't you understand?"

"I don't understand at all what is going on here."

I put my arm round her shoulders. She rests her head on my shoulder and cries, abjectly and with abandon.

"None of it makes sense," she says when she's able to talk. "What's happening here? How did I get here? What's happening? Please. Please."

What will validation do for us now? There's no cozy pretend world to slip into, averting our eyes from the present, taking refuge in dementia-fantasy, stepping through into dementia-time. What else is there to tell her but the truth? If it were me, that's what I'd want.

"Here's the thing," I tell her. "You have a condition. Your memory doesn't work properly. You don't remember things.

That might seem like something quite trivial but, actually, it undermines your whole life. It means that you don't really know who you are."

She snuffles through the handkerchief and tells me her maiden name.

"That used to be your name, but when you were about thirty, a little over thirty, you got engaged to a nice chap called Morris. You got married to him and you adopted two babies."

"But I don't remember that. I don't remember any of it," she says.

"That's because you have this illness and . . ."

"I am not ill. I am absolutely fine."

"You have a condition that lots of old people get. You're in great health otherwise, fit as a fiddle, but your memory is almost gone. Lots of old people get it."

"Am I old?"

"You're seventy-nine. Nearly eighty."

"Am I? Am I? I'm not. I'm not eighty. Am I?"

"Yes. Nearly."

"Oh my god. That's right, is it. I'm eighty." She laughs nervously. I consider taking her to the mirror but then think better of it.

"Yes. Do you remember living in Edinburgh?"

"That's where I live. Edinburgh."

"Do you remember the apartment by the canal? Feeding the moorhens and the swans with bags of bread?"

"No. I don't remember that."

"Do you remember going to work, your little car, your rack of navy blue suits and shirts? Doing your nails every night?"

"No. Not really."

"Do you remember the children? Getting the children, the babies?"

"No. No."

She looks at me as if hopeful that the two of us might be in this mess together.

"That was forty years ago, more. You're retired now and you live with us. With your son and his family. Morris is here, too."

"Is he?"

"Yes. He's the man sitting through there."

"Can I see him? I've been wondering where he was." She starts to cry again.

"Come on. Quickly. Come and see him and give him a kiss."

We go through the kitchen and up the step, through the second door. When she sees him, Nancy goes into reverse, trampling my feet.

"No! No, no. You're wrong. That isn't Morris."

"Of course I'm Morris," Morris says.

Nancy turns to me. "That. Is not. Morris."

"Yes, it is. That's Morris. He's got old, just like you. And he's disabled. His legs don't work, remember?"

"You're all mad. You're all mistaken. That isn't Morris. You think I don't know who Morris is? Well, I do and that isn't him."

All this is horribly upsetting for Morris, and his confidante has been counseling him at length in the mornings. The rejection is hard for him to bear. Nancy seems so hard-hearted, so impermeable suddenly. Morris tries to talk her round, to jostle her memory, insisting on the truth.

"But darlin'! It's me! You must know me! You must!"

"I most certainly do not. You're all liars."

"Nancy, please. Please don't say you don't know me. Please."

She goes and sits on the edge of her bed for hours and hours, refusing to eat or drink, sitting looking hopeless in her cold bedroom; me going in from time to time and trying to coax her to come back to the fire. Sometimes I find her in bed fully clothed, the duvet pulled up over her mouth, her shoes sticking out the other end, flat on her back and deeply asleep. Sleep is good. Sleep is her friend. The event is wiped clean away. As long as I don't use the words *Morris* or *husband* when I reintroduce her to her sitting room, things are fine for a while. If only Morris could resist asserting himself and conjuring up their shared history, things would stay calmer for longer, but he can't.

The rages spill out of the sitting room. There begin to be rumblings from day centers. They cope well at the Tuesday one, where they are trained to deal with Alzheimer's old folk and have others with dementia attending. Dementia's meat and drink to them. But the Thursday club, held in our own village, is a different matter altogether. It's a social club for over-sixties. They are kind, good-hearted people, the people who run the Thursday club, and they try diversionary tactics first, before they call. If Nancy's stroppy, somebody takes her out for a walk. They might go to the shop and get her an ice cream and go look at the boats in the harbor. If diversions don't work she's brought home early, delivered to the door, she and Morris alone in the bus, Morris embarrassed. "She's not had too good a day today," the helpers say. "Not too happy today." Sometimes she comes home wearing borrowed underwear and I am full of admiration for the volunteers who deal so stoically with that.

In May, we experience the first of the major Thursday club upsets. It's heralded by a phone call after lunch, from one of the helpers, who happens to be the mother of one of our doctors.

"I'm afraid Nancy's in a terrible state," she says. "Do I have your permission to take her to the surgery?"

"What on earth's going on?"

"She's . . . well, she's just in meltdown, really. We can't do anything with her and I, um, think she might need medical intervention."

"You mean she's having a tantrum, she's upset? Is she being rude to people?"

"You might say."

Everyone's far too nice to be explicit. I have visions of Nancy going at the other members with a hail of china-saucer-fire, a volley of cutlery artillery, kicking old men in the groin and felling them with karate chops. Nancy is whisked off and given emergency sedation. They keep her there until it kicks in and then she is driven home, arriving monosyllabic and irritable. The doctor rings me later. "That was quite something," she says. "I've never seen her like that before." A frank conversation follows. Nancy is prescribed a mood-improving drug to add to the galantamine, the blood pressure drug, and the aspirin in the dosette box. Though we don't give it to her beyond forty-eight hours, as its principal effect seems to be to tranquilize her in the daytime and make her more restless and agitated than usual at night.

Can I cope with this? Should I be trying? These are the questions that whirr in the brain at five in the morning when the long, gray summer days of the far north dawn early. We are already way out of our depth and we've been here for less than a year. How much longer will this go on? How much longer can I stand it?

Internally, I'm fervently apologetic to all those unknown, anonymous people I ever maligned for *dumping*. Dumping their parents in nursing homes, when they should have been clasping them to their familial bosoms, for better or worse. Movie grannies, with their crumpled-and-smoothed tissue-paper faces and gray plaits worn Heidi-like across their heads, and tea dresses and crochet cardigans—the kind of grannies who are pliant and hygienic, who dispense old-world wisdom to the children of the house, and are amusingly direct—they have a lot to answer for. Movie grannies don't refuse point-blank to clean their teeth. They don't yell obscenities at their grandchildren or accuse their daughter-in-law of stealing all their money or tell outsiders they're being kept a prisoner. They never pull down their trousers and touch their toes and ask you if their bottoms are clean, or get sent home early from the Thursday club for disruption.

I am out in the garden tackling the weedy borders and planting new shrubs quite a bit of the day, having abandoned the novel, again. It isn't something I'm happy about. It's not been a matter of choice, but writing isn't possible with Nancy on the rampage and the constant interruptions. Nor is writing possible when so much unhappiness is at large. Nancy's. Morris's. My own. So instead of struggling on, there will be reading and gardening and strategies for psychic survival. Weeding is good for impotent rage. Old neglected borders full of grass and dandelion are gone at with energy. I take Nancy into the garden with me for part of the day and try to filter out her wittering, and try to be calm about her standing in the middle of the flower beds, trampling new plants. Her white skin is sun sensitive and burns in a trice. She is dressed in her customary elastic-waist slacks, a long-sleeve cotton shirt, and a wide-brimmed hat. She smiles, when she's outdoors. There's Nancy in the photographs, flushed pink and grinning. It's indoors that she hates, the terrible boredom of indoors. Outside, she gets all my attention. And maybe it's more than that. Perhaps it's Nancy who's found a relationship with the Sublime.

Clinging to the idea that we ought to make her days as fulfilling as possible, and having given up on work for now, I try to include her, like mothers of preschoolers do, in the daily domestic tasks. It's exhausting work: "Now here's your peg, here's the sock—see, you open the peg like this and put it on the line and when you let go it grips it. See? No, don't put them all on top of one another, they won't dry. Ah no, see, you've got the peg upside down, that won't work." On Mondays, when Morris is out at the day hospital, I make a special effort. Then, having spent five unbroken hours together, I put her in her chair and go to make her a coffee and when I get back she is purple-faced with rage.

"I've been left here all day on my own! People have been going by and not speaking to me! If I'm not wanted here you had better just say so!"

I've been reading a book that claims to explain consciousness and its neurological mechanisms as something entirely animal. The writer pulls off the disarming logical trick of spending the entire first chapter disparaging Descartes, and the rest of the book coming face-to-face with a series of pro-Descartes (Cartesian) scenarios—suggesting in their various ways that there *is* a ghost in the machine, operating the machinery—and dealing with them, one by one, by pointing out that since Descartes must be wrong, because his ideas are preposterous (a favorite authorial word), there must be some other explanation. It is, weirdly, a book that seems unconsciously to be prey to subconscious tides pulling its conclusions in opposite directions to those intended.

I also come across some rather startling research to do with the electrical impulses that carry information between neurons. Apparently, studies of the *action potentials* have found that they fire up *before* we decide they should be doing whatever it is that we've asked of them: for instance, to turn a page or flip a fried egg or pick up a stone on the beach. Experiments showing this to be true were begun by the research scientist Benjamin Libet in the 1970s, and continued in 1985 in a scientific trial done with people who flexed their wrists at will and signaled the moment of deciding by marking the position of a rotating disk. Extraordinarily, it was discovered that the appropriate neurons fired up a full half second before the moment the subjects "decided." The interval is known as Libet's delay. In terms of the speed of the electrical impulse, a half second is a very long time. What seems to be happening is that

something below or aside from consciousness is making decisions before we think we are making decisions. Something else
in us, backstage of our deciding, appears to be deciding before
we decide. It reminds me of a British TV series called *Yes Minister,* in which civil servants manipulate a member of the government, convincing him that he's in charge when the truth is
that the real decision making is going on elsewhere. In April
2008, an experiment using fMRI scanning not only confirmed
that Libet's delay exists, but went further, showing decisions
can be predicted up to *ten seconds* before deciders "decide." (Of
course, it's possible to argue that these are ten seconds in which
the subject is observed in readiness, preparing to do something
as instructed by the experimenter.)

I DON'T KNOW what all this has to do with Alzheimer's. Probably nothing. But it increases the sense of there being some
other self beyond the one we're confident of living within, that
feels contained and definite—an alternative self that in our
more exhausted moments, in my mother-in-law's case, we've
taken to calling Nancy's evil twin. The interesting question,
for me at least, is whether this new Nancy's simply a part of
Nancy that's always been there, long suppressed and now un-
leashed by loss of inhibition, or is it something properly new?
The validation thesis suggests that it's the former: that Nancy's
self is still intact; it's just that we're seeing a different part of it
now, one kept at bay previously by the frontal lobe but given
liberty by dementia—the rise of aspects from her subconscious, perhaps. It's quite a Cartesian idea when you think
about it, the idea that Nancy's self is still intact but trapped
within failing machinery, and it's just her superficial way of
dealing with the world in the old way that's been lost (if thinking can be said to be superficial). But my own suspicion is that
it's something new—that the amygdala and more primitive

parts of the brain, dedicated to survival, selfish and aggressive, are being allowed to come forward and create a new self; one that, in the circumstances, we can only continue to call Nancy. I'd always hoped, until recently, that I had a soul that would survive me, but I see now that I will have to locate it somewhere hidden from consciousness, unknown by what I think of as my self, if what I know now about the consequences of brain damage isn't to have the effect of extinguishing that hope. Reading about caregivers' experiences of looking after loved ones—husbands and wives, but particularly husbands—who have suffered catastrophic head injuries in accidents or assaults and have become *different people* isn't reassuring.

The weather's quite outstandingly foul for May. A hailstorm in May seems like the end of the world. Though the gloom is mitigated by being offered more paid help, by one of the other aides. After a brief crossover period the first aide bows out, Morris's confidante, citing tiredness and illness; I've no doubt that Nancy's sniping was the cause of both. It's difficult (that's putting it mildly) to find people who can work with Alzheimer's sufferers and not become short-tempered, bewildered, bored, exhausted, or demoralized. Our second aide is one such, someone who doesn't and isn't. She's cheerful, assertive, robust, and unoffendable. But she also has young children, a farm to run, is the school cook, and caters for weddings. We squeeze extra hours out of her when we can but that's the most she can offer.

There are seasonal signs of hope in the garden. The wood is teeming with bluebells, thousands of them in a purple haze, and a melancholy bluebell scent drifts up the garden. People have been along in their cars to visit them. Nobody thinks to ask us if it's okay to wander in there, but we don't mind too much, at least not until we see, one late afternoon, somebody standing on the drive with his hands on his hips, looking up

toward the house, standing guard it turns out, while his ac-
complice is at work. They see me at the window and retreat.
But when I go down there, the earth has been disturbed in
several areas under the trees. It was the whole plant, bulb and
all, that they were after, and they've made off with armfuls.

Chapter 20

ELSEWHERE I DESCRIBE MEMORY BANKS AS A LIBRARY that we can visit in our heads. That's the traditional way of seeing it, but it isn't remotely accurate. Memory is an activity and not a vault. The brain stores different aspects of any one memory in different parts of the brain. What was seen, what was heard, the smell, touch, taste, the emotional input— all are contributed by their specialist areas. Visual memory's called up from the occipital lobe, auditory memory from the temporal, working together in a synchronized way. It's not a place, but a process, and a process not unlike music made by an orchestra. In short, it works in just the same way that consciousness does.

Why do some people have good memories and others bad? My sister has an extraordinary memory for our shared childhoods, which puts me at a disadvantage, when I'm quoted at age eight in a fight over an ice-cream scoop. Partly, the reason some people retain the "film" of the past in such vivid detail is that they use their memories more. To keep a memory you have to keep having the memory, revisiting the memory, using it, so as to keep that collection of neurons imprinted and those synaptic connections in place. If they're not used, then they wither. To remember things you have to go through the process of remembering them again. You make a new memory each time you remember, revisiting the route from neuron to neuron. Researchers have discovered that there is an actual anatomical change in the laying down of long-term memories. The axons grow new synapses and new proteins are made in the nucleus of the neuron. There's a change at the cellular level, something that doesn't occur in the making of short-term memories. In his book *In Search of Memory,* Eric Kandel, who was awarded the 2000 Nobel Prize for medicine, elaborates on this idea that in order to convert a short-term memory into a long-term one, we need to care about it enough, whether for happy or unhappy reasons, and that our caring has physiological effects. One hit of neurotransmitter and the synapse is improved. Five hits and the cell is alerted to this (whatever it is) being something important. It sends the information, via a protein, to the nucleus that triggers the genetic switch for the growth of the new synaptic port. There are two ways in, it seems, via quantity or quality: either via repetition, thinking about something over and over, or by means of the intensity of a shock or equivalent emotional event.

The things that stick aren't always the obvious things. Odd, oblique, incidental, tangential things stick. As the writer Elizabeth Bowen said once in an interview, "The charm, one might say the genius, of memory is that it is choosy, chancy, and temperamental: it rejects the edifying cathedral and indelibly photographs the small boy outside, chewing a hunk of melon in the dust." Montaigne, in the sixteenth century, was more succinct but less alluring, as is his way, in writing that "[t]he memory represents to us not what we choose but what it pleases." What you care about isn't necessarily what you think you care about.

When you remember, it's a memory of the memory that you're having. You don't go into the library of your memory and pick up the book and read your past. In a sense, you write the book all over again. And research shows that if you don't take the trouble to rewrite the books, the books disappear. It's rather like those wardrobe nannies who insist that anything not worn for twelve months ought to be put in a bin bag. *You haven't thought about this for years so I'm chucking it out.* It sends the nanny in and chucks, and it's only when you open the wardrobe that you discover your fake fur jacket/caravan holiday memory is missing. Or, to use another analogy, we need to keep digging out paths in the snow. If we don't, snow eliminates them. Get out there and dig those paths. Maintain them and you can keep walking on them. Don't maintain them and they are gone. How does the brain do this? The nanny in question's an enzyme called PP1 that removes the phosphate from the target protein and deactivates it, in effect wiping a particular memory from the slate.

There are four levels of memory. The first, sensory memory, isn't really memory at all. It's stuff that the eyes see, that the brain may know (far more goes in than is retrievable), but the conscious self doesn't notice. Take the scene in front of my eyes just to the side of the laptop, right now, for instance. The books and papers, used coffee cups, the tin of salted almonds, the box of old photographs waiting to be put into albums, the postcards, pens, mobile phone, plus the jewelry and homework the children left there—everything that's spread on the coffee table beside me as I write this—made a brief sensory imprint in my mind, but hadn't been processed any further until I turned my attention tableward. Perhaps a probe could find it in my head, if probes and scanners grew that sophisticated. Perhaps I might be an unwitting witness to a crime that my eyes saw but I didn't register, while looking out of the window in the city at the cherry blossom on a busy street, where among the traffic and pedestrians, somebody was quietly and efficiently killed with a knife. I saw it but I didn't register it. It was among the things my eyes were seeing while I was concentrating on something else. That's the first level of memory.

The second level is the working memory. This is the material we *hold in mind,* temporarily, like part of a mathematical calculation we put aside while doing the second part, ready to add the two numbers together, or a phone number we need to remember that was given to us when we didn't have a pen. It's recited in the head and retained for as long as we need it. Then we forget it. Nancy is beginning to forget things that have just happened, things that have just been said to her, and how to finish a sentence she's only halfway through speaking. She's losing her working memory and is unable to hold things in mind. The man known only by the initials H.M., a neurologically much-quoted epilepsy victim—run over by a bicycle at age nine, and in his twenties at the time of being a research subject in the 1950s—with his temporal lobe function diminished and hippocampus removed, could still remember new things done or said for a few minutes. His working memory survived although his short-term memory, ordinarily the next phase in the process, no longer functioned.

Scientists classify short-term memory differently according to length. Neurologists tend to talk about it as short-to-medium term. The things we did yesterday, last weekend, even the wedding we danced at the weekend before that, can be described as held in short-term memory. The process of converting a select few of these into long-term memory, forming strong memories that survive, can take weeks, and it's thought most of the work's done while we sleep.

Memory making is a single-track road. To get from the sensory memory stage through working memory into short-term and thus into long-term memory is like going along one of those winding narrow routes that stretch out into the fingers of the coast of Argyll in remote western Scotland. There's only one road from the village of Sensory to Long Term. To get to Long Term you need to go through the other three villages first. In other words, if there is a break in the road, a flash flood, say, and then a road slip, a section of the road sagging and tipping down the hill, and the road becomes impassable, nothing can get to Long Term. That's what happens in Alzheimer's. The short-term memory fails, is gone for good, and so nothing new can be processed into long-term memory. The poor old village of Short Term is obliterated entirely. The brain has an alternative route *out* of Long Term, though not in. Eventually it, too, will be obliterated.

Once you get into long-term memory, the road branches. Down one road there's implicit memory, and down the other, explicit. Explicit further branches, into episodic and semantic. Implicit is another way of saying procedural memory, the one that deals with the things that we do as if automatically. Riding a bike, driving a car, knowing a dance, playing the flute: these skill memories are taken care of by the cerebellum in league with the basal ganglia, four clusters of neurons at the base of the brain that help initiate and control movement. Serotonin is the neurotransmitter of choice in the making of implicit memories, and dopamine in the creating of explicit memory. Researchers think that implicit memories are laid down while we're in REM (rapid eye movement) sleep, in which our dreams are most vivid, and that explicit memories are made during non-REM sleep.

Explicit memory is the sort we need actively to call up, "thinking" in the familiar conscious sense. Episodic is autobiographical, and locates things in time and sequence: "I ate eggs for breakfast, went to the life drawing class in the village, and after lunch Nancy and I took the dogs to the beach." That's episodic memory. Semantic memory is encyclopedic, intellectual, for facts.

Alzheimer's damages the episodic (autobiographical) memory first and worst. The semantic survives longer. Sufferers might know very little about themselves, nothing whatever about what happened ten minutes ago, and yet might be able to talk at length about the history, the battles, and the princes associated with a ruined castle visited on a Sunday afternoon outing, using long-term semantic memory. Alzheimer's sufferers of a certain generation, taught screeds of poetry by rote at school, find they can still recite their twenty verses of Longfellow with perfect accuracy, until quite late in the disease.

Because memory is a process, relying on neurons to fire up in the same sequence each time we remember, memory can be wrong. Memory, indeed, is notoriously unreliable. Why should it be, though, when we rely on it for survival? Perhaps that's the point. Perhaps our brains are more dedicated to our psychic health than to the truth. What we see, the way that we see it, and the way we remember it are essentially subjective. The process of making memories and then remembering them is both technical and personal. The synapses may not reproduce their original pattern. It's like the old fable of the bad carpenter's table, in which leg number two is drawn from leg number one (and is a bit out), and then leg number three is drawn from two and is even more wrong, and number four, drawn from number three, isn't anything like the same length or shape as number one. Something we thought, imagined, doubted, added on one occasion of remembering distorts the memory for next time it's called up. How then can I be sure of what I have done and experienced in my life? There are some slices of time, moments, collections of moments, from the deep past that are unlikely, eccentric, unaccountably preserved, and which I treasure. But are they accurate, or are they a story I tell myself for my own reasons? There's no way of knowing for sure. Not only do you, the reader, perhaps suspect that not all of what I write about life with Nancy is exactly as it happened, but strictly speaking, knowing the mechanism to be emotional, I ought to suspect the same. Our memories of things are never objective. We interact with them and add meaning; highlight certain aspects and throw others into shadow.

The brain is selective about memory. Not only about the

details, but about the quantity. This selection and editing is important in life having a shape. The truth of this is illustrated by the problems encountered by people who have too much memory. There have been neurological cases of people who can't forget things. Their brains can't filter out or edit and everything is retained. They can tell you in detail exactly what was said or done on this day last year. What happens to them is that they lose the big picture, a sense of perspective, and are overwhelmed by detail. No choices can be made, no judgments. Everything is of equal importance. Because of this, they don't always function well as humans. So it appears that in principle and in moderation, forgetting is important. As Nietzsche wrote, "There could be no happiness, cheerfulness, hope, pride, immediacy, without forgetfulness."

Chapter 21

Between the acting of a dreadful thing
And the first motion, all the interim is
Like a phantasma or a hideous dream.
—WILLIAM SHAKESPEARE

I FIND, ON A ROUTINE SELF-AUDIT, THAT I HAVE BECOME very low. Nancy is succeeding in sucking the optimism out of me, a strange new place to find myself in the middle of summer: flat in the heart, empty in the head, craving solitude and sleep. Peninsula sunshine is blinding, uninterrupted by geography, reflected and magnified by the sea, but I am peculiarly unmoved by the sun at the edges of the curtains in the morning. It's worse, in a way, when the weather is good. On top of my own lowness is overlaid recrimination. Here it is, a summer day at last, and I don't want to have anything to do with it. Worse, I don't seem to be *able* to have anything to do with it. I can't step into it and be warmed. The heat on my skin is an irritant, the warmth on my head provoking. It's best if I keep my distance.

What I want is a sofa to myself. I want to be left alone to read, reassured by the sun pouring in at the windows, which is a novelty in itself, but Nancy's reaction to the arrival of something like summer is an inability to sit still. Daily she wanders the hall. Up and down to the conservatory and back. Through one kitchen door and out the other, twenty, thirty times a day. Up and down from bedroom to sitting room. In and out of the bathroom with an absent expression, her mouth drooping, her eyes blank and hooded. She's taken on what's called the *lion face* of Alzheimer's. But if sunshine makes her twitchy, it's worse, far worse, on the bad weather days that follow, which come as we know they will, a wind and rain corrective. Seasons arrive and depart in self-contained daily chapters that seem to have little to do with one another or with the conventions of the calendar.

"Hey, you. Hey. What you doing?" I say cheerily. "Wandering again? Can't we find something for you to do?"

The voice of doom speaks in monotone. "There is nothing to do. There is nothing at all to do. It's just all meaningless. It happens again and again and it doesn't mean anything." She goes to the window, gestures out at the bay, the headland, the sea roaring and the wind howling in another midsummer gale. "Look. There's nothing there."

She's right, I find myself thinking. We must get back to the city! Though it's my mother-in-law's thought, this Edinburgh-craving thought I'm having. I'm channeling my mother-in-law. She has possessed me and I am diminished.

After the gales recede there are days of gray mugginess, the midges gathering in clouds on the road beside the wood. Then there's a cold snap, which coincides with the B and B booking of two women from New Mexico engaged on a European tour. They live in perpetual drought at home with a cactus garden, and though they say that they expected Scotland to be cool, their idea of cool is 68 degrees, a temperature regarded as sweltering hereabouts. The house isn't warm enough for them, even with all of our inadequate heaters blasting on max. They huddle by their coal fire in three layers of thermal and fleece. One of them wears a bobble hat for breakfast. They go out on a cool June morning wearing all the sweaters and coats and ear-muffs and scarves and gloves they could find in an emergency dash to the knitwear shop in town. Nancy meets them in the conservatory and makes a fuss of their itchy Fair Isle acquisitions. "Oh, that's just brilliant!" I hear her exclaim. "Where on earth did you get it? Because I want one just the same! Can I try it? Can I? Can I if I'm extra nice?"

Written feedback arrives from Nancy's April respite week. It seems that she was a happy bunny at the residential home. "She taught some of the other residents to dance." She "only became distressed when the time came for her to leave." Next, feedback arrives from the care manager, verbally over tea and biscuits. There's bad news from the bed allocation committee. Our attempt to get Nancy onto the list bounced back with little consideration. "More help could be offered at home." Seven words. Nancy's not anywhere near eligible even for the waiting list yet. Meanwhile, following more day center shenanigans, and spurred on by this bounce back, one of our doctors writes a letter saying that in her opinion Nancy has already reached the point of requiring twenty-four-hour medical care. This cuts no ice whatever.

It's getting more difficult to persuade Nancy to take her clothes off at bedtime. Underwear is a particular bone of contention. She's physically as strong as ever and holds on tight to her underpants with both hands as they descend.

"Come on, you know you don't wear underpants in bed," I say.

"I've never heard anything so ridiculous in my life," she thunders, Miss Jean Brodie to a T.

SHE BEGINS A concerted series of kitchen raids. She seems to be hungry all the time. This is explained when I go back into the in-laws' sitting room one morning and find Morris eating Nancy's cereal. He has a rabbit-stunned-by-headlights look when he sees me coming.

"Morris, you really shouldn't eat Nancy's breakfast," I tell him. "I can get you another bowl if you're hungry."

"It's not that. It's just that she won't eat it and she's anxious about it, so I'm helping her out."

"The thing is, we need to know how much she's eating."

"Okay, boss, I hear you."

"It's important that she eats properly. I can find her something else to eat if she doesn't want Weetabix."

"You're the boss."

He's also helpful when she decides that she isn't going to take her pills any longer. More than once, I approach their door and hear Morris saying, "Quick, she's coming, give them to me." I find them cupped in his palm, the five little pills that Nancy doesn't want to take.

What does he think, that this helps Nancy? What does he think, that I'm the nasty matron who will insist on cod liver oil, and ought to be outwitted? That's how it seems. His attitude produces a twin. Mine. Cast in the role of nagger.

"You have to be in charge of Nancy eating enough, and Nancy getting her medication," I tell him.

"Uh-huh," he says, not taking his eyes off the television.

"Morris! This is serious stuff. This is important."

"All right, all right! I hear you!" he snaps.

When I leave the room, they mutter together. The word *she* begins to be heard a lot. I am she. She is me. The nasty matron.

NANCY'S DIET BECOMES difficult to manage. She is rejecting most of the things I present her with. Morris gets given them when I leave the room. Her breakfast cereal, her toast. Her lunch. She'll eat the potato chips and the yogurt but not the sandwich. Morris gets first dibs on that, and if he declines, it's offered to a passing dog, and if the dog turns his nose up, it goes into the fire. I find the evidence in the grate among the cinders—a jumble of foodstuffs, tipped and scraped. Sandwiches, grapes, baked potato, small heaps of rejected salad. I fill up the

biscuit barrel on Morris's side table every day, and every day it
empties again. Every day, hungry, Nancy comes into the kitchen
when I'm not there and carries out a snack raid. Things begin
disappearing that nobody can account for. Packets of biscuits,
packets of nuts, half-pound bricks of cheese, a bowl of straw-
berries, tomatoes brought in from the greenhouse and left in the
colander. Things put out on the worktop ready to cook suffer
random losses. An aubergine with give-away bite marks appears
in the wastepaper basket. I come into the kitchen one afternoon
and find Nancy standing in front of the stove, stuffing buns into
her mouth. They'd been left out to cool on a rack ready for the
children coming home. She has one in each hand and her mouth
is full, working hard at another. There are four others missing
from the tray. I'd been gone from the kitchen for ten minutes,
gone to bring washing in. I'm beginning to understand what lies
behind her constant opening of the kitchen door, and her retreat
when she sees I am in there.

"Oh. Oh, there is somebody. Well, it doesn't matter. I'll
come back."

"Something you want, Nancy?"

"No, no. Just wondering if there was anybody here."

"I'm here. Just reading the paper."

"Yes, yes. Well, then. I'll come back."

"Sure I can't get you anything?"

"No, no. It's fine."

Occasionally she's caught red-handed. She's defiant about the
buns.

"Oh, Nancy—no. They were for later."

Nancy (through a mouthful of cake, spitting liberal
crumbs): "What's it got to do with you?"

"I made them. For later."

"Well, then. Well, then. Enough of your nonsense."

She reaches for another.

"Nancy. Leave the buns just now. Go and see Morris. Here,

take some peanuts with you. How about some cheese and crackers?."

Nancy ignores these offers. Her beady eye is fixed birdlike on the cakes.

"Leave the buns till later, Nancy."

"I will not. They're just as much mine as yours."

"Actually, no, because I made them."

"Oh. Oh, sorry."

But when she leaves the kitchen she takes one with her.

She picks things up and inspects them even if she doesn't eat them, which is worse in a way. Bathroom hygiene has been abandoned, so nobody else in the family wants to risk eating food that Nancy has touched. The fruit bowl becomes unpopular. Jack will only eat bananas and oranges, things that have to be peeled.

There are several alarming toilet incidents. The kind that make a person gag when called upon to deal with them. By "a person" I mean me. Chris is made of stronger stuff and this is chastening. I didn't have any problem dealing with the children's bottoms when they were little, after all. I try to think of Nancy as a big stroppy baby—one shouting, "I didn't do it! I didn't do anything! It's nothing to do with me!" But it doesn't help. One morning we come down to find—and I'm sorry to be so graphic, but this account is only of any use if it's honest—what can only be described as a trail, leading from the day bathroom out into the hall. The beige-colored carpet is smeared. Turds have been deposited at intervals and then trodden in. Opening the bathroom door, the floor is awash. Chris steps in and rolls up his sleeves and deals with it. I offer to go and have a look at the perpetrator. She's fast asleep. The feet are easily sorted out, courtesy of a series of wet wipes and a supermarket bag, breath held and eyes averted. The carpet will never be the same.

It's not a good month for bottom issues. Morris has been given a toilet aid, a mobile lightweight frame with a higher seat. One day when I'm cleaning, I move it away from the toilet in the day bathroom and forget to put it back again. Nancy, not able to understand the significance of its being moved, goes in and sits on the frame rather than the toilet, and pees gallons on the carpet. She's getting enough to drink. That's obvious. The kitchen door is often open in the morning and I suspect she's sleep-snacking. Sleep-snacking and filing her nails. Having refused tea, coffee, juice, squash, or water all day, she's possibly waking thirsty and going to the kitchen tap. But how? She can't any longer manage a tap. Nor find a glass in the crockery cupboard. Nor find the cupboard, come to that. Not when she's awake, at any rate.

The worst day with Nancy, the worst ever, comes unexpectedly as disasters tend to. One morning, when everybody is out of the house except Nancy and me—Morris has gone to the day hospital, the children are at school, and Chris is away—she summons me to her bedside with shouts. I can't be sure of this, but it might be *"Service!"* that she's shouting. When I open the door to her room, she's red faced, her eyes blazing. It's 9:00 A.M. and twenty minutes ago she was snoring. The twenty minutes have been spent profitably. She's lying in bed wearing miscellaneous layers of clothes: a shirt and a pair of trousers next to her skin, followed by a bra (backward, clips across the bosom, cups flapping behind) and another pair of trousers, then underpants, then a cardigan worn round her waist like a skirt, another two cardigans worn properly, her bathrobe on top.

"Where have you been? What time do you call this, then? About bloody time, too," she says to me.

It takes almost an hour to get her undressed and showered and redressed—she's soiled and peed herself in bed—by which time she is in pugnacious form.

"Is that all you've got for me? It's not very much, is it?" she says when I light the fire. "Is that all you can do?" when I put her television on. I ask if she'd like a cup of tea.

"Not likely, not if you've anything to do with it," she says. "Get me somebody else. Go on! Go on! Fetch me the manager because I want to complain."

"Look," I say. "I do not work here. For your information. I live here. This is my house. You are my mother-in-law and that's the only reason that I put up with you."

She looks taken aback.

"Well," she says with great theatricality, "I've never been so insulted—"

"Really? It's early yet," I shout, leaving the room and slamming the door.

I sit at the table, heart thumping. What am I doing? Why am I so angry? My hands are shaking.

I get up and open the door. Smiling like a maniac.

"Nancy! How lovely to see you!" I trill. Ordinarily, this tactic would work. Short-term memory loss can work to a caregiver's advantage. But Nancy isn't going to be bought off anything like that easily. This is a seriously bad day, heroic in the pantheon of Bad Days with Nancy. Ordinarily an immediate about-turn of mood on my part has an almost magical effect. Ordinarily she would grin at me and greet me back. "I've not seen you for so long! My friend! Come and see me, come and sit by me." Patting her lap as if I were six. This would be a normal about-turn and all would be well. But today is different.

"I'll just get your breakfast, back in a tick," I say.

I take her a bowl of two Weetabix with milk and sugar and a piece of jammy toast for her tray, a glass of orange juice and cup of tea for her side table. She stares forward, rubbing her hands together. She takes her pills without comment, without resistance, still staring ahead and rubbing. I stand in front of her for a moment. She doesn't seem to see me. I crouch down. "Nancy," I say. "Here's your cereal." She is rubbing more urgently now and her eyes are wide. I put the spoon in and offer a little to her lips. I offer up the toast. She takes no notice.

Righto, then, I think. Just leave her be. Get your own breakfast. I eat some porridge and drink some coffee and read yesterday's *Times*. Then I go back into her sitting room.

She's sitting in her armchair with that same unseeing stare, hands rubbing rhythmically. Her lap tray is on the table by the window. Her orange juice has been drunk, and her tea, and her bowl is almost clean.

"That's great, you managed it all this morning," I say. Then my eye is caught by the fireplace. The Weetabix is on the hearth in a scraped milky heap. As I approach I see that the orange juice and tea have been poured onto the grate among the cinders, over a wigwam of toast. Nancy sits rubbing her hands quite frantically together, the pace increasing as I approach, her face streaked with crimson and blue, her expression defiant.

"What on earth have you done?" I say. "Why on earth did you do that?"

"What?"

"That. Look. Cereal all over the hearth." I poke it. It's setting into quite a useful Weetabix-based cement.

"I didn't do that. It was that other woman. That bitch, the other woman."

"Come over here," I command.

"I told you, I didn't do it," a high wavery voice insists. "It's nothing to do with me."

"Come over here. Come here. Come here," I say, attempting authority.

She gets up, sighing.

"Look," I say. "You did that. You made that mess and I want you to clean it up." I give her the coal shovel and brush.

"I'm not doing anything of the kind," she says.

"Yes. You. Are," I say.

"NO."

"YES. YES YES YES." I'm shrieking now. I'm losing it.

Months and months of holding back and being reasonable have their price and here is their invoice.

"I am sick of you!" I yell. "I am so sick of you and looking after you and the endless bloody drudgery!"

Nancy roars. That's the only word for it. She roars like a lion, like an old skinny lion with a mangy coat, left behind by the pride to starve. She's dangerous. She's a cranky old lion and still has teeth. She swings the shovel toward my head, and I make a reflex movement and it misses. She throws the shovel against the wall, where it breaks into two pieces and falls. She brandishes the brush and jabs forward with it at my chest. I grab it and we're struggling. She lets go of the brush and has me by the upper arms with tight white fingers. She pushes suddenly and I fall backward. She's shouting incoherently; I can't make out the words. I barely hit the carpet before I'm up again and grabbing her. I have her by the upper arms now. Now it's her turn to topple backward.

"Don't you ever, EVER, get aggressive with me, you vicious old cow, or you will be in a nursing home before you can say *tea bag*!" I screech. I can't catch my breath and it occurs to me that I'm going to have a heart attack and die. All I can think is, What if it had been one of the children? What if she'd taken a swing at Jack and the sharp edge had hit home, across his cheek, his ear, his eye?

By the time she falls, in graceful slow motion, onto her bottom on the carpet, still holding on to my arms, rolls onto her back, and is pushing herself upright again, one knee and one foot braced, I am screaming. I can't remember what I say. I remember that I step backward and am holding on tight to the door handle. I don't trust myself not to hit her. I'm yelling my head off. She's standing up by the fireplace now—thank god, thank god that neither of us fell toward it: I have a flash, a vision of Nancy cracking her head on the hearth and going limp. She's rubbing at her upper arms with both hands and saying, "Oh Christ, oh Christ."

I slump onto the floor, my back against the door. I'm shaking violently. I can't believe that I threatened the nursing home as a punishment. Elder abuse. Elder abuse is all I can think of. Strictly speaking it was self-defense—or retaliatory, at least, as she pushed me first—but even so. She has Alzheimer's. What in hell am I doing?

The rest of the day is spent making ostentatious amends, singing songs, taking her on walks and garden visits, and brushing her hair and making her laugh, all upset forgotten. But when I put her to bed I see that she has bruises. Small, faint fingerprints encircle both arms. Mine are sore to the touch but are unmarked. She bruises easily, dramatically easily these days, but even so. These I inflicted. Aristotle in the *Poetics* describes how *hamartia,* a serious lapse of judgment, can all too easily lead to *peripeteia,* a calamitous reversal of fortune. The dark shadow of *peripeteia* is hanging over me. Guilt, in other words.

I pour myself a (large) glass of malt, noting idly that daytime drinking is becoming the norm, and administer a self-directed pep talk. There's no point in rising, in engaging, in any of the negative energy because it's only me who suffers. I give away my power, and I'm not going to do it again. Tomorrow, if the same happens, I will scrape the breakfast from the hearth and leave the room and go find other things to do. I'll do it quietly and without comment. I will find a way of not minding. It's not caregiving that's exhausting, but minding. It's minding that will make me ill.

I get it all out of my system in the classic modern way. I write e-mails. How could Weetabix lead to violence? In the calm of the aftermath, in cold words on the screen, it's hard to say. Pauline, a good friend, replies almost immediately. "Course it's not the breakfast cereal. It's the incessant drip drip

drip, the relentlessness of it. Not surprising that you should crack. She's okay, I take it, and blessed with goldfish memory, so that'll be that as far as she is concerned—but dear god, this is real lulu for you. You still sound pretty shaken up. I wish you better things for tomorrow. Poor you. Poor battered soul."

It occurs to me to worry that the aides will see those faint amulets of bruises and will imagine that they know the truth. It isn't the first time I've worried about what people might think. Nancy is constantly in the wars, walking into doors and tables, tripping over steps, falling out of bed and blackening her eye; do the paid caregivers ever mention the bruising that ensues to the social work department? I launch an Internet hunt on the question of caregiver abuse, and the words in the search box bring up other, unexpected results. Abuse *of* caregivers, and not just by them. Here's a dementia victim, a husband who killed his caregiver wife with a hammer. Another woman, assaulted by her Alzheimer's husband, who declares herself afraid of him, describing him as "cunning, nasty, aggressive, menacing." On the Web pages I glance over, though, these stories are outnumbered by attacks by caregivers upon the demented. Most of them detail a "snap" moment. Most appear to be about male caregivers attacking wives. Some of these have been dubbed mercy killings: a wife strangled by a husband who said he couldn't any longer bear her to suffer, another with her throat cut. More often, though, the attacks are attributed to rage. Faced with an impossible situation, people can fail in a dramatic manner to cope. Here's a man who smothered his wife because she wouldn't stop taunting him, in her demented, perseverating way. Another who tied up and gagged his wife after she'd kept him awake for days and nights on end roaring and shouting; she died. All elicit a mixture of horror and sympathy, the two vying feebly for precedence.

I read wider and come across the Greek myth of Eos and Tithonus. Eos, goddess of the dawn, falls for Tithonus, a hunky

Trojan prince. She asks Zeus to grant him immortality, and he does. But she neglects to ask for immortal youth. Tithonus gets old at the usual rate and then keeps on getting older. He becomes senile, and stays that way for eternity. Eos, driven to distraction, locks him up in a room. In some accounts she turns him into a grasshopper.

Ralph Waldo Emerson wrote, "Finish each day and be done with it. You have done what you could. Some blunders and absurdities no doubt crept in; forget them as soon as you can. Tomorrow is a new day; begin it well and serenely." This is good advice, though he also wrote, more pertinently, "Sometimes a scream is better than a thesis."

Chapter 22

Between the essence
And the descent
Falls the Shadow

—T. S. ELIOT

HER MIND IS OPAQUE NOW, HER MOODS IMPOSSIBLE to read. Does she know that, as Iris Murdoch put it, she's "sailing into the dark"? Does she spare us this knowledge as a kindness, by speaking in metaphors?

"I want to go home," she says over and over, and she doesn't mean to the bungalow we rescued them from, that lonely suburban isolation, the washing piling up, tea made from the hot tap and packets of biscuits for lunch. She means home to her old self. She's aware that she's lost her somehow, the woman who was a company secretary, with long painted nails and a wardrobe full of blue jackets, who made raspberry jam every summer, who knitted exquisite baby clothes for each of the children. She knows, but she can't quite put her finger on it. There are days when the delusions are full throttle. In the throes of the hospital one, she has begged me for medicine for the dying patient in the next bed, all the time standing in her nightdress in the hall.

THE SUBLIME SEEMS of no use to me now, in this dark time of bright sunlight. I go out into it desperate for something good, for a taste of the Epic, for help: hoping to encounter something even mildly similar to Wordsworth's "spots of time / That with distinct pre-eminence retain / A renovating virtue," but come back feeling far worse. I can relate, at the least, to his pre-visionary moments.

> *O'er my thoughts*
> *There hung a darkness, call it solitude*
> *Or blank desertion. No familiar shapes*
> *Remained, no pleasant images of trees,*
> *Of sea or sky, no colours of green fields;*
> *But huge and mighty forms, that do not live*
> *Like living men, moved slowly through the mind*
> *By day, and were a trouble to my dreams.*

On bad Nancy days, the really bad days, the beauty out there seems tainted, all of it, by her animosity, which begins to seem like a misconceived fight against disease, against the lights going out, like a misdirected energy in her struggle to emerge from the dark. The anti-Sublime, purposelessly and destructively ruminative, reveals a landscape full of death. Death we think trivial. A broken cat in a ditch. A seagull neatly bisected on the side of the road. A baby seal dead on the beach, and then a dolphin, part eaten before it was washed ashore. I begin to feel an overwhelming, disproportionate pity for the sheep and the bullocks that watch me from their pasture as I pass. It's all suffering and cruelty out there, I think, stomping along the beach in a summer dress and raincoat and Wellies; it's cruelty disguised by landscape, by our fetish for views. I blame Wordsworth for that. I come across the archconservative Joseph de Maistre—a man named by philosopher Isaiah Berlin as one of the six Enlightenment enemies of liberty. "In the whole vast dome of living nature," de Maistre wrote, "there reigns an open violence, a kind of prescriptive fury, which arms all the creatures in their common doom; as soon as you leave the inanimate kingdom you find the decree of violent death inscribed on the very frontiers of life." Unsurprisingly, this doesn't help much.

I read that Charles Baudelaire said that de Maistre taught him how to think, and find this quotation from the poet: "We are weighed down, every moment, by the conception and the sensation of Time. And there are but two means of escaping and forgetting this nightmare: pleasure and work. Pleasure consumes us. Work strengthens us. Let us choose." Yes, I think, that's so true; work is all that will keep me afloat. I must work and make everything else secondary. Though it's slightly disheartening to discover that Baudelaire died at forty-six.

I dip in and out of books, following dementia trails like snail tracks across the paper, but seem unable to settle on anything new. I revisit John Bayley's magnificent account of life with his wife, Iris Murdoch. Her demise seems to have illustrated the fact that though highly educated people are somewhat less likely to get Alzheimer's, when they do succumb it tends to be an aggressive, fast-acting, fast-forward disease. Iris Murdoch's Alzheimer's first presented itself as trouble with finding words. It manifested itself in her last book, *Jackson's Dilemma* (1995). Neurological study has found her vocabulary much reduced in it. She died in 1999, three years after diagnosis.

More care meetings, more assessments. The professionals come and settle themselves in chairs; they drink tea, they talk to us and make occasional notes. Conversations with Nancy are brief. Nancy is produced, and as is usual when faced with a social situation is utterly charming. Some emergency facility, buried deep, is mined and polished: that of the social bluffer.

"So. Can you tell me your date of birth?"

Nancy's grinning. "I've absolutely no idea. But I can tell you it was a very long time ago; my memory's terrible."

The professionals are reassured. They give us quizzical looks. She's really not at all bad. Crisis, what crisis?

Rita Hayworth (1918–1987), the Hollywood film star, developed Alzheimer's early. She was diagnosed formally in 1980 but had been ill five years, since the age of fifty-seven, and her daughter says in interviews that she had shown the first symptoms twenty years earlier. Alcoholism confused the issue, but reported agitation, hand rubbing, paranoia, mood swings, vacancy of the gaze, obsessive reorganizing of cupboards— this all sounds like Alzheimer's. Her daughter reports that even quite late in the disease, her mother continued to turn on the charm with doctors. Asked a direct question like "Who's the president?" she'd switch into flirtation and change the subject. The performance was remarkable, it's said; it was as if she was constantly auditioning. That sounds familiar. Nancy's winning smile and stock of phrases dredged from the past are a form of doctor repellent.

JULY BRINGS A series of bed-and-breakfast food sensitives. They bring their own tea bags and ask for hot water at breakfast. They want to discuss what's in the bread, the provenance of the bacon, and they have a raft of food aversions. *Rhubarb? Sorry. Wrong sort of acids. Oops, no, I don't do fungus. Is the coffee fair trade? Are the mushrooms organic? I'm a celiac, didn't I mention? Do you have any gluten-free bread?* And then, as plate goes down on table, *Ahhh, sorry, but I can't actually eat tomatoes, or anything that's been in proximity to a tomato.*

It's warm some days, but the wind blows. The wind blows most days. It's so much our default weather that the days when it stops are puzzling. The silence takes its time to penetrate the senses. Being here in quietness is a different experience. The landscape is different. The air hangs heavy over it and its shapes settle into quadrilaterals—broad stripes of sky and sea, thinner strips of garden and wall, layered, irregular blocks of headland—all of this replacing its customary dynamic wild-ness, the sea in ferment, clouds scudding, the sharp diagonals of trees blowing. An elderly neighbor I meet one chilly morn-ing down on the road while dog walking (in the Barbour, in midsummer, with head-wrapped scarf in place and Wellies) tells me that she has decided she can't face another peninsula winter and is moving down to Somerset. "Make sure you get off frequently, regularly; quarterly if you can manage it," she told me. "You have to get off sometimes."

Off?

"Away south. Four times a year. It's important. Otherwise you get unhappy. Cabin fever."

I've lost all sense of where my feelings about caring for Nancy and Morris end and where those about living out here begin. The longer we're here, the more the two things, the social isolation entailed in caregiving and the physical remote-ness of the house, seem bound up in one another. Words-worth's exalted observation, "How exquisitely the individual Mind / . . . to the external World / Is fitted:—and how exqui-sitely, too— / . . . The external World is fitted to the Mind," seems unintentionally close to taunting.

I go out into the landscape and see it all externalized: Nan-cy's panic and my own resentment. The view is soaked in both varieties of unhappiness. I am beginning to think that I will love the peninsula only after I've left it. Flaubert had a similar relationship with Egypt, which bored and depressed him when he was there, at twenty-seven, but grew in his mind in all the years afterward, some forty years of ripening. The Egypt of memory, his idea of Egypt, followed him to the end. He was thinking of it, longing for it, just before his death. That's probably what will happen here and it's all down to elemen-tals. The sea and sky, beach and cliff, meadow and wall and wood. These will prove irresistible, once memory has charge of them.

★ ★ ★

SCHOOL BREAKS UP and the summer holiday stretches lengthily ahead. On days when it's grotty weather, bucketing rain, autumnally cold, we struggle to find things to do indoors that Nancy will tolerate. I invite her to come and do some art with me and the children at the kitchen table one afternoon.

"I can't really do it. I'm terrible at drawing," she tells me.

"Doesn't matter. But would you like to have a go? Play with some color on the paper?"

"I'd love it. Just show me how."

We sit down with a still life between us, a jug with flowers, a cup, a glass. Quietness descends with concentration. Nancy sits with an oil pastel in her fingers, looking uncertain.

"What do I do?"

"Just draw what you see. Or part of it. Or whatever you'd like to draw. Anything at all," I say. "Or just make colors on the page." She looks more uncertain. I've given her too many instructions. "Just use the crayon," I tell her.

The rest of us have settled into a slow breathing rhythm, glancing from objects to paper and sketching in the shapes. Nancy looks at the jug of flowers, the glass, the cup, and at her paper, which is a large white sheet. The oil pastel makes contact at the left-hand side and she begins. What emerges is very like her signature, what her signature's become, repeated with variations: a long unbroken series of what look like *n*'s and *v*'s interrupted by the softer contours of what might be *m*'s and the occasional punctuating *y*. It goes across the paper and up, forming a ribbon of letters about half an inch broad. All the time that she's writing, she's looking, as the rest of us do, toward the still life grouping and back at the paper, as if what she's doing reflects what she sees. She talks to herself as she draws, murmuring along. "There, that's up and away and here's the next part, and there it goes, and it's like that, and it's like that again, that's right." The children maintain a tactful silence. "There," Nancy says, putting her oil pastel down. "That's it, I think."

The American abstract artist Willem de Kooning (1904–1997) died of Alzheimer's. His late work, his dementia art, is very different from the hectic, intricate colors and anxiety of the art of his prime. It's much simplified, has curving open lines (lines dominate), allows generously for white space, and fills in the shapes created by intersections with color. It's as if Jackson Pollock turned into Mondrian. In a series of huge canvases the white field is interrupted by curling tendrils, "ribbon paintings" that tangle their ribbons together, and more than one critic has said, rather tactlessly, that they resemble the tangling of tau protein in the Alzheimer's brain. There had been symptoms as early as 1980, when the output is visibly taking on its dementia-period look. In that same year a friend reported that de Kooning, formerly a voracious eater-up of books, had given up reading entirely. Instead he painted and drew all day long obsessively. He gave up preparatory drawing in 1983 and used old drawings as the basis for compositions. He was extraordinarily productive: 340 paintings were produced in the 1980s alone.

There's been much debate about whether de Kooning's 1980s work is properly art or not. Some critics have raised issues of intention. Is the demented de Kooning still essentially himself, still giving of the same self that made his pre-eighties work so valuable? (Be in no confusion. This is a question about value. About money. His canvases sell for many millions of dollars.) There needs demonstrably to be an artist in control of his material, especially in the modern art market. In terms of value (monetary), the artist's brand is more important than the material. The self that is implied by the work, that is sold in the selling of the work, has outstripped the power of the work itself. In the age of Damien Hirst and Tracey Emin it's the artist that's the artifact. The artwork is secondary.

De Kooning wasn't diagnosed until 1989. In that same year, another friend reported that though he remained physically robust, affable, appeared to recognize people, and was still painting, when asked questions he'd give answers that were utterly unintelligible. Images remained with him but word and meaning were lost. He gave up painting in 1990. What would the art world have thought about that final decade if de Kooning had died undiagnosed? Mightn't there have been a rather different tone to the discussion, talk of an old man's retrospection, his sense of peace and optimism? Funny you should mention that, for lo and behold, reevaluation can take us there. The late works are beginning to be exhibited and written about as complex marvels, and in this spirit of reassessment de Kooning's dementia is given quotation marks and spoken of as irrelevant. There is plenty of evidence that he was a happier man in these brief years, having recovered from the alcoholism that precipitated a breakdown in 1980 and seemed to bring Alzheimer's on.

Nancy begins to pick on the dogs. Perhaps it's a pecking order thing, and this is her only remaining outlet for the exercise of authority. Asked if she'd like the dogs in her sitting room, Nancy will always claim that she does, warmly and with apparent sincerity. The dogs have spent a lot of time in the in-laws' room this year. Nancy asks them in, blocks off their exits and bosses them about. The terrier prefers to be by the fire but Paddy goes and sits by Nancy's feet, enjoying having his ears fiddled with, tolerant about the ranting. They get biscuits, they get sandwiches, are bemusedly offered orange peel, and they get told what Nancy calls *stories*. That was the case until recently at least. Now, though, they're unwelcome. Doors open and dogs are evicted.

"Out! Out! You're a bad dog. You don't deserve to be in here. Off you go you little bastard. Away with you, you bad dog."

Paddy and Sparky are untroubled by "bastard" but they know what "bad dog" means and are suffering intermittent crises of self-esteem, slinking out with their ears held flat and tails pulled in tight.

A fortnight of summer respite looms and the care manager is preparing a dossier, again, on Morris and Nancy. Chris, in consultant mode, gives her the full consultation, though I'm not convinced that the comprehensiveness of his reports is appreciated. I join in with anecdotal examples and occasionally quite daring moments of honest noncopingness, though I don't like myself much for doing this. The care manager doesn't respond emotionally to anything we have to say. She is a highly trained professional, unflappable, has no doubt heard it all before, but we are new to the business of dealing with social workers and find her stoicism unsettling. Well, I do. And I find I might be exaggerating the problems slightly, in order to get a rise out of her. (It doesn't work. You could say to her, "Nancy is eating dog poop now," and she'd say, "Is she? And how's that impacting on the rest of you?" She is unshockable.) We're listened to with sympathy but very little is written down. She's a conduit of the system, and the system is only after one thing: the facts of the matter, and translating these into a score on a sort of geriatric Richter scale. The assessment is printed up and returned to us for checking. It amounts to ticked boxes, mapping what's possible and not in terms of their physical and mental status.

The assessment has a dual purpose: It will go to the bed allocation committee (we're still trying to get onto the waiting list for a nursing home) and to the home where residential respite is being offered. Because it's also for the respite home, the report strives to be positive where possible. The temptation to minimize Nancy's problems so that a home without dementia facilities will take her is irresistible. We've been warned that the residential care waiting list is long, two years long or more, and the situation is worsening. I know I won't last another two years without cracking. So it's important that this assessment is frank. Can this assessment, the one assessment, do both jobs? No. It's a bit like being self-employed and preparing one set of annual accounts. These are rounded down as much as possible for the tax man (small income, please don't bill me). But they also need to be bigged up for the mortgage company (sizable income, we can afford the house). Which way to jump? A happy medium is best in most things, but possibly not in the case of social care assessments. In the case of social care assessments the report is left dangling, nowhere, compromised, full of euphemisms. Reading over the report is a disheartening business because it bears very little relation to the reality of all our lives.

Morris is to be in the seaside home again, and Nancy is to go into the town home. Then Nancy loses her place in the town home, thanks to bed blocking, which happens when there are no new beds available because patients who have nowhere else to go continue to occupy a spot for days or weeks (or in some cases years). The care manager is frank about the problems. Sometimes people don't go home again. Sometimes families refuse to take them back. We've been asked to sign a statement pledging to collect Nancy on the agreed date. The care manager says she's hoping she's got Nancy into the same home as Morris. *Hoping.* The stumbling block is that Morris's home has no Alzheimer's unit. Luckily the compromised report does the trick. At the time, a week before our holiday is very nearly canceled, this seems like the most important thing. We can go. And we do, though expecting, even at the gate to the aircraft, an announcement over the loudspeaker calling us back to duty. *Would the woman who's abandoned her mother-in-law please come to the information desk. . . .*

Reading up on neurology on holiday, I find that the buzzword in brain talk is *plasticity.* The brain can be molded, reshaped, even in adult life; it responds to demands made on it.

An experiment done with adults taught intensively to play the piano, from scratch, who were then brain-scanned, showed that their motor cortex had expanded significantly to cope with the workload. Not only that, it was commandeering neurons in neighboring zones to help with the job of learning and playing the piece in question. Cabdrivers in England doing "the Knowledge," which involves learning the entire driving map of London, have been shown to have enlarged hippocampi.

Brains that are damaged try to compensate for their losses. They set up connections elsewhere, get adjacent areas to set up lost functions, march in to other bits and clear the desk and lay down the law. It's a situation rather like that of soldiers interrupted in their task by a higher ranking officer: "Yes, I know you're supposed to be in North Africa but, actually, we need to move you into Crete. No arguments!" (Groans in background.) "There's a war on and we need to pull together, be a bit adaptable." A damaged brain is a war zone and its efforts to keep pushing on, delegating jobs to other areas, opening up and staffing new fronts, appear nothing short of heroic.

Size isn't everything. It's wiring that matters, connections, pathways. The wiring process is called myelinization. Myelin is the "white matter" that forms the insulating sheaths that coat the stems of the axons and ensure the signals are full strength when they're emitted from the end. Without insulation there would be seepage and slowness and incompleteness. It's a slow and steady process, and has its own sequence. Section by section, parts of the brain are brought online by being myelinized and connected. Motor functions are first in the infant human (we hold our heads up), then touch, better vision and hearing, and language skills. The frontal lobes (the executive self) and the memory-forming hippocampus are the last to be brought onboard, beginning at about three, when most people's earliest memories commence. Frontal lobe evolution is still taking place in teenagers. By the end of the teen years, the pruned neuronal forest has its myelinization completed.

One hot potato—hotly fought over—is the question of when we come to consciousness. The answer seems to be that consciousness grows as we grow, and that the experience of being alive is what makes us more and more conscious. Thus is consciousness linked inextricably with memory, not just in the process of knowing and doing, but *knowing* that we know and have done. Once we're on the move and encountering the world, our consciousness grows rapidly, until at about the age of three we're fully conscious beings. As Nietzsche wrote, "Only then, through the power of using the past for living and making history out of what has happened, does a person first become a person."

The reason I'm telling you all this is that Alzheimer's reverses the processes of turning from baby to toddler to child to adult in a way that's almost pointed. Almost uncanny. In Alzheimer's there's a gradual loss of intellectual ability, stage by stage in grotesque mimicry. There's a last-in-first-out kind of logic to it. The two "adult-making" brain zones, last to develop in children, the hippocampus and frontal lobe, are decimated first, the basic motor functions last. The memory goes, the memories that form the context for all our adult judgments, our own hard-won experience of what's right and what's good, what works and what doesn't, what we like and don't, what's safe and dangerous. The self that debates these things, that uses memory as an intellectual tool, as a consequence is pared away. We're returned to a second childhood, one jammed in reverse gear. The intellectual capacity of the teen is lost, and then that of the primary school child, and we are returned to toddlerdom. Toddler milestones go last. The power to govern oneself, to dress, go to the bathroom, manage our own eating, the things all learned and perfected then, begin to falter and disappear. Finally the Alzheimer's sufferer, should she live long enough, is returned to a state of infancy and to incontinence. Language and recognition of language, then the infant powers of walking, bending, grasping; the ability to sit up, to lift the head and to smile, all these are lost. Advanced Alzheimer's cases resemble newborns in their total dependence on others.

Chapter 23

We live in the mind, in ideas, fragments. We no longer
drink in the wild outer music of the streets.

—HENRY MILLER

NOTHING IS HARDER THAN COMING HOME FROM HOLI-
day. Having undergone the serene psychic rebooting
that comes about, mysteriously, by means of daily immersion in jade green water, the return to the house and its
duties is shockingly difficult. The sense of dread starts at the
airport. By the time we get in the car I am properly nervous. So
much of coping is contained in its being got on with, prompted
by adrenaline, habitual and unconsidered. It isn't always helpful to be allowed to step away and see the big picture. The
hawk's-eye view, hovering above the landscape, is likely to
induce an abrupt case of vertigo. Now, with Aegean salt still
crystallizing on my skin, driving north through a cold gray
summer, the return to the battlefield seems too difficult to
contemplate. We have a day before the in-laws' return from
the nursing home and it's spent feeling ill at ease. We're all
subdued and I'm barely talking. The unspoken questions come
round in a loop. Can I do it, keep doing it? What if I can't
switch back? What if, perversely, relaxation and refreshment
and that renewed sense of self I had on a Turkish veranda have
been destructive after all? What if that transforming alchemy,
the one brought on by aimless fiction reading and grit between
my toes, has made me intransigent? Am I prepared to give it all
away again? It may not even be a question of that, of choosing.

I fear I may have lost the knack. When Morris and Nancy's bus trundles up the drive, it's hard to assume a welcoming face. I smile but I'm close to revolt. Morris looks glad to be back, but doesn't ask about our holiday. Nancy and I have one impulse in common, at least, one that's instinctive but lacking in specifics. Within a half hour she's telling Morris that she's leaving.

"You can stay here if you want but I'm not staying here. I'm going home."

"What are you talking about, you daft woman? This is your home."

"You think I don't know where my home is?"

"Yes! That's what I think!"

AUGUST IS ALL about doors. All the doors must be locked as Nancy is intent on escape. Every morning she is asking, even before breakfast, when she can go home, if she can go out, if it's time for her to leave yet; have they come for her, is her father coming, is it time to take the train, are the friends here yet? Morris shouts her down in his customary manner. That's usually the spur to action.

Until the school holidays arrived, the outer doors were locked all day and the keys were left in them. When we arrived here, Nancy couldn't manipulate a key. But now, apparently illogically, she can. She seems to have learned how, and retains the ability, day on day. She gets better and quicker at it, opens doors and is off. How, in someone lacking a functioning memory, is this possible? The answer may lie in the history of H.M., of whom we heard earlier, the epileptic research subject run down by a bike. He had his hippocampus removed and other bits of his brain modified, as a typically gung ho 1950s approach to defusing the extreme severity of his fits, and couldn't remember things. But when scientists asked him to draw, to copy the image of a star, following its outline, and then do the exercise again and again and again in the days following, H.M.'s performance improved. He couldn't ever remember, from one day to the next, that he'd seen the star before, but he got significantly better, progressively better, at drawing it. The answer lies in the cerebellum. The procedural memory appears to be able to learn, bypassing the conscious mind and the ordinary routes of memory. And this, I suppose, is what's happening to Nancy.

So now, official policy is that the key is taken out of the lock and hung on a hook. She can't manage to get the key off the hook and into the lock; she doesn't identify it, hanging on its hook, as the key to the door. It's the school holidays, however, and the children are constantly in and out of the house. Neighboring children are in and out of the house. There are bikes piled on the lawn, alien sneakers and sweaters in the boot room, strange strident voices on the stairs. And the doors are hardly ever locked.

Nancy's escaping becomes a big part of our lives. It wouldn't, of course, be an escape, if it weren't imperative that somebody always be with her. How lovely it would be for us all if she could be left to saunter round the garden picking the tops off flowers and chewing random stalks of found rhubarb, shutting the hens in their house because they've been naughty, telling her troubles to horses. Alas, this isn't possible. Thirty seconds after getting out of the door and into the world, anxiety descends. Some days we find her walking round the laundry green in ever diminishing circles, wailing; on other days, standing tightly, closely in to the elbow of a wall, chewing on her cardigan and paralyzed with fear. But then she starts leaving the garden. She begins to make a beeline for the road, charging down the driveway with whatever possessions she has judged vital to take home (cardigans, the address book, a singing toy kestrel I brought from the airport, the blue handbag) and out onto the lane, without pausing to look out for traffic.

She is found one afternoon in our nearest neighbor's garden, talking to workmen building his extension, asking them if they know where she lives. She is discovered on another afternoon lying on the road.

On this occasion she is found before we realize that she's lost. Her habit of going to her room to be alone, two, three times a day, and the taking of lengthy afternoon naps: these are to blame for our not noticing. Morris doesn't raise the alarm if she disappears anymore, assuming, like the rest of us, that that's where she's gone. A stranger ringing at the doorbell is the first alert in this instance. Are we missing an old lady, she wonders. There's a white-haired old lady in a red cardigan lying on the road by the farm, and they've already called 999. We rush down there, two hundred yards down the lane toward the beach, and sure enough, there's an ambulance, parked; two ambulance personnel crouched by a seated figure, freshly cloaked in a tartan rug; and three cars pulled into the verge, with concerned (nosy) locals, waiting to see what happens next. They assume she's been run over, although statistics suggest not: Their three cars amount to 60 percent of the local traffic, from houses on the headland beyond us, and they're intimately related to the drivers of the other two cars. If somebody had bopped Nancy, word would be out by now. As Douglas Adams, the author of *The Hitchhiker's Guide to the Galaxy,* observed, "Nothing travels faster than the speed of light, with the possible exception of bad news, which obeys its own special laws." The ambulance people are just about to whisk Nancy off to hospital, when we come running up. We have to explain that dementia makes her do this kind of thing. She has no apparent injuries and is determined about not going anywhere. We bring her home and keep an eye on her as promised. The first hint of illness, and she's to be whisked off to the emergency room.

I bring her back into Morris's orbit, the TV room, his occupied chair and her empty one, the afternoon movie in full flow, and tell Morris where we found her. Nancy interrupts me.

"That's just a pack of lies and you know it."

"Nancy. You were down on the road. Don't you remember?"

"No."

"You were lying on the road. The ambulance came along. They sat you up and put a blanket round you."

"Lies. It's all lies."

"Look. You've got a scrape on the side of your hand. I'll clean that up. I think you must have toppled off the sidewalk."

"It's a load of nonsense. I haven't been anywhere. I've been here the whole time."

The weather's peculiar and the hens aren't laying consistently. Some days there are five eggs, other days none. The trouble is that when both guest rooms are occupied, we need four eggs a day. On one particularly grim and windy morning, there are four Canadians to feed and no eggs at all: none in the fridge, all backups depleted. It's too early for the shop. Before the guests appear downstairs, we nip off in the car to a neighbor's roadside honesty box and are saved by the half dozen eggs sitting in it. It's only later that afternoon, following Chris's hunch, that we find a pile of fourteen eggs in the herbaceous border, and another pile of twenty-two among some brushwood on the lawn. I ask Nancy to help sort them, inventing a task I think she'll enjoy. She crouches down in front of the hoard of twenty-two, sitting on her haunches, and talks her way through it. "Two piles," I tell her. "Brown and white." I start her off. "Brown in this pile, white in this. See?" She murmurs her assent. I clean the chickens out and watch, with horrified fascination, as Nancy fails to be able to do the task. She can't seem to distinguish brown and white, can't make two piles. The browns and whites are mixed up again. But she enjoys handling the eggs, so delicately and gently, in cupped hands, and seems absorbed in her task.

AUGUST BRINGS NANCY'S eightieth birthday. I speak to Morris about this great event a week before the day. Would he like me to do some shopping on his behalf?

"I don't think so, dear, no."

"But Morris, her eightieth. Surely you want to get her a gift. Look at all these mail-order catalogs. Wouldn't you like to choose something? A new cardigan, a bracelet, some of these Velcro slippers?"

"Nup," he says, not tearing his gaze from his television quiz show.

I buy him a card to write and stand over him. His handwriting is affected by age, though only insofar as greater concentration on signing has exaggerated its sweeping ascenders and descenders. Nancy's attempts to sign her name—on bank things, for instance, since she and Morris still have a joint account—have become stressful and also hilarious. She's the one who's amused, laughing till she cries as she tries and fails to write her name. I give her a practice few goes on a blank piece of paper, and these aren't too bad. They don't look like a name but at least they are done with brio. It's when the form is produced that the trouble starts. No matter how many times I explain that the name has to go in the box, resting my fingertip as a guide, Nancy can't get it in there. She signs above, below, or on the wrong part of the sheet entirely. Nor can she sign in a straight line. Morris doctors her signature afterward, adding vowels.

"What shall I write?" Morris asks, his pen hovering over the card.

"Oh, I don't know. Something about her birthday." What does he mean?

Happy Birthday Nancy, love Morris, x. That's all she's getting. Not that it really matters.

Nancy enjoys opening her cards, but insists on putting them back in the envelopes afterward, and needs help getting them in. She carries the stack of mail around with her all day. She admires her Fair Isle cardigan, her new necklace, but won't try them on.

"These aren't my things."

"Yes. They're new. We bought them for you. And the chocolates we ate earlier, remember? And the bath bubbles. For your birthday."

"Is it my birthday?"

"Yes. You're eighty."

"Am I? I'm not. You're joking. You're funny. Eighty, she says!"

When we bring her cake in, crowded with candles, and sing to her, she claps her hands and her eyes fill with tears. "Oh! Look at that! It's so beautiful. I haven't seen anything that beautiful for many a long day."

She joins in with the singing, eats three pieces of lemon sponge, sips at her champagne, and sleeps most of the afternoon.

But the day after, she's noticeably tired. And that evening, when I've taken supper through to Nancy and Morris, and have settled down to our own meal, there's a sudden explosive ruckus from next door.

"Just leave them to it," Chris says, mid-potato.

I eat a leaf of salad and hear the door from their sitting room out into the hall closing with a slam, Morris remonstrating, "Nancy! Please!"

I rise from the chair. Chris puts his hand over mine. "Just leave it. Eat your supper," he says.

"Na-an-cy! Nancy!" Morris shouts. I put my head round the door. "What's up? Nancy stomped off?"

"Yes, and she's taken her plate."

This is a first.

I check the bedroom first. No Nancy. Nor is she in the bathroom. I go round the ground floor calling. No response. I can't see her. She must have escaped, I think: Is there an eighty-year-old woman inching down the driveway with a plate? Then I hear a noise. Scraping. Coming from the library. Sure enough, there's Nancy, standing in the dark tipping her supper into the bookcase. Sausages, potatoes, radicchio, off the plate and onto the paper tops of a row of novels. I'm only grateful there isn't any gravy, though vinaigrette has already bled its way into Richard Ford and Edith Wharton.

I take Nancy back into her sitting room by the elbow and the moment she sees Morris, before I can speak, she turns to me pointing her finger and says, "This woman's a liar." She sits and fumes. But when I take her to bed she's all smiles.

"You're wonderful. You're my friend," she says.

"Well, thanks, Nancy. That's nice."

"I can't tell you how grateful I am that you look after me so well. You're a lovely person. No, I mean it. A really lovely person and kind."

"You're very welcome," I say, smiling at her.

"Not like those other ones. Those other people here. I don't like them."

Chapter 24

When ideas fail, words come in very handy.
—GOETHE

MORRIS IS CONFIDING IN CAREGIVERS BUT NOT IN US, and now the contrast has become explicit. His favorite stays on past her duties to talk and I overhear things I wish I hadn't. Standing in the kitchen making a shopping list, I hear the aide's voice from next door, raised slightly, arguing a point. "But it's your home, too, Morris." I'm beginning to wonder if factions are forming.

He's ill, with ongoing kidney problems, and has disappeared somewhere within himself that Prozac can't reach. He no longer makes an effort to speak to the children. Any of the grandchildren who dare run the gauntlet of Nancy's heckling and threats and go into their grandparents' sitting room find that not even Granddad seems happy to see them. He has nothing to say to them and has lost all curiosity. On Millie's birthday he is unforgivably morose. Nancy's quite chipper: Presented with a slab of cake and a dog on the next sofa cushion, begging for a bit, she seems perfectly content. She has a lengthy conversation with the terrier about whether he's a good boy and deserves pudding. Morris sits in his chair and looks at the carpet. He eats a bit of cake and leaves the rest. He doesn't talk. He doesn't wish Millie a happy birthday until prompted. He pointedly doesn't take an interest in her gifts. This makes the whole day seem heavy. It's hard to rise above the heaviness set by such unwarranted indifference.

Nancy's nighttime restlessness has a new flavor to it, one of strident noncompliance. Nancy's ranting into the wee small hours and Morris is at his wits' end. We check up on them every half hour, standing outside their door and listening.

9:30 P.M. Nancy's voice, chivying Morris, trying to galvanize him to get out of bed.

"We've got to get out of here, come on, we've got to get home. We need to go. We've got to get up and get dressed and go now. But you aren't listening. No. You're not listening to me. You never listen. You just lie there, a useless lump. All the people here hate you but you don't know that. They hate you. They hate me, too, but that's beside the point. I'm used to it. I don't say anything. They tell me what to do all day. All day I have to do the work. They should do the work but I have to do it. You just sit there. And they—they have got you all wrapped up. All wrapped up. Yes, miss, whatever you say. She thinks she's in charge but she isn't. She's going to get a shock. I'm going to surprise her one of these days. I'll sort her out once and for all. She doesn't know the first thing about it, not a thing."

10:00 P.M. Nancy is moving around. We can hear her dressing. She is pulling clothes out of the cupboard. The wire coat hangers tinkle and clank as they fall. We hear her walking, her heavy breathing, and her continuing monologue.

"This is what we need. We need these things to go home. We need to go home now. I have the things, the things and the other things and the rest of the things. You have to get the other things now. But you won't do that, will you? No. You just lie there, doing nothing. Doing nothing as usual. I have to do everything."

The door opens. I'm standing in the corridor. Nancy looks at me and closes it again.

"She's there. She's standing there," she says to Morris, who doesn't respond. "I need more things to get the things. She is going to take them. She will take them away and sell them.

She doesn't want anything or anything but the money. She will take the money. That's right. I know that. I have always said that but you won't listen. You don't say anything to her. It's all left to me as usual."

The door opens cautiously and Nancy peers out.

"Hello, Nancy," I say. "Time for bed now, isn't it?"

"No," she says. "It isn't time for bed. I'm just going out for a walk."

I go in and open the curtain a little. "But look out there," I say. "Look how dark it is."

"Oh. Oh dear."

"It's very late and everybody's going to bed."

"Oh."

"Time for you to go to bed now."

She gets into bed, muttering under her breath. I close the bedroom door and put an ear to it.

"She's such a bitch. A bitch, and you don't say so. You don't do anything about it ever."

10:30 P.M. Nancy is still talking, though more quietly. I can't make out individual words but they pour out of her in a stream. She sounds as if she's sitting up in bed.

11:00 P.M. She's out of bed again. I go in and take her to the bathroom—usually her bedtime cup of tea has caught up with her by now—and put her back to bed. "Good night, then, have a lovely sleep, see you in the morning," I say, tucking her in firmer.

She glares at me.

"Don't even talk to me. Don't you dare even say a word."

I should walk away. Usually I do but sometimes I don't. Sometimes I mind having my evening fragmented. On those days I have to have the last word.

"Well, that's charming," I chide. "That's very good manners, isn't it?" As I leave the room, the low monotone starts up again, the words "she" and "bitch" just audible.

11:30 P.M. Nancy's wandering the halls. She looms in her

white nightdress out of unexpected directions in the dark like a phantom. She's not keen on returning to her room. Morris speaks up. "For god's sake, for pity's sake, Nancy, shut up and get into bed. I'm not sleeping and I'm getting really fed up with you now."

"Oh right then. Oh fine," she says, getting into bed and pulling the duvet over her nose. Two affronted rheumy blue eyes stare at me from the covers.

Midnight is the fighting zone.

MORRIS: Nancy, I've told you, I need to go to sleep now. Will you just shut up and go to sleep?

NANCY: I certainly will not. Who the hell do you think you are?

MORRIS: I'm your husband and what I say goes.

NANCY: Oh are you. Are you indeed. Well, we'll see about that.

MORRIS: Be QUIET.

NANCY: I'm going home. I can't stand another minute of this place.

MORRIS: Get back into bed RIGHT NOW. I mean it.

NANCY: You're a fine one to talk. You just do everything she says. She tells you what you can do and what you can't do. She has everything she wants and you have nothing. You don't have any of it anymore. You just lie there. You are never helpful to me. You never do what I say. But she. Oh she. She is ever so that way, and you know it. She has you wrapped round her finger.

MORRIS: What are you talking about now? Who does?

NANCY: You know very well.

MORRIS: You're talking rubbish. Shut up and go to sleep.

NANCY: I won't shut up. Not until you tell her. You must tell her, this is my house.

MORRIS: Who? Who are you talking about?

I know who she's talking about. And so does he. But when he's exasperated he can't resist reminding her of her failing memory.

NANCY: I don't have to tell you her name.
MORRIS: You don't know it, do you? You don't know anybody's name.
NANCY: Don't be ridiculous.
MORRIS: Go on then. What's mine?
NANCY: You know your name very well.
MORRIS: I do. But you don't, do you?

12:30 A.M. Morris is quiet again, probably asleep. Nancy rants on undauntedly. At this point Chris might give her a spoonful of something prescribed to help her sleep, though we try to minimize its use because of the hangover that will follow. If she gets sleeping syrup, she'll doze most of the following day and be awake all that night angry, which demands another dose, another day of dozing and another wakeful night, leading to more and larger dosages. So is it that a care facility syndrome is born.

In any case the sleeping syrup doesn't always work. What she needs, I tell Chris, is rhino tranquilizer. We stand outside her door and whisper and stifle our giggles at the idea of a rifle with a tranquilizer dart. We're not quite ourselves. Later, I look up sleep disturbance in dementia and find that melatonin levels in the pineal gland fall in Alzheimer's sufferers, who as a result no longer take darkness as a cue. Melatonin can be given as drops, apparently, but you can't buy it over the counter in Britain; caregivers on message boards get theirs from the United States. As Alzheimer's progresses into the final dark phase there will be a complete turnaround, and sleeping will be the norm, as the disease goes further and deeper and cell damage is such that wakefulness can't be supported. The brain is then so damaged that it demands unconsciousness in order to muster all its forces of repair.

1:00 A.M. Nancy's monologues are sleepier, with more pauses. We go to bed, hopeful of rest. Most nights now there is another breakout, or a succession of them, typically at 2:00 A.M., 3:30, 5:15. Chris jumps out of bed and goes blurrily off, insisting I go back to sleep. I hear their two voices echoing up the stairway.

"No, Mother. You're not going anywhere."

"I'll do as I please."

"Be quiet, you're waking the children."

"I will not."

But when he's away working I have to get up and do the night shift. This is difficult. There's a reason, other than for filial duty and husbandly kindness, that otherwise it's always Chris who goes off to sort his mother out at night. Nancy has taken against me, me specifically. She's dramatically less cooperative with me than with anyone. She sees me coming and bristles.

There's been an abrupt switch around. I've gone from most favored to least. "And who the hell do you think you are?" she asks when I take her elbow and try to steer her bedward. "This has always been my house, do you hear, and I want you to leave RIGHT NOW." She turns, her face set with hatred, cheeks reddened, mouth turned decisively down. "You, you are not worth anything, do you hear me? Nothing. You think you're somebody, don't you? You really think you're somebody. Well, you're not. You're NOTHING. NOTHING. You're not worth the shit on my shoe."

The home aides are getting some of this treatment, too. Nancy wakes in a foul temper most days, and the appearance of the home care team, cheerily wishing her a good morning as they go to get Morris out of bed, is the trigger for ranting verbal abuse. "She's a bit upset this morning," the ladies say to me, looking rather shaken. "Not a happy bunny." "Nancy's been crying and upset and she's set Morris off." Morris is wheeled through with red eyes, a wet hankie.

"You know it's just the Alzheimer's talking, don't you?" I say to him. "It isn't you she's having a go at. It's just the disease speaking."

"I know, dear," he says, his voice cracking, "but that doesn't make it easier to take."

How hideous this is for him. How intolerable and cruel, to spend your seventies in this state (he's three years Nancy's junior), witnessing the death of your wife by slow degrees and having to deal with this protracted and ongoing grief, a predeath bereavement spread over a decade. Not for nothing is Alzheimer's known as *the long good-bye*. Other people in their seventies go traveling, have adventures. What's worse, having Alzheimer's or being handcuffed to it and forced to watch? If it *is* just the Alzheimer's talking and Nancy is already gone, then Morris's seems to me much the worse of the two fates.

Some mornings, Nancy gets in the way of his routine and one of the aides brings her out of the bedroom and chums her while Morris is dressing. I hear Nancy's voice, monologuing away as if it were still 1:00 A.M., as if she'd not paused for breath. "And I say so but he doesn't listen to me. He's useless. He just sits there and won't come home. And he won't stand up to her. Oh no. The bitch has it all her own way. Yes. She says what goes and what doesn't go. He won't say a word. Not a word." The aides don't comment but I can see from their reactions that they know the bitch is me. They shut the kitchen door so I can't hear. What they don't know is that when they leave the house, even before their fingers have left the door handle, Nancy's delivering her parting shot toward their receding footsteps. "She's a terrible bitch, that one. Don't let her in the house again. I'll not have her in the house. Coming into my house and talking to my husband like he was hers. She should get her own husband."

Husband is a word she uses only when cornered, these days. *Husband* is a word available only by means of the emergency generator, the same one that powers conversation with the health visitor. *Husband* is a concept dredged up under pressure. We're all a threat, as she perceives us, all the other women who populate the house, to her marriage and her matriarchal rule. I come to realize that the days in which Morris has more protracted contact with the home caregivers, the days they hang about and are animated and make Morris laugh—those are Nancy's worst days. She sits in her chair watching, and rubbing her hands, saying nothing until they are gone. Then she'll be foul and ungovernable all morning. She'll likely as not be foul all day.

THE QUARTERLY ASSESSMENT is due. We sit in the conservatory and take tea, as is habitual.

"I'm afraid I have bad news," our care manager tells us.

"Oh?"

"We failed to get Nancy and Morris onto the waiting list again."

"Oh, what? How come?"

"It's bounced back from the bed allocation committee. I'm sorry. I was sure they'd get onto the list this time, but no."

"But why?"

"It's just the way it goes. There is a lot of competition. There aren't enough beds."

"But we're not asking for a bed," I say, more emotional than I would like. "We're just asking to go on the list."

"Can you tell us what criteria are applied in the decision-making process?" Chris asks.

"What happens is that they look at the assessment, and at other reports, and we talk to them, and they look at all the evidence, and then they make a decision. Once they've made it, there isn't a lot we can do. Just put the application in again. Do a new assessment. Have another go. I realize this must be very disappointing, but we'll keep plugging away for you."

"What other reports?" Chris asks.

It transpires that our care manager had visited Nancy and Morris while they were last in respite. A conversation was had with Morris about the future. The care manager confirms this much but won't comment. Can't comment. Disclosure would be against the law. Nonetheless it seems pretty clear to Chris and me that Morris, whether intentionally or not, has ambushed Nancy's route onto the residential waiting list this year. It's our guess that he's done this by taking advantage of our absence to insist that she's no trouble at home.

"I thought this may be of interest," the care manager says, holding out a large brown envelope. Inside there's a glossy brochure for a swanky residential community, one that's geared to active retirement, Florida style. Everybody owns their own property within its walls and pays annual premiums to fund the social life, the golf, the recreational facilities. Chris and I look at this prospectus when the social workers have gone and are rendered speechless. They can't really think, can they, that this clinically depressed, poorly wheelchair-bound old man and his demented, aggressive wife would fit in here, into this tea-dancing, bowls-and-bridge-playing culture? Have they been here, really been present, the social workers, at these quarterly meetings? Have they been listening to us at all?

Nancy, meanwhile, has taken to carrying her turds around the house. She no longer recognizes them. She carries them in her hands and brings them to us. "I found this and I don't know what to do with it" or "Somebody put this thing in my underpants and I don't know who it was but when I find them there'll be words, I can tell you that." She's begun using her bedside chair as a toilet in the night.

All of which has a curious effect. I am becoming squeamish

about dealing with the B and B guests, about cleaning their bathrooms and de-hairing the plughole and changing their linens. I find, in my demoralized state, that I am beginning to resent the poor holidaymakers and their ordinary holidaymaking habits. Their leaving jammy knives on the tablecloth, coffee rings on the bedside table, and sticky kitchen refuse in the raffia wastebasket. It's too like dementia, this behavior, this not knowing what's appropriate. I'm not related to them, these paying guests. I have no burden, no duty, I don't have to be tolerant. I fume at their flushed, toilet-blocking sanitary towels, at novels that have had their spines bent; rage about books that go missing because somebody "inadvertently" packed something plucked from our library, a £20 full-color guidebook the same weight as a brick. Muddy footprints on a pale carpet provoke immoderate tutting. I bridle, not always silently, at luggage dragged along corridors, against newly painted walls and off the dressing table, leaving characteristic black smears.

The promised Indian summer doesn't materialize and the weather is gray and sullen with a stiff breeze. We wrap up and go out on the boat, leaving Morris and Nancy locked in the house. It's the only way we can go out on our own at the weekend, just the five of us, since our private care hours have shrunk to the minimum. It's also a complete no-no, leaving them alone and locked in, something I'd guessed even before the phone call, the caller tipped off by one of our aides. Locking in is unacceptable. What about the fire risk? It's a mustn't in the lexicon of don'ts that surround geriatric care.

"But what if I can't find a sitter?" I ask.

"Well, it's obvious, isn't it?" the voice on the phone says. "You'll have to stay at home."

We decide that we'll fish for mackerel but have no clear idea how to do it. We make fishing lines out of string hanging from twigs plucked from the wood. We can't buy hooks in the village, so we have to settle for safety pins, which are difficult to fix. The bacon won't stay on the pins. We go out for two hours and catch nothing. Bacon doesn't seem to be very desirable to ocean life. Or perhaps there's just nothing there, the sea a vast empty bowl. That has become my suspicion.

Our assigned October respite week is canceled, and this time our begging falls on deaf ears: There's no money available, not enough staff, and that's that. It means there'll be no half-term Turkish trip. I put my bucking bronco up for sale and buy a horse unseen on the Internet. He arrives in a borrowed lorry late at night, huge and brown and quivering with alarm.

Chapter 25

World is crazier and more of it than we think,
Incorrigibly plural. I peel and portion
A tangerine and spit the pips and feel
The drunkenness of things being various.

—Louis MacNeice

I AM LOSING IT. LOSING MY GRIP. THE THINGS THAT ARE various are spinning out of control. One afternoon in October, as I'm sitting in the drawing room in my pajamas, working hopelessly but with energy on the fiction project, surrounded by dogs and dog hair, toast rinds, watermarked coffee cups and old newspapers, the doorbell rings out. I decide to ignore it. Then it rings again. I fling the laptop aside on the sofa and go to the conservatory door, muttering loudly about bloody visitors.

Two people stand there, unmistakably American. A shiny rented Peugeot sits parked in the B and B spot. Light dawns. And there seems no other option but to respond with a sharp expletive.

"I'm sorry. I'm so sorry," I say, opening the door. "And sorry about swearing. I completely forgot you were coming."

Chris keeps them talking in the hall until I can tidy the drawing room. Then he keeps them talking in the drawing room while I hurtle round the apartment.

We spend that weekend moving a woodpile out of the old stable. The woodpile fills it floor to ceiling. People here are hoarders, particularly of anything that will burn, as trees are so few and stunted, and this pile amounts to the accretions of an era: wormy limbs of furniture, old sash windows, planks, logs, twigs picked up for kindling that are brittle and silvered with age, rotted-out joists, wartime ships' boxes with faded stenciled labels.

The respite booking system seems to have turned into a form of roulette. We're awarded six days in October at the council-owned home. Then these days are canceled again because of staff shortages. Then, out of nowhere and at short notice, we're awarded two and a half weeks at the privately owned Victorian home in the town. Though it's a private home, the social work department (under pressure, no doubt, from relatives who have had their respites canceled) has made the decision to buy in extra placements. We hadn't inquired about permanent care at the private home because the truth is we'd not wanted to use it. It doesn't have Alzheimer's provision, which is crucial, but in any case we'd heard unflattering reports. The private home is glad of the business and a representative begins chatting us up about permanent places even before the in-laws' stay.

Two and a half weeks later there is unexpected news. It comes four hours after Morris and Nancy were due back and, weary of hovering at windows, we phone the home to see what's happening. The reason for the delay, it transpires, is that Morris doesn't want to leave. Chris goes off to see him. When Chris appears, Morris backtracks. He wants to go home, please. No, he doesn't want to stay here. It's hard to know whether this is properly considered decision making, or whether he feels in some misplaced way embarrassed for electing to be in residential care, as if he is rejecting us and our hospitality. These are the only two possibilities that occur to us at the time. Chris reminds his father that last night he had cried and begged to be allowed to stay (according to the home). All Morris will say now is that he feels quite the opposite. He wants his chair and his fire. He doesn't want to stay here where everybody is old. It's fixed that Morris and Nancy will come back the following day.

The chap from the home rings again, to reiterate that Morris has had a lovely stay and (until Chris turned up) was heartbroken at the prospect of leaving. He says he'll talk to Morris again. Then he rings back and we have almost the identical conversation, word for word: Morris is adamant he's coming home and does, with Nancy in tow looking baffled. The chap rings to see if they're happy to be back. Then he rings the following day to advise me that the twin room is still available, but that they can't hold it for long. I tell him not to hold it. I don't think Morris will change his mind. He rings the day after, and the day after that. Finally, I'm short with him and he stops calling.

"He's a persistent character, isn't he?" Chris says.

"Odd, how he keeps on calling," I say.

"Makes you wonder just how keen Dad was on staying on permanently," Chris says. "And whether the guy was trying to cover himself, in his insisting that it was all Morris's idea."

This is a shocking idea but rings true. It occurs to me that it was just business.

AT HOME IT'S business as usual. Morris tells one of the aides, on Nancy's day out in town, that he doesn't know how much longer he can go on; that he thinks he made a mistake, preventing her going into care. He doesn't say so to me, though, even when I've been tipped off and prompt him directly. Chris is barely communicating with his father by this point, so there's no prospect of confidences arriving via that route.

When Nancy comes back from town she's all smiles, but the peace is short-lived. Caitlin finds her heading out the door to the garden, asks her to come in, and is slapped hard. She suffers a volley of verbal abuse from her grandmother, which is overheard by Chris. He takes Nancy into the sitting room and sits her down and tells Morris how angry he is with her. Morris isn't altogether impressed with this. He reacts rather like a mother at the door, when another mother comes to complain about her child being beaten up. He's not quite sure how to react or whose side he's on. But later, he seems surer. I'm in the kitchen preparing supper and overhear him reassuring Nancy.

"It's just you and me, you know," he says to her. "All we have is each other. It's just you and me against the world. Do you believe me? Because there's no one else. When push comes to shove, there's no one else that matters to me but you."

MY HEART IS hardening. I can feel it hardening and contracting. I begin handling Nancy's kitchen incursions differently. I turn the radio up louder and mouth, "Sorry, can't hear!" If she comes into the kitchen in a rage I don't say a word, just turn her round and open the door and eject her. If she comes back in, I have taken to shouting, "No!" just as the door opens and her angry red face appears. This is usually enough to prevent another annunciation for a while. I can hear her ranting about me next door, but she is in rant mode most of the time now anyway, so it doesn't matter. None of it matters in the least, I say to myself, turning the radio up louder. The radio is on in the kitchen all day now, radio or the CD player. Hendrix turns out to be an excellent granny-repellent. Mozart brings Nancy in asking questions and Sinatra sparks something that has the tone of reminiscence, but is a random putting together of words and ideas, presented as urgently true.

This may sound harsh and uncaring. Maybe it is. But it comes after a long, long campaign. Take battle weariness into account. The only way of continuing with this is to disengage emotionally. That is what has happened here. Self-protective distance has kicked in. I no longer intercede unless it's necessary—and even then only briefly, to call for a truce and move on. I no longer feel I have to wade in and referee. I no longer have that old burning impulse to convince Nancy of anything. I've spent a lot of time this year in trying to help Nancy to orient herself. However well intentioned, the information that she is ill was a mistake, misguided. She didn't believe it; she saw it as a form of aggression, as another lie from a hornet's nest of liars.

What I do now is keep my distance. I service their physical needs. I make sure they are warm enough, not too warm, that they have everything they want—newspapers, books, possessions, food. They are passive and need prompting. The television might need retuning. Phone calls may need to be made and shopping commissioned. Morris would never ask, but is grateful to be second-guessed.

What's upsetting and awkward, what begins to be seriously upsetting and awkward, is that Nancy's ranting about me to helpers and caregivers has become ubiquitous and vicious. *She's only after the money; that's the only reason she's here. She steals things and has to be watched. She hits me. She shouts. She smells. She hates everyone and nobody's her friend, nobody loves her. She's thinks only ever of herself. She's greedy. She eats all the food. She doesn't feed me. She's lazy. She makes me do the work. She's nasty and cruel but nobody knows that, nobody guesses. Don't be fooled, it's all pretend. Somebody should tell the manager. Somebody should tell the police.*

They ignore her, let her rant on, which is considered the correct response, but that doesn't seem the most important thing suddenly. Why is she the only one with rights? What about mine, not to be slandered and bullied? I want the aides so badly to intervene and tell her off. It would do my soul good to hear someone just once saying, "Don't talk about your daughter-in-law like that; she looks after you and works hard, and it isn't fair to call her names." But nobody ever does. They

don't mention it to me, either. Which makes it more embarrassing. Chris gets told what she's been saying about me, but
never me, and it's a distinction that seems close to pointed.
Why wouldn't they mention it to me directly? Is it because
they don't want to upset me? Or is it because it's their judgment that there's rarely smoke without fire? I get to wondering
if Nancy's allegations are mentioned in a file somewhere. My
continuing and deepening depression, my evident detachment,
these might lend a little weight and credence.

Old friends call them from time to time. Nancy's friend
Carol is on the phone again, and Nancy chats away to her as if
it were fifteen years ago, her voice spookily youthful. Only the
content is lacking. She has nothing to say for herself and what
emerges is a string of clichés strung together. "She couldn't put
a name to me," Carol says, "but she knows my voice and knows
enough to treat me as a friend." Carol's an excellent antidote to
the correctness of professionals, quite ebulliently partial. She
says she's come across "this bitch thing" before. Her mother was
the same. "It's not you, you know," she says. "It's hatred of your
being young and able-bodied and running the household."

Nancy's brother Angus rings from Australia once every
couple of months. Nancy takes the phone and starts off well.
"I'm not too bad, thanks, plodding along, you know how it is,
life is never simple, you better look before you leap, but you
know, wasn't that always the way?" Then she runs out of steam
abruptly and hands the phone over to Morris midsentence.
"Here, you take it. You do it."

Our little sailing boat's parked out in the bay in front of the
house for a few days, halfway on its journey to its winter berth
in the town marina. While it's here, the weather turns wild
and the boat is smashed against the pontoon. Her rudder is
broken and Chris says he'll have to organize a lifting crane.
Before he can do this, the storm winds worsen and we wake to
find, looking out the bedroom window one morning toward

the mooring, that only the top of the mast is showing above the surface. The rest of her is wedged down tight, badly holed and her fin keel ripped off. Poor Chris is submerged in gloom. Mahler's Fifth is on the CD player.

The weather turns apocalyptic, with floods, hail, schools closed, the horses cantering in hysterical circles in the road as we try to bring them up from pasture. It abates for a few days and we think it's over, though the truth is that we're at the eye of the storm. By Halloween wild gales are battering us, windows banging in their housings, the house creaking, sea in uproar. The house itself appears to undulate, rising and falling in queasy ocean-liner rhythm. Chris is out wrestling with the horse fencing—the electrified white tape is blown out of its posts and flies about. The wheelbarrow and henhouse are both blown across the garden, the hens roosting cluckily in the *Hebe* bush.

Nancy changes into her outdoor shoes and rattles the doors. She sits on her bed in two coats and a hat. She's bolshie at the village day center. She gets brought home early one Thursday afternoon, having verbally abused the other members, having denounced Morris, having taken off her jewelry and thrown her full complement of rings across the floor. But that's not all. It seems there has been an incident. The day center manager rings. "When Ruth tried to take her to the bathroom, she went for her," she tells me.

"She tried to hit her?"

"Afraid so."

"I think the time may have come to expel her from the center," I say. "I know it's harsh, but I don't think you should be expected to put up with this. It must be spoiling everybody else's day."

"We're okay, we manage fine most of the time," she says. "We'll continue as we are for now."

Chapter 26

Any idiot can face a crisis; it is this day to day living that wears you out.

—ANTON CHEKHOV

WINTER CREEPS IN MUNDANELY, UNSPECTACULAR with a gray wind. Wallace Stevens wrote that "the mind is the great poem of winter." Nancy's mind, perhaps. It's somewhere frosty winds moan, earth stands hard as iron, water like a stone. All human warmth has gone.

She's passed beyond some unnamed, unmarked point. She's unhappy and angry nearly all the time, and when that's true, the power of unhappiness and anger is lessened. They begin to seem inauthentic. As caregivers we become desensitized. Unhappiness and anger are Nancy's defining characteristics, and the few residual things that made her herself are fast fading. Her knowing her Christian name, and her hanging grimly on to the idea that she lives in Edinburgh: these are really the only two things she any longer knows for sure.

I've done a lot of research on dementia, but this doesn't make me any better at excusing her behavior. I do excuse it, intellectually. I know what it means and what it doesn't. But emotionally it's much more difficult, and I find that I'm behaving accordingly. Her being angry all the time, her seeming to single me out for particular contempt, has switched off something in myself that used to feel responsible for her being entertained, for her life having *value*. I might have observed something causal in the chain that's got us here. She becomes more difficult to handle and thus harder to like, and I react to this by being less friendly and less keen to spend time with her, which (possibly) makes her more difficult to handle.

It's hard to love somebody who hates you. It's hard to care for her, in either sense. The Book says it isn't Nancy to blame—not really, not in any meaningful sense—it's the plaques and tangles. Validation theory disagrees. It says that people with dementia become angry because they are trying, before dying, to express feelings and ideas they have long suppressed, which validation workers help them to release. It seems that Nancy might hate me, after all, might always have hated me. I've asked this question before and don't feel any closer to an answer: Is the person that Nancy has turned into as a result of the disease someone new, or someone who appears new because previously hidden? Validation has it that dementia exaggerates aspects mined deep from the buried self. I'm not sure how much credence should be attached to this idea. After all, how could anyone know what was or wasn't buried deep? And what does this say about human nature? Almost all of the Alzheimer's sufferers I've heard of have become abusive and contrary. Is it really possible to make a case for the greater part of humankind suppressing feelings of rage all their lives, feelings only let out of the box by the loss of inhibition that dementia brings?

Looking for more on this, I read a book about dementia caregiving that takes the playing-along-with-delusions approach, and simplifies it into three golden rules. It insists that all that's wrong with Alzheimer's sufferers is the loss of short-term memory, and all that's needed to make them happy is to stop asking questions, to stop contradicting anything they say, and to live in the past with them unquestioningly, using sympathetic conversational techniques, because the long-term memory is still intact and working perfectly logically in its way. It claims that there cease to be behavioral problems and upset once the caregiver acts accordingly—for instance, in going along with a loved one's impression that it's 1970 and they're both teachers at a school—and advises that the caregiver brief everyone else the ill person comes into contact with, so that others can join in with the dementia drama. Caregiver, family, friends—all should agree to leave the world of real time and engage with an individual's "dementia reality," another dimension in the present where time is more bendy than even theoretical physicists imagine. Could the ballad of Morris and Nancy be rewritten as an illustration of the truth of this? I doubt it. Not only because my experience of Nancy's dementia convinces me that memory loss was just the start of her story, and not the story itself, but because Nancy wants only very rarely to engage with her past self. She's much more concerned with grappling with the present, caught at the meeting point of the two worlds, a place at which neither past nor present makes sense, and that seems insoluble.

In terms of keeping her occupied, I'm a burnt-out case. Nancy doesn't remember making pastry/collecting eggs/listening to Beethoven; not a trace of it survives the subsequent five minutes. Is there a point to having experiences we don't remember? Yes, probably, in terms of mood. But Nancy's mood is no longer improved by my giving of myself. Quite the reverse. That being the case, I have justified my withdrawal. There are other demands on my time. Children and work, preeminently, both of which have been neglected in the last eighteen months. But it's more than that. I'm bored with Alzheimer's. I'm bored with her decline. I'm bored with being yelled at. I'm bored with dealing with it all.

Unfortunately for Nancy, this is the last thing she needs. What she needs is twenty-four-hour, one-to-one love, and new ideas about what she might do in the great and engulfing boredom that comes from not remembering. The problem of keeping her happy is desperate and paradoxical. Her presence

in the moment, where she now lives, is one of constant quest-
ing for something: something to do, the *something* that she
should be doing. The last thing I tried to do with Nancy was
over a month ago. I took her into the dining room and asked
for help with setting the table. She couldn't put the plates out.
She couldn't put the cutlery at the sides of the plates. She ended
up throwing the forks on the carpet. I think that might have
been the moment at which something in me gave up.

DOWN. MID-NOVEMBER.

I've woken in the morning lately feeling heavy. It's hard to
get out of bed. I can't face the day. I surprised Chris by saying
to him, "Life is just work, isn't it, hard work, unrelenting and
hard. I'm beginning to wonder if it's worth it."

I feel as if I might be vanishing. My physical weight might
just be imaginary.

"All I do is service other people's needs," I say to him. "I
don't think I really exist. Not as something independently. Just
a function."

I start thinking about being dead. Not thinking about it,
but imagining, fleetingly, what it would be like not to be here.
I have transient longings for life to stop, but what I mean is
This Life. It's just a way of despairing. The idea of life really
stopping—a terminal illness diagnosed and definite—would
be quite a different matter. There'd be constant pleading with
a hoped-for deity, then.

I am beginning to find it difficult to make housework happen. Physical objects are becoming more powerful than I am. It's
a huge effort to rearrange them in the usual everyday way. Cups
and books and laundry have become uncooperative. I am not any
longer sure that I can bend the world to my will.

I am no longer a person who speaks freely. There's a lot that
can't be said and plenty else that can't be said in the public spaces

of home. I have secrets, though I'm not sure what they are. The framework of secret keeping is present but not the content. No one who lives here is frank any longer. Unsaid things become a kind of pollutant. The things that some people won't say. The things that other people daren't.

I begin to be convinced that I have early-onset Alzheimer's. I'm losing my memory, groping for words. I forget easily, can't seem to hold things in mind, need to make lists, have become mathematically illiterate. I begin to understand what a train of thought is, the sequential synaptic journey from one carriage to another. I lose my train so easily now, grasping for a foothold; if I could only get back onto one carriage along the sequence, I'd be able, surely, to revisit the whole train, but it's not happening. I think about things and think about them and develop them and tell myself I'll remember and on the way to find paper and a pen they're gone. There's a name for this syndrome but I only discover it later. Caregiver's dementia.

I write long e-mails. Some of them are sent, though most are severely edited. I reread before pressing Send and think, What *tedious* self-pitying drivel; you can't burden your friends like this. Some days I do burden them and their kindness in responding is almost unbearable. It can't be done every day. It's boring for people to hear it and keep hearing it. Not when there isn't any resolution possible other than death of the aged dependents. Nobody could be so crass as to hope for that.

And I mind people knowing. I don't want pity. I think of my state of mind as failure: Looking after aging parents is a normal fact of life for millions of people, after all. And it's the right thing to do. It's impossible to argue otherwise. Life has a circular shape. First we are helpless and mothered. Later, the mothers are helpless and mothered in turn. That's how it works. It's ungrateful, selfish to abstain from obligation. It smacks of the worst kind of individualism, of duty overthrown by the will. Me me me.

Gandhi said, "The best way to find yourself is to lose yourself in the service of others." Which is ironic, because I begin to feel an indefinable loss of substance. (It isn't, of course, ironic in the least. I refuse staunchly to lose myself and thus will never experience Gandhi's revelatory self-dissolved identity.) I'm becoming intolerant. I feel bad about my tolerance levels dropping. Protest is a source of shame. I should put up with verbal abuse because the abuser can't be held accountable. If I don't tolerate it, if I shout back, then I know that I have put myself into the wrong. I put myself in the wrong more and more. I'm bad-tempered and demanding. I'm sarcastic with Nancy, impatient with Morris. I become sour with the children, with Chris, with people on the phone.

All this has physical repercussions. I eat the wrong things, drink to excess, put on weight. Exercise feels like it will take too much out of me. There isn't enough of me left to play with the children or ride a bike. Taking the dogs to the beach feels like a major undertaking. Coming back is exhausting, my heart racing and thumping up the casual hill. I collapse on the sofa and sleep.

"It feels like a life sentence, this task we have taken on," I say to Chris, and then, in a silly accent, "We should not have made this bargain," a *Star Wars* joke. It's important to go on making light of things.

How to bring up the subject of permanent residential care? It's not easy when your relationship has dwindled to the surface dwelling and pragmatic; even less so when your relationship has *always* been surface dwelling and pragmatic. Morris doesn't want to face the inevitable. Big subjects are shrugged off. Attempts to talk about the future are repelled: The future's the future; it will come and then we'll see, won't we?

"Can we cross that bridge when we come to it?" he says, exercising his most boyish smile.

The thing is, he'll never come to that bridge—not in his own mind, anyway, even though I can see that we're standing on it right now, and have been for some time.

I read and reread all I can find about dementia. The grim books are piled by the bed. What I'm looking for, though I don't admit this even to myself, is reassurance that this will all soon be over, that we are entering end game. I want to see it in print, that we are approaching the beginning of the final phase, and that somebody soon will see that Nancy needs to be elsewhere. "Once the turds are in the cardigan pockets and she will only eat biscuits. . . ." is how this craved-for paragraph will start. But I wouldn't wish the final stage on anyone, not least my mother-in-law. What I want for her, really, is to die peacefully at home in bed before getting to that point. That would be the best thing for her. And for those who love her. Her life seems to have become a prolonged form of suffering. "You wouldn't leave a dog in that state," Nancy's voice says from the past. Among her papers in the desk, we find a yellowing membership pack, at least twenty years old, from the Euthanasia Society.

IT'S OFTEN SAID that people don't die from Alzheimer's, but from complications arising. It's true that many dementia sufferers die of the conditions that overwhelm the old: blood clots, stroke, water infection, pneumonia, or blood poisoning from infected bed sores (Auguste Deter died of this). But people do die of Alzheimer's. If patients live long enough, brain atrophy will get them in the end, the brain stem under attack, the body-maintenance circuits going down like city zones in a power failure. It makes the hairs prickle on the back of my neck, watching the film *2001: A Space Odyssey* and hearing the quiet panic of HAL, the onboard computer, talking as he's being dismantled and saying, over and over and in a determinedly quiet and rational way, that he can feel his mind going, and then admitting that he's afraid.

The Internet is thoroughly trawled, in search of camaraderie. Camaraderie at arm's length. I'm looking for others who wish their loved ones would die and feel degraded by their hope. Instead, I find the opposite. I come across the blog of a woman—let's call her Marigold—who has decided against institutional care for her Alzheimer's-stricken husband, and has kept him at home throughout a terrible final stage. She reports going through a phase of profound doubt about her decision. But then her story takes an unexpected turn, about which she's evangelical. She's found a way through, by embracing her role as caregiver, and, unlikely as it seems, finding joy in it. She sees her role as a privilege, almost a sacrament. It's become a spiritual awakening for her. I read all this avidly but fail to be convinced. I find myself agreeing with her friends, the ones who plead with her to find residential care and not let two lives be spoiled when only one need be. That's how I am now. Hardnosed about numbers. A utilitarian.

People ask me how I am. "Oh fine, fine, though Nancy's hard work," I tell them. This is the person I've constructed: the cheerful coper. A forgery.

Sydney Smith, the essayist, farmer, and founder of the *Edinburgh Review,* wrote a letter to his friend Georgiana Morpeth in 1820, advising on a twenty-point plan for dealing with depression. "Always take a short view of life—not further than dinner or tea," he advocates, which is good advice, at least if somebody else is cooking. He also suggests that she live as well as she dares, take tepid baths, get as much exercise as possible, and see people who amuse her. "Avoid poetry, dramatic representations (except comedy), music, serious novels, melancholy, and sentimental people," he writes. He tells her to confide in

her friends. "Low spirits," he says, "are always worse for digni-
fied concealment." He adds, "Don't expect too much from
human life, a sorry business at the best." Nothing is said about
vodka, but I suspect he may have disapproved.

I disappear whenever I can into a book, taking solace in
other lives and others' eloquence. I am hungry for proxies. I
become particularly keen on people in trouble. Biographies of
the besieged, bankrupted, and maritally abandoned are particularly welcome. I have repetitive, variant dreams about being
trapped in buildings. I try to negotiate broken stairways, stairs
that turn into steep ramps or ladders with rungs missing. I
need to escape out of windows onto ledges, down onto lower
roofs, walls, slipping unseen into dark gardens. I'm chased by
faceless, unknown enemies, from whom I must hide.

I am supposed to be working when the caregivers are here.
I try. I give every impression of working. But it's all done
without breaking the surface of imagination. I'm one of those
water boatmen whose long feet straddle the top of the pond,
indenting it like a skin, deep water stretching away beneath. I
can't seem to go beneath the surface of the novel anymore. It
occurs to me that perhaps this is how I am now, this is what I
am, and what I will be when caregiving is over with. I've
changed for good. I'm no longer a writer. Marigold's transformation has taken place, a darker version of that, inverted, its
subject ungrateful and in revolt, like one of Milton's rebel an-
gels.

I go out onto the headland, getting as close as I dare to the
cliffs, which are bronze red and steeply raked, the sea crawling
up them with agitated gray fingers. I go down onto the beach,
enduring the wind's ranting and roaring, showering me with
stinging sand, and sift through stones on the shoreline, looking
for something perfect and lovely. Tennyson comes into my
head.

Strange, that the mind when fraught
With a passion so intense
One would think that it well
Might drown all life in the eye,—
That it should, by being so overwrought,
Suddenly strike on a sharper sense
For a shell, or a flower, little things
Which else would have been passed by.

Time moves very slowly with Nancy, unendurably so. Empathy takes me into her world and I don't want to be there. Wherever she goes, fear goes with her. How will it end, this hideous ticking-away day? There is no relief. She has begun to be severely carsick and throws up even on a trip to the village. The caregivers are housebound with her. The weather's increasingly stormy and she paces like a caged cat, growling at the world outside her bars.

Chapter 27

One's real life is so often the life that one does not lead.
—Oscar Wilde

I'M BETTER THAN IN NOVEMBER, BUT I CAN'T SEEM TO stay in a good mood, or in any mood. The alarm clock, set to local radio, switches on at 7:30 every morning, and the room fills with dread at the prospect of the day. Chris and I lie in bed listening to the presenters in the dark. Cattle prices, sheep sales, council controversies, travel news, sporting and artistic triumphs, lengthy descriptions of lost and found cats. The wind howls round the house. It's black dark when the girls go to the end of the drive to meet the high-school transport.

I'm beginning to feel afraid, though it isn't clear what there is to fear. That I won't be able to do it anymore, perhaps. That Nancy will hurt one of the children and that I will hurt her. That she sees through me, my plastic attempts at love. That this is a test of character that I'm failing, D minus. That I will say something to Morris I will always regret. I'm irritable with him and his apparent not caring. I'm having thoughts and feelings of which I'm ashamed. Dislike. Resentment. Regret. Things a caregiver isn't allowed to feel; our moral relationship isn't individual, but universal, cultural, social. Morris is so far in denial now that he no longer registers Nancy's behavior as anything unusual. Oblivious, he affects puzzlement if I bring the subject up of his taking more of a role in entertaining and watching over her. He sees a magazine piece I wrote about our lives with Nancy and is shocked by it—not because I wrote it, but because, as he tells me, he'd no idea that things had got so serious and gone so far.

December contrives to be both vile and uplifting. The weather's atrocious but Christmas with children is a guaranteed solace. I am busy and the calendar fills up and I find, on some days, some half days or half hours, that I feel almost normal. The downward spiral is also an upward one. That's how spirals are.

I like the peninsula Christmas, the modesty and gusto of its series of concerts and events, its precommercialized spirit. The village lights are unshowy in primary colors. The tree in the square is tall and twinkly, and held down by guy ropes so that the wind can't take it. The official village tree lighting is preceded by the Salvation Army, at length. There was no music last year (we gathered, the lights were switched on, we funneled into the hall for mulled wine), but this time the band swings into action with a program of carols to get through, out in the square, and we're all caught out, in thin coats and hatless, shivering as we sing along.

Nancy has a new friend. She finds her, unexpectedly, standing at the dogleg from rear passage to hall. An expanse of wall there has been enlivened by an Arts and Crafts mirror, a large rectangle with a carved oak frame. Nancy finds her new friend here, three-dimensional and in color, backlit by the glass outer door. It's shocking to discover that she no longer recognizes herself. A year ago, compulsively washing her hands (this urge has passed), she would have a good look at her reflection while doing so, adjusting her hair and muttering her displeasure at being so dilapidated. The year before that, she could still be funny about it. "God, but you're ugly," she'd say, laughing. Self-recognition is a major hallmark of consciousness. Chimps, dolphins, and apparently also elephants recognize their own reflections. Elephants are the newest additions to the list: an experiment in 2007 at a New York zoo found that once they got used to the mirror, they'd use it to have a good look inside their own mouths. Nancy's loss of self-recognition is, it seems, to do with severe right hemisphere damage, right frontal lobe damage.

Not that talking to herself in the mirror is alarming in itself. People talk to themselves all the time, with or without a reflection on hand. When you think about it, this is rather odd behavior. Who is it that's talking and who listening? Perhaps it's simply and unmysteriously true that we're all two people, two in one. One of us, the actor, is out there in the world, interacting and reporting back, doing things and saying things, out on a limb, a free agent. This self might behave badly, be easily led, go astray, come back with ludicrous notions or shameful confessions. The other one of us is deeply embedded, the sum of everything we know, and thus is infinitely wiser and more cautious. That's the editor. While the actor's out shopping, the editor stays at home in the mind, and makes judgments.

"You were so stupid to buy that jacket."

"Shut up, it was half price."

It's undeniable that there's a dialogue going on.

People refer to this internal double act all the time. "I'm not myself today," they say. "What was I going to do?" "Why did I do that, why do I do these things?" and my personal philosophical favorite: "What do I think I'm doing?"

Sometimes, we're hard on ourselves. We speak of ourselves as dual creatures: self-knowledge, after all, requires a self and a knower of self, which seems to leave the field wide open for Team Descartes. The Cartesian view isn't needed, though, if you accept that consciousness and self aren't strictly equivalent; that self extends beyond and below what we know of it. Aristotle said, "We are not able to see what we are from ourselves." We do what we can. Polonius, in *Hamlet,* tells his son, "[T]o thine own self be true, / And it must follow as the night the day, / Thou canst not then be false to any man." *I know you better than you know yourself* is probably the most irritating thing anyone can tell you (other than stuff about Aristotle).

It's universally agreed that having a dialogue is better than having a war and perhaps that's the point of the inner conversation. Different parts of our selves, instinctive and rational, conservative and liberal, get to debate things. That's how the mind seems to work. That's how information is presented and assessed, teased out, opinions formulated and actions decided upon. The editor doesn't always triumph. Sometimes other parts of the brain win the argument. The gut instinct, for example, which is delivered via a red phone from the limbic system.

"This man's trouble."

"Nonsense. Just because he has tattoos."

"This man's trouble, shut the door on him."

"He showed me his card, don't be so paranoid."

"He's trouble. Look, I'm shutting the door if you don't." Slam. Locks are shunted into place.

"Well, I hope you're happy now because you look like an idiot. He was from the electricity board."

"He was a fraud. Couldn't you sense it?"

"Ridiculous."

It seems sometimes that Nancy is traveling through what survives of her life asleep. Life is so odd, so unaccountable, so disengaged from reality to her brain-damaged perceptions, that it might be like being in a dream. The once Amazonian-sized forest of nerve cells and axons and synapses, its millions, trillions of connections, seems now to have reduced to just a few well-trodden tracks through a wood, a few broad footpaths that have been worn into deep ruts. The rest looms dark and unknowable. Things seem out of control, bizarre, to her. People around her look familiar but unfamiliar—I think sometimes that it must be like a constant process of déjà vu. They make statements that cannot be true. She can't convince the people in the dream that her life is elsewhere and that they are all, all of them, engaged in the joint hallucination that takes place through the looking glass. The dream goes on and on, for months and years, and there's no waking up. Jung wrote that it's likely we continually dream, but that consciousness makes so much noise that we're not aware of it. What if Nancy's consciousness has stopped making much of a noise? Is it a kind of waking dream that takes its place?

NOW THAT SHE'S found the woman in the mirror, Nancy's talking to herself for much of the day and her mood is miraculously lifted. I find her there one afternoon as I come in from outside. I come up behind her.

"Hello!" I say. "Looking in the mirror again? How are you looking today?"

"Here's my friend!" Nancy says, gesturing toward herself and looking absolutely delighted.

"Hello, there," I say to the grinning reflection. "And who are you?"

"She won't tell you that," Nancy says. "I keep asking her to come in, but she won't."

"How's she going to come in?"

"Through the door," Nancy says. "Through here." The mirror is a doorway. She takes a step backward and her arms are raised, beckoning. "Come on then. Come on. Come in for a little while. Won't you come in? Because I'd love it if you would."

"This is a mirror, isn't it, Nancy?" I say. "Look." I knock on the glass. "It's a mirror, and that's you."

Nancy looks at me as if I'm really idiotic. "I know that. I know that. Do you think I'm stupid?" She laughs at her reflection and it laughs back. "Look! Look! She's laughing at you," she says.

"But that's you," I say. Why can't I let it go? I don't really know. Perhaps it's to do with being a mother, this habit of correcting people's misapprehensions. Or perhaps it's something worse.

"That's you, isn't it?" I say, waving at her in the mirror. "Look. I'm waving at you. See, here's my hand waving"—she looks briefly at my hand—"and here's my hand again, waving in the mirror."

"That's my friend," Nancy says.

"Why don't you wave, too?" I say.

The woman in the mirror is frowning.

Nancy's face falls. "She doesn't like it," she says.

"Okay, then." I am conceding defeat. "I'll leave you two to chat."

When I pass by again an hour later, seeing to laundry, Nancy's still there, chatting away to the mirror. And she's smiling, laughing, giggling with her friend. I go into the kitchen and make a pot of coffee and sit staring at the cup. Nancy isn't always unhappy. Nancy still has her moments of fun. She's getting something out of life. She doesn't always hate you. She doesn't hate you at all. What on earth made you think that? How could you be so deranged? And how—oh dear god, this is appalling—how on earth could you wish her dead?

WE DECIDE NOT to do any more bed-and-breakfast, a decision sparked by discovering that one of our guests this year has stolen quite a number of DVDs. We're not sure how many. We only cotton on because Chris asks if anybody knows where the Humphrey Bogart films have gone—all of them are gone, it transpires—and then we discover more films are missing, another twenty or so classics. The idea that somebody friendly, somebody who wrote admiringly in the visitors' book, put thirty or more DVDs in his suitcase, shook our hands and thanked us very much again for the fantastic weekend, and drove off with our stuff, is fatally dissuasive.

By mid-December, I have a permanent sharp pain in my head and neck and the doctor diagnoses tension, bad posture, a trapped nerve. He prescribes a muscle relaxant (tranquilizer), which I daren't take. Jack is ill with one of his epic bouts of tonsillitis, and in mid-December he's admitted to the men's ward at the local hospital—there's no children's ward—to put him on a stronger regimen of drugs and monitor him. I don't sleep. I sit downstairs in the in-laws' sitting room, warmest in the house, at 5:00 A.M. with herbal tea. Nancy is up and wandering the halls. She comes in the sitting room door, then goes out through the kitchen saying, "Well, you're no use, are you? Typical, typical," and puts herself back to bed. We go to the hospital in the morning and find Jack up, dressed, playing PlayStation. They've found a heart murmur and will want to see him again. He's discharged and comes home. Purple and white and gray.

Jack, the trapped nerve, the stresses of the night shift, anxiety about making the children's Christmas happy—evidently it's all too much. December's recovery turns out to be veneer. One day when Nancy has been making the perfectly routine complaint that I'm the only person that's nice to her, but that the children who live here are nasty and call her names, my facade suffers a small additional crack. Small but structural. I leave her sitting on her bed and go to find Morris, landing in Nancy's chair with a thud.

"I'm at the end of my tether. I can't stand any more. I can't. Stand. Much. More. I mean it," I say. Morris looks appropriately alarmed, which is to say that he looks just the same but his eyes are wider. I seem to be having a breakdown, right there in the middle of *Cash in the Attic*. "Why don't you respond? Say something!" I tell him. "Are you listening? I'm telling you something important, Morris. I can't go on with this. I'm at the end of the road. Do you understand me?"

"Yes. I understand you," he says, looking at me as if he's the bank teller and I'm the madman with the gun.

I'M ON THE Internet a lot, finding refuge from the too-specific gravity of life in the weightless world of e-mail, which floats free of consequence. But Alzheimer's has its teeth in me and before long I find myself trawling dementia forums. There's a lot of guilt out there: blame, self-blame, and confused thinking. A physician in the *New York Times* remarks that, though American citizens believe that the modern generation of elderly is being dumped in vast numbers in care facilities, the reality is rather the opposite, with a huge percentage being cared for at home. I think about that word *dumped* all day. All across the World Wide Web there is praise for those who keep caregiving in the family, and the widespread assumption that opting for residential care is a kind of failure, only mitigated by personal circumstances. Rita Hayworth's daughter, interviewed about the care of her mother and whether she'd considered an institution for her says no, never, not even at her worst, and the interviewer hands out the appropriate admiration. Even I, the battered soul and incipient alcoholic, whose blood could be used to inoculate others against the taking in of parents, can see that hers is the right answer, the honorable answer. Recognizing this, people agonize on the dementia forums about whether they can go on, looking for permission from their peers to capitulate. Among caregivers who have capitulated, who've gone for the nursing home option after years of keeping loved ones with them, there's almost unanimous self-loathing for giving up. The words *giving up* are used a lot. That and *dumping*.

Dumping. Do we *dump* people in hospitals when they're ill? Is that the language used? I worry that we're all confusing a physical disease with natural aging, believing that we ought to be able to contain aging and death within the family, recognizing the failure and stigma of doing otherwise. We confuse dementia with old age, and it's a moral given that old age oughtn't to be punished by exclusion; put in those terms, there's no argument.

I sit close to two girls in a coffee shop. One says to the other, "Is it true your gran has gone into a home?"

The other one nods. "My mum said she couldn't cope with her anymore."

"God, your poor granny, those places are terrible."

"I know. I'm so angry with my mum for putting her in there. We went to see her and she was crying." She's blushing a deep red.

There's a strong whiff of shame about parents going into a nursing home. I worry that the medical profession colludes in this. I see them colluding all over the Internet. One American woman reports that her Alzheimer's-suffering mother, at about Nancy's stage of the disease by the sound of things, has four doctors and a therapist, all of whom have agreed that putting the mother into residential care would be "like killing her."

The weekend before Christmas we have our party. Nancy and Morris go into respite at the private home for the weekend and appear to enjoy it. Nothing is said about staying on, this time, and there are no sales calls. We have two hundred guests, a magician, a movie-and-pizza splinter group upstairs for those under four foot six, and tipsy teenagers gathered round the pool table.

"It looks pretty likely that Nancy and Morris will go into residential care next year," I find myself telling people when they ask (and everybody asks). I don't seem to have any other form of conversation. I seem to feel the need to brief everybody there, individually, about the situation. I'm properly defensive about the reasons.

"And if they do go into care, will you be moving away?"

That's what everybody wants to know. Will we be staying or not. There's a strong chance we won't be, but I hesitate to admit this.

We're an odd assortment of souls, gathered here together tonight. Most of us are *incomers* (less charmingly, *blow-ins*), who have come to live on the peninsula from the outside—outsiders and not locals. The sheer intrepidity of incomers is impressive, like the organic farmer over the hill, who persists in trying to grow vegetables on an economic scale in these weather conditions, despite constant setbacks. Some people I've met came because they're artists and because it's relatively cheap to buy an artist's house on the shore; many are here because of house prices. There's a lot of sea view, a lot of fresh air, a lot of unspoiled wilderness on offer per pound spent. And very little crime. People don't lock their cars in town. People don't lock their houses. But once people are installed, many of them become possessive of the place. They don't like to hear it criticized, and leaving is seen as rejection. They're openly perplexed by people not staying on.

"Don't tell people you might not be here more than two or three years," somebody says to me at the party. "They won't bother to get to know you."

"It's irritating when you make friends and then they leave," someone else tells me. "You invest all this time in them and then they're gone."

The occasional local die-hard grows donnishly disapproving. "Why come here if you don't like extreme weather, though?" they ask, in a tutorial manner. "But why come here at all if you didn't intend to stay?"

Living here can be a trial of strength. That's one way of looking at it. The challenges of meteorology, of isolation, of making a living are looked upon by long-established residents as a test of true grit. "Naah, they left after eighteen months, they couldn't hack it," they say, at one of the many village socials, dismissively of some poor soul. It's important to show that you can hack it, that you relish hacking it, that you're man or woman enough.

"It's only a force nine, what are you talking about; that's just for drying your washing." "Call that winter? That was only a shower. You just wait." As Sydney Smith observed: "No nation has so large a stock of benevolence of heart as the Scotch. Their temper stands anything but an attack on their climate." But the joke's on Sydney Smith. Almost everybody I know who feels this (on occasion quite savage) defensiveness of the superiority of *here* and the inexorable decline of *there* is English. Adopted Scots.

NANCY AND MORRIS come back glumly from their weekend, and remain glum over the holiday. On Christmas morning we gather in the drawing room for the children's present-opening ritual, something my in-laws would once have enjoyed, despite carping about the overgenerosity, the waste of wrapping paper. Nancy is kept busy with a tin of gaudily wrapped chocolates and Morris is silent. At Christmas lunch Morris picks at his food in silence and Nancy is occupied trying to eat gravy with her fingers. Afterward, I give Morris the option of an afternoon by the TV with a box of chocolates, and this is gratefully taken up. The two of them sit by a roaring fire in paper hats, eating truffles and drinking from the various bottles I put on the tray, flicking between Christmas Day programs, and seem almost jolly.

After Christmas, friends come to stay for New Year's Eve, another family of five. One evening while the ten of us, crammed round the kitchen table, are having supper, and

Nancy's supposed to be eating hers with Morris, she appears at the door, hands on hips, nodding slowly at us all, her face bright red, veins pulsing in her neck.

"Nancy! What can we do for you? Have you finished eating?"

She stares at me and then says, "So, you're all still here, then?"

"Er, what?"

"I said. I said so you're all still here, then. You're all still here."

"What are you talking about? We live here. And these are our friends, visiting for New Year."

"I'm not having it. You all have to go now. Now. I mean it. Out. I said now."

I bundle her back into her sitting room and close the door. I am angry.

"Now listen to me. Don't you dare embarrass me in front of our friends. I've had quite enough of your mouth lately. Stay in here just now. Stay here. Stay put," I snap at her, and then I return to the kitchen, aware of a subtle shift in mood. I'm embarrassed by my own reaction as much as by Nancy's rudeness. Everybody heard me shouting at her. Various explanatory sentences are born and die in my head, particular, and then at last general: None of it makes any sense if you haven't been here and lived through it, though saying as much sounds trite. I shrug it off, as I have learned to. Mr. Bennet in *Pride and Prejudice* flashes into my mind, chastened by his part in Lydia's disgrace, and feeling, despite Elizabeth's soothings, that morally he ought to suffer. "I am not afraid of being overpowered by the impression. It will pass away soon enough." And even while I'm thinking this and feeling bad, I'm also feeling grateful that I have this store of associations on hand, and the healthy brain that delivers them up.

On New Year's Eve, Morris expresses a positive disinclination toward staying up late. They'd rather go to bed at the usual time, thanks, he tells me. We drink a lot, have champagne at midnight with a dozen or so neighbors, watch the fireworks going off out on the headland, and wish each other, with greater sincerity than is ordinary, a very happy New Year.

Chapter 28

This long last childhood
Nothing provides for.
What can it do each day
But hunt that imminent door
Through which all that understood
Has hidden away?

—PHILIP LARKIN

T HE NEW YEAR BRINGS NEW DEVELOPMENTS. THE FIRST of these is that Nancy begins to declaim. She's a mobile declaimer, addressing herself to each of the rooms she walks through. As she walks she makes three statements. She hasn't spoken to me directly since Christmas. Instead, she has fixed on three repeated lines:

"And I will never be.

"And I will never know.

"And I will never be again."

If I'm in the kitchen when she passes by, she doesn't seem to notice me. She looks straight ahead. "And I will never be."

"Hello, Nancy," I say. Even when I address her she doesn't look toward me.

"And I will never know."

"Just having a walk? Morris's through that door there, straight ahead, if you're looking for him."

She goes up the step and rattles the handle of her sitting room door.

"And I will never be again."

When she gets tired, she goes and sits by Morris and needles him.

"I've been waiting for you for twenty-five years!"

"It's forty-seven years, actually, that we've been married," Morris corrects her.

"I've been waiting for you and you haven't said anything to me."

"What do you mean? We spend all day together. We talk to each other all day."

"You haven't said a word. Not a word. A real word, I mean, and not one of the other ones."

"What are you talking about?" he bellows. "I'm always here and you're always here and we're always talking."

Much later, passing by their door, I find the same conversation's still going on.

"You never talk to me. I sit here and I talk and you don't answer," Nancy's saying.

"That's rubbish," Morris says emphatically. "That's total rubbish. Think before you speak. Think what you're saying because it's rubbish and you know it's rubbish."

"I talk and I talk and you don't listen."

"Shut up! Just shut up, will you," he cries.

"Don't you dare to tell me to shut up."

"Well, be quiet then. I want to watch this TV program."

"I want to watch it but you won't let me."

"What do you mean? You're sitting right in front of it."

"You won't let me do anything."

"Can you just be quiet so I can watch it?"

"I didn't say a word."

SHE'S DISCOVERED THAT the mirror in her bathroom also has a friend in it. She goes there in the evening and talks to her reflection in the moonlight.

"Oh yes, and I always said so. I said that about you but nobody believed me. That's what happens, though. To me, I mean." She pauses as if the reflection is speaking. Perhaps it is. "Oh my goodness, yes. You're quite right and no mistake."

"Hello, Nancy, what are you up to in here in the dark?" Chris asks amiably, putting the light on.

He doesn't often call her Mother anymore. She won't answer to it, might query it, might want to make declarations that are best avoided.

"That's my friend," Nancy says, smiling at herself. "I only have one friend and that's her."

BLACK SUNDAY. NANCY'S in a state of perpetual rage. Jack is threatened. He has the temerity to touch the dog in her presence.

"What are you doing that for? Get out of here. Do as you're told."

He leaves the dog and goes to stand by the fire.

"Get out of here, you little bugger."

"What? Why, Gran?"

"Come closer to me and I'll get you. I'll kill you. I will. I'll kill you. I mean it. You filthy little bastard."

We don't talk to her about these outbursts anymore. There's no point and everybody gets pointlessly upset. Morris pretends he hasn't heard and Nancy's determined she didn't do anything wrong. She'll be difficult for the rest of the day, if she's told off. The reason for the telling off doesn't register. Nothing is learned by it and nothing is gained. If she isn't told off, chances are her rage will subside pretty quickly. So, strictly in terms of the balance sheet, it's better to ditch the moralizing. Though this is difficult to explain to Jack.

Like an anorexic girl finding power over her mother in not eating, Nancy begins to decline food, any food, whether left out for her to forage in the kitchen or offered on a plate. A fish pie with a mashed potato top, served to her in a bowl with a dessert spoon, is rejected untasted. I go and kneel by her chair and try to spoon some of it into her.

"I don't like it! I'm not going to eat anything if I don't like it!"

"You need food, though, Nancy. Usually you love fish pie. It's got lots of cream in it, and prawns. Just try it. Just have a bit."

She takes a spoonful from me then talks with her mouth full, spitting haddock. "You've given me far too much! Ask them and they'll tell you straight. There's too much in my mouth."

"Just stop talking and eat it."

She chews and chews, looking pained.

I offer another spoonful. A protective, shielding hand goes up, her fingernails an ominous dark brown.

"You've got to eat something or you'll get ill."

"Don't make me laugh."

"No, I mean it. You can't live on biscuits. You need some protein and some vitamins."

Nancy's head goes back disdainfully. "No no no. No, they don't. That's stupid. You don't know what you're talking about. You really have no idea about anything or any education."

"I mean it. You need some real food or you'll get poorly."

Her hand is slammed on the dinner tray.

"Well that's *not* what they do in Edinburgh."

"Perhaps you should go back to Edinburgh, then, where you could eat biscuits all day."

"Yes. Yes. I'm going back tonight."

Morris mutters something that I half hear.

"Is that what you want?" I say to him. "I can arrange an Edinburgh residential home if that's what you'd like."

"I'd go tomorrow if I knew where to go," he says.

★ ★ ★

NEXT, THE WHISPERING starts. It's curiously disconcerting, this whispering. Nancy talks to herself under her breath all day and for much of the night, rehearsing imagined wrongs. Almost all of what she has to say begins with "she." The whispered undertone follows her, precedes her, announcing her arrival at the half-opened doors of other rooms. It's difficult to make out what's being said unless you're up close to her face. I find her early one morning inserted tight behind the wide-opened door of the day bathroom, pressed hard between the wall and the door, a length of toilet paper held up to her chin, and only know she's there because of the whispering. "She can't and she won't, it won't be like that, I'll find it again, I'll take it there, and there will be the end of it, and then they will come, and I will tell them, and they will be glad, and I will be there again, and then I will come home, come here, or not here, where is here, I don't know, and then we will know, we will all know, and I will be right, and she will be wrong."

Then Nancy stops washing or wanting to wash. The caregiver arrives for the Monday morning session and finds that she can't get Nancy in the bath. The bath is run but Nancy won't get in it. Nancy gets her way. The caregivers feel that they can't pressure clients into being clean if they don't want to be. I step in. I pressure without a qualm.

"Come on, Nancy, time for your bath."

"I'm not having a bath. I don't need one."

"You are. You smell."

"I do not. Don't be ridiculous. I never smell."

"I hear what you're saying, Nancy, but unfortunately you're going in the bath anyway."

"No, I'm not." A little scream. A foot stamped hard.

"Yes, you are. I'm not taking any nonsense from you about

this, you have to have a bath every now and then, and you are beginning to smell bad."

"It doesn't bother me so why should it bother you?"

This is actually a really good question and surprisingly sophisticated in the current scheme of things.

"It bothers me because you smell and I have to look after you," I tell her. "It bothers me because you are making the house smell. And you will get ill if you stay dirty. So come on. None of your nonsense [historically, a favorite child-chiding phrase of her own]."

"You're NOT LISTENING." She's shouting now. "I'm NOT GETTING IN."

"Yes, you are. Get your clothes off. Get in the bath. You're filthy. Your underwear is filthy." Inspiration strikes. "Everyone can smell you. They will talk about you and say how dirty you are."

As ever, alluding to what the neighbors might think does the trick. She starts to take her sweater off, kicks off her shoes.

"Well, all right then, but I'm not happy."

Once she's in the bath she loves it. She starts to sing, warblingly.

"When all the men are dead now, and the world has come to me, and the way I bring home and the sort I do then, and it's the same for me. . . ."

She plays with the bubbles, purrs when her hair is washed, and is reluctant to get out. And she can still rhyme.

Eating problems escalate. Like a choosy toddler in a high chair, she clamps her lips shut and then her eyes and turns her head away from the spoon. The Battle Royal of the Baked Beans is typical. When she's refused meals for more than twenty-four hours, beans usually break the fast. But not any longer.

"I'm not having it! I'm not," she cries, jumping to her feet, throwing her tray across the room and exiting. I find her in her usual retreat, talking to her bathroom mirror, a stray thread of moonlight reflecting off one eye.

"And she says the same; always the same bloody lies. . . ."

Then she sees me. "And what do you want?" Her most imperious tone.

Later, after she has consented to toast and jam, eaten a quarter of a slice and passed the rest to Morris, I find her in the corridor.

"Hello, Nancy," I say cheerily. "How nice to see you. How are you?"

The Book insists that a caregiver's tone is paramount.

She stares. "I'm not. Speaking to. You."

Chris appears and takes her by the hand: "Come and find Morris, come on," steering her through the kitchen. I go into the hall and *bouf,* there's a small explosion. Chris, renowned for not losing his temper, has lost it and is yelling. "Don't you dare, don't you ever, ever call my wife a bitch again!" I go into the kitchen and make a vodka tonic and hear them at it through the door. I'm thinking that I'll go in and change the subject, offer whisky, get Chris out of there. But Chris is in full flow. He is talking, and then Morris, and then Nancy, and all of them calmly, taking their turn. A most bizarre half hour ensues in which Chris and his father talk Nancy through her recent behavior.

I hear Nancy responding in her shrill defensive voice. "What have I done to anybody? Nothing, nothing at all."

MORRIS: You've been very rude to people and you're upsetting them.

NANCY: When have I been rude to anybody? I wasn't rude. Who told you that?

CHRIS: Nobody told me, Mother. I was there, standing right next to you. You called my wife a bitch and it isn't the first time and it has to stop.

NANCY: I've never done anything of the kind. I've not used that word my whole life.

"Why did you bother?" I ask him when he emerges, having enraged Nancy into sulking and silence.

"No point at all, not for her, but it was good for my father. He got to air some recent grievances."

This is true.

"You've been very rude to me, too, and sneering; you sneer at me and I don't like it," Morris told his wife.

THE DAY AFTER this, I wake feeling certain that I'm at the end of the road. I have to do something. I can't go on, can't physically. My legs are leaden, my heart heavy. I can't face another day. I ring the surgery, and the doctor on duty says he'll call by. He'll reassess Nancy and perhaps prescribe something else. Her drugs may need adjustment.

The drug regimen of Alzheimer's patients is one of the chief bugbears of their and their caregivers' lives. The neurotransmitter breakdown inhibitor that boosts communications in surviving brain cells and at best slows the sufferer's decline, the one that has four manifestations, four brand names: that's the only drug available. Everything else an Alzheimer's sufferer is prescribed is tried out from a menu of drugs developed for other conditions, tackling individual symptoms. That's the best that can be done. Antipsychotics, benzodiazepines like Valium, epilepsy drugs, mood stabilizers, antihistamines, antidepressants, sleeping pills, Parkinson's disease drugs, in rare cases even Ritalin: all might be dipped into, on a suck-it-and-see basis, and every Alzheimer's patient has her own cocktail and combination. Every individual is an individual drug trial. Things are tried, don't work, are adjusted. That's how it is.

"You sound like you're at the end of your tether," the doctor says.

"Not quite," I tell him, "I'm not quite there. But I can see it now, the end of it." It's in my mind's eye, the end of a fat sailing rope, looming frayed up ahead.

The doctor has been in touch with the social work department, and so have we, and a care meeting has been fixed for tomorrow in town.

When the doctor arrives, I take him into the drawing room—respectably tidy, coal fire lit—and go and fetch Nancy. She is civil when she shakes his hand but begins to look suspicious when he sits by her on the sofa.

"I'm just going to ask you a few questions, Nancy."

"If you must you must. But be quick about it." Her disdain is penetrating.

The doctor has the laminated sheet out of his bag, the standard Alzheimer's memory test known as the MMSE (mini mental state examination). Points are given out of thirty. There aren't thirty questions. Ten marks are given for orientation to time and place, three marks for registering three words, five marks for attention and calculation, three marks for remembering three words, eight marks for language, and one for visual construction.

"Right then. Do you know what year it is?"

"No idea."

"What is the month?"

She thinks a moment, shakes her head.

"What's the date today?"

"Haven't a clue."

"What day is it?"

"No idea at all."

"Right. Do you have any idea what the season is? What season are we in?"

She looks blank.

"Do you know what a season is? What's a season?"

She purses her lips and looks straight ahead.

"I do, of course. It's one of those things that's over there, which is to say it's one and two and three, that kind of thing."

"Right. Next I'm going to give you three words to remember, and in a minute I want you to remember them and tell me what they are, okay?"

"What would I want to do that for? I don't want anything to do with your things, it isn't anything to do with me."

He gives her the words, three short common nouns. Ball, car, man. "Can you say them for me? Ball, car, man."

"I'm not remotely interested in that," Nancy tells him.

"Can you repeat this phrase for me? No ifs, ands, or buts."

She stares at him.

"Say this: No ifs, ands, or buts."

She keeps staring.

"Do you know the name of this house?" the doctor asks her.

"No." Annoyed. "And don't ask me that again."

"Where do you live, where is this house?"

"Edinburgh!" exasperatedly. "It's Edinburgh! That's where I live."

"What's the area called? This area we live in?"

"Edinburgh! Are you stupid? Edinburgh! Edinburgh's where I live."

"What floor of the house are we on? Are we on the ground floor, or upstairs?"

"Not a clue." With some satisfaction, folding her arms.

"Can you spell this word—*world*. World. Like the world we live in. World."

"What?"

"World. Can you spell it?"

"No, and I don't want to. What would I want to do that for? All stupid questions! You and your wode."

Nor can she spell it backward, or remember the three words

he gave her to remember. The math test is skirted over quickly. It's pointless, really, asking Nancy to subtract seven from one hundred.

"Right. Here's a piece of paper. I'd like you to hold it in your right hand."

Surprisingly, she can do this one and is happy to oblige. "This is my right." She extends her right hand and picks the paper up.

"Can you fold the paper in half?"

She can do this, too. Two points have been earned. She puts the short sides carefully together and smooths the fold crisply and precisely in place.

"Now, put the paper on your knee."

"Where?"

"Put it on your knee."

She leans down to put it on the floor.

"No, put it on your knee."

"This is my knee." She lifts her left knee up and looks puzzled. The paper drops to the ground.

"Right, Nancy. Can you tell me what this is?" (It's a pen.)

"Yes, of course, it's one of those things that's for you, and that's yours, and it's for holding and it goes along there. It's yours, just take it yourself. Why are you asking me?"

"And can you tell me what this is?" (It's a watch.)

Very irritably and shrill. "I've told you already, it's yours, just take it, if you want something you just take it, don't you, you don't ask stupid questions about it, just take it!"

The doctor is sounding properly nervous now. His mouth is dry when he speaks. Nancy's intimidating. Wild-eyed, spittle flying.

"Can you write a sentence for me—a short one, absolutely anything?"

"Like what?"

"Anything you like. A short sentence of your choice. Just a few words. Whatever you want."

"But what do you want me to do that for?"

"It's a test. I just want to see you write something down. Just write one word if you like."

He gives her the pen. She holds it, looks at the paper. Her fingers work their way round the Biro. She pauses and considers. Then she hands the pen back.

"I've got absolutely no need to do that and no interest in doing it, either." High dudgeon. "Why should I do these things for you when you do nothing for me?"

The doctor clears his throat. He holds out the laminated sheet. "Okay then. Can you read this?"

"Where?"

"Just here. These three words. Can you read them?"

She looks at the sheet, at where his finger indicates, for a moment.

"That's a *c*. And another *c*. And that's an *o*. There's a *c* and an *o*."

"Right. Do you still have that block of paper? Here's a pen. Can you copy these shapes onto the paper?"

"What shapes?"

"These shapes here, on the sheet." They're intersecting pentagons.

She looks at the pen and at the sheet of paper and her hand hovers. She looks at the sheet and at the pen and at her hand, frowning.

"Why would I want to write that down? I don't want to," she says eventually. "I don't see the point and the point and not that at all."

"It's just a short test. It's over now."

"I know who did this," she says, putting her hair behind her ears. "I know his name. I know why he did it but I'm not going to say, oh no. I'm not telling anything to any of you at any time."

Less than twenty-four out of thirty indicates substantial cognitive impairment, the Internet tells me. Healthy people over the age of eighty should be able to score twenty-five. Nancy scored two. Just two out of thirty.

The Alzheimer's Society says in its MMSE fact sheet that a patient should score twelve or more for there to be any point in taking the dementia-specific drugs. Nancy's galantamine is to be phased out with immediate effect and a new drug given in its place, one recommended by the psychogeriatrician at the city hospital for mood swings and aggression (one we give her for less than a week as it makes her ill at night, comatose in daylight).

The final thing the doctor wants to do is to check Nancy's blood pressure.

"No, I don't think I want to do that."

"It will only take a moment. Just want to check your blood pressure."

"You're not taking any blood from me, I can tell you that."

"I'm not taking blood, just checking it," he reassures her.

"Well, if you say so, but I'm not happy about it."

She consents to her sleeve being rolled up. The plastic is wrapped round her upper arm. He begins to inflate it. Puff puff. Puff puff.

"Christ, that's cold."

"Sorry. It's been in the car."

Puff puff. Her face droops, her eyes close.

"You do that one more time," Nancy says in her low warning voice, "and it will be the worse for you. And I'm not joking. I'm not kidding around. You will regret it."

He puffs another puff and her other arm comes up with the fist balled tight. The doctor ducks.

Chapter 29

The very tones in which we spake
Had something strange, I could but mark;
The leaves of memory seemed to make
A mournful rustling in the dark.
—HENRY WADSWORTH LONGFELLOW

THE EMERGENCY CARE MEETING IS HELD IN THE TOWN, at the swanky new social work offices that look, appropriately enough, like a cross between a medical practice and a solicitors' group and smell pungently of carpet. There are four of us present. Me, Chris, our care manager, and the care manager's boss, whom we're meeting for the first time. The first thing the boss has to say is that we can't see the file because Morris would have to give consent. (Why would we want to see the file? Is there something in it that's material? We'll never know.)

"So how are you, and how are things?" we're asked.

"Desperate, and desperate," I say.

"We need to establish why Nancy isn't on the residential waiting list," Chris says, "and how we can get her onto it."

"We can do another assessment," the boss says. "Things seem to have deteriorated badly since the summer."

"All that's changed lately," I tell her, "is that she's no longer so charming with outsiders, and doesn't mask her condition so well."

We talk about Nancy's MMSE result, which the doctor has

been in touch about. "That really is quite a marked deterioration," the manager comments. I point out that she hasn't had the test before.

"We're confused about what the criteria are for getting onto the waiting list," Chris says again.

The sea change is coming. It's seconds away. And it happens by accident.

"The thing is, we can no longer cope," Chris says. "We can't do it anymore."

"Every day is a struggle," I concur.

"Are you saying you can't go on?" the boss asks.

At once, I begin backtracking, feeling as if I'm about to be judged inadequate.

"We're at the end of the road," Chris tells her. "We can't any longer care for them, unfortunately."

"So. You're saying that you can no longer look after them. Is that what you're saying?"

"Yes. That's what we're saying."

"It's much more difficult now," I add, "to manage Nancy at home, because she's threatening the children, and hitting them."

The professionals look at each other.

"Well, in that case, emergency respite will have to be arranged with immediate effect," the boss says. "We'll have to consider the long term. And the Family Division will have to be informed."

Family Division? I have visions of cars arriving at dawn, the children hauled off, and protest energetically. There's an instinctive fear of social workers, the extravagance of their powers, buried just below the surface of all my dealings with them. The social workers say, with regretful finality, that they have no choice, now that the abuse has been reported; they have a legal obligation to report violence upon children.

No care places are available locally, so respite will involve a journey into the next county. We mention that Morris is keen to return to Edinburgh, and they tell us they can get names onto the Edinburgh waiting list. In the United Kingdom, it's worth campaigning to have the list placement done by the social work department, rather than just going ahead and finding somewhere yourself. If it's their referral, the nursing portion of the fee is paid by the sponsoring council. This isn't to be sniffed at, being £150 or so a week *each,* saving £15,000 a year. Even so, it will be around £35,000 a year for the two of them (by national standards, this isn't expensive). Discreet inquiries are made about means.

"They have the money to pay their own way for the first few years," Chris says. "They have their life savings. The rest of it's invested and will have to be de-invested." It's our house we're talking about; that portion of it that Nancy and Morris own. The house will have to go on the market. All assets count. Their savings, investments, all of it will be liquidated into a pot from which the state will drink hungrily. It will leach away, month by month, until there's £20,000 left. Only at that point will the state begin to contribute. At the time of writing, the rules dictate that only the final £12,250 will be left intact, untouchable by the state. This information hits Morris hard. It's a disheartening thing to face, for those who've always been frugal. The people who held on to their ancient washing machine until it gave out, who were content with the old linoleum in the kitchen, who put money by for a rainy day—their rainy day has come. The make-do-and-mend philosophy was all about providing an inheritance for Chris and his sister. But getting old and ill will take almost everything. It's raining hard now.

Once you have it clear in your mind that Alzheimer's is a disease, whose sufferers are ill, and that what's needed for it is treatment, the idea that a nursing home is optional, a luxury, and will be invoiced on that basis, is deeply offensive and wrong.

Next, the care twosome pays a house call. It's Morris they

want to talk to and they go into closed session. He's anecdotal-izing and hoots of appreciative laughter boom out under the closed doors. On this occasion laughter isn't a good sign. It means, almost certainly, that Morris is illustrating that the problems, such as they are, are blackly comic at worst. Later, Chris tries to talk to his father about the meeting but is met by the usual studied vagueness.

Three days later. The phone rings. Our care manager. Can she come out today to talk to Morris again? She'd want us in on the conversation this time. "Will you sit in? Because he doesn't seem to believe that there's a problem." She asks me if I will be frank with Morris about being at the end of the road, at the end of my tether, and needing the two of them out. No, I can't do that, I tell her. I'm not going to be a part of any staged resolution, no emotional pleas, no histrionics. I'm cer-tainly not going to confirm anybody's dark suspicions that this has all been about me.

Nancy's up all that night, wandering, rattling doors, and ranting. She won't take the sleeping syrup; she clamps her lips together and flat refuses to comply. Her nocturnal narratives begin to remind me of somebody with a head injury trying to keep herself from losing consciousness. One foot is put in front of another, literally but also verbally, without there being any really strong thread at work. Just keeping going is the thing, keeping walking and keeping awake, with whatever words come to hand.

She has extraordinary stamina. Nighttime sleep is intermit-tent and daytime naps have been given up but she keeps on going nonetheless. She badgers Morris all the next day and is still badgering when I deliver the afternoon tea.

"I've told you already, I want to go for a walk."

"You can't go for a walk, it's dark outside," Morris tells her.

"I have asked you a hundred times," Nancy says.

"What are you talking about? I can't walk. I have a wheelchair. You'll have to push me. We'll do it tomorrow. It's too late now."

"It was the same with my father. He was standing at the door and he said something to me and you closed it."

"Your father?"

"You closed the door on him when he was here. He was talking to me."

"Your father's been dead for thirty years."

"I know the truth and you don't. He died last night."

She's weeping now.

"Thirty years!" Morris roars. "He's been dead for thirty years!"

"It all comes to money," Nancy tells him. "They want my money."

"*Who* does?"

"They know who they are and where they went and you don't."

"I haven't the faintest idea what you're talking about."

"Well, that's what I'm saying. You're my father."

Morris (apoplectic): "I am *not* your father. I am your husband."

Nancy's whimpering. "I've told you a thousand times but you don't listen. We could go home if it wasn't for you."

Morris is yelling now at the top of his voice. "I've told you! I can't walk! You'll need to push me in the chair." And then, calmly, "It's dark now; we'll do it tomorrow."

ON THE MORNING of the assessment I have a brief conversation with Morris.

"You know that it's coming, don't you? We can no longer cope with Nancy in the family. You know that, don't you?"

"Yes."

"And you will want to go with her, yes?"

He pauses. "I think so."

He's decided against Edinburgh, though. He'd rather stay up here. He doesn't think the old Edinburgh friends would visit them, he says. Not once the novelty had worn off.

The care manager and the boss arrive, and ask, ominously, if they can talk to Chris and me first. We repair to the drawing room. The boss appears to have a speech prepared. She tells us that it's going to make this whole process a lot more difficult if Chris and I won't speak to Morris directly about our feelings and won't agree to go on the record as having done so.

She's talking about the phone call, the one in which I was asked to tell my father-in-law that I need him to leave, in circumstances (social workers present) that might look engineered. But this isn't about feelings. It isn't about Morris. It's about Nancy, and Nancy's unhappiness. Nancy's health. I don't think the social workers see that. I don't think they understand Alzheimer's. I think they look at us, Chris and me, and see people giving up, capitulating, *dumping*.

Morris needs to give permission for Chris and me to sit in on the meeting. He says he wants a confidential talk with the two ladies first. I say to him that I feel at this stage of things that he ought not to have anything to say to the social workers that he couldn't say to us. This angers him. The social workers are hovering so I leave the room, embarrassed. Foolishly, I pause at the door, and hear Morris berating me for wanting to know everything, wanting always to be consulted, for wanting to be in charge, for being interfering and bossy.

Fifteen minutes later, we are admitted to the room. Nothing's said about the confidential talk. Long explanations follow about how the waiting list works—not as a queue, it turns out, but strictly according to need. Every time a place comes up, the whole list is consulted for the best match. And it's possible that a double room will become vacant this spring.

Morris is emotional, his eyes brimming, his voice quavery,

when the boss asks if he is happy to go into the nursing home. I feel like I might cry myself. Pity and relief are fighting for top billing.

"Not really," he says, "but what's the alternative?"

"You could stay here. We could offer more help. But I think you're aware that your family are having difficulty coping."

"Well, if that's the case, then there isn't any choice," he says.

The boss says something about confidentiality. Morris's reply is surprising.

"There's nothing you say to me that you shouldn't say in front of my son and daughter-in-law. They have looked after us magnificently. . . ." The phone rings out and I have to excuse myself to answer it, so I miss the rest of this tribute.

The day before they're to go off to respite, Nancy is spoiling for a fight. By lunchtime she and Morris are in open warfare.

NANCY: You are getting on my nerves, I wish you'd clear off out of here.

MORRIS: Oh that's very nice. We'll both shut up, then.

NANCY: You talk to me as if about I was a child.

MORRIS: No. I talk to you as if you *were* a child. There's no "about" in the sentence. That's what you should have said. Why don't you rub your fingers together?

NANCY: Why should I do that?

MORRIS: You do it all day. Rub rub rub. I'd like to know why myself. Why don't you twiddle your hair?

NANCY: That's just ridiculous. I do nothing of the sort.

MORRIS: Why don't you stick them up your nose?

NANCY: That's completely ridiculous.

MORRIS: That's right. I'm being ridiculous again. Which is another way of saying that I'm totally fed up.

Cases to pack. Morris doesn't want to be involved in this. He watches television and I take suggested clothes and books through for approval.

When I go into their sitting room later that evening to take Nancy to bed, she has that look on her face: the warning look, pinkish violet, with lips in a tight purse. She goes to the bathroom and I sit on her bed to wait for her, feeling uneasy. Things can get out of hand at this point in the day. She sits on the toilet and free-associates. At least I think that's what she's doing. But it occurs to me after a while that she might be talking to her urine.

"You're going to go there and do the right thing and go down, and that's right. And I will have to talk to her about you and where you need to go next."

Now she is having trouble with her underwear.

"Are you all right in there?" I call through.

"Yes. No. I'm coming. I'm coming, I tell you. I'm telling you straight." Her head bends to deal with errant clothing and her voice is muffled accordingly. "You don't go on right anymore. You used to know where to be but now you don't. And she will have something to say about that."

A few minutes later she trundles through.

"Right then," I say. "Let's get you changed for bed."

"I'm not getting changed, I'm bloody freezing."

"It's warm in here, Nancy, with the heater on. I'm really warm. Aren't you warm?"

I start to unbutton her cardigan. An old veined hand clamps itself over mine.

"Now come on," I say. She just stares at me. She is as ever astoundingly strong. "We just need to get your nightie on."

"But I've spent all my life trying to get it and it isn't there. You don't know the first thing about it."

I have her cardigan off now and she consents to her sweater coming over her head.

"Now that'll do fine. I'll just go like this," she says, holding on to her blouse hem tight, her knuckles white.

"Look. Your nightie and your fleecy bed jacket. You'll be warm as toast."

"Hum huum, hum huum, hum hm-hm." Her favorite tune. She hums it now. She can no longer rhyme.

I whip the vest off and get the nightie on, the zip jacket. "You're going on your holidays tomorrow," I say, grinning at her.

"I am not."

"Yes, you're going away on your holidays, with Morris."

"Who's Morris?"

"That's your husband."

"Oh. That's what you say. That's my husband, is it. You don't look like my husband."

"No. I'm married to your son. Yours and Morris's."

"I don't have a son. I never had children and I'm glad because they just disappoint you."

Here comes the crunch. The trouser and underpants removal from under the long skirt of the nightdress, pulled quick and altogether like the magician's tablecloth. "Oh Christ! What the hell do you think you're doing?"

"Good night, Nancy! Sweet dreams!"

Chapter 30

Life is the continuous adjustment of internal relations to external relations.

—HERBERT SPENCER

MID-FEBRUARY. THICK SNOW, BLUE SKIES. THE RE-turn from respite is delayed by transport problems, and Chris has a series of phone conversations with the nursing home manager, in the course of which she says, "Can I ask, are you thinking about permanent care for your parents?"

Chris launches into the abridged story of our lives in the last two years and then gets to the point and confirms that he is.

"Because they could stay on, you know," the manager says. "They seem pretty happy here."

"Well, that would be ideal for everyone, if that were the case," he tells her. "Let's take it a step at a time. Let's wait and see what Morris has to say to the social worker when she calls by."

Next, we hear that Morris has booked to stay on in the nursing home for another fortnight. The extra fortnight morphs, within twenty-four hours, into the real possibility of perma-nence. Morris likes the nursing home. Nancy has been moved into a single room in the Alzheimer's unit and he sees her at mealtimes. He doesn't tell us about his plans directly; a mes-sage is conveyed through our care manager, who's also in-structed to tell us that he hopes we aren't offended.

There's a phone call from The Charity manager, Mary, who's a good egg and empathic. She mentions that she had a run-in with someone in authority at the council about Nancy's not being on the waiting list. The someone had maintained the until recently unanimous stance that Nancy wasn't severe enough a case to be on the residential care list.

"Not severe enough?" Mary had echoed, incredulously. "She's a lot more severe than plenty of the people you do have in nursing homes. You just try spending a couple of days looking after her. You'd see what she's really like."

Then she makes an illuminating point about the fundamentals of how these things work. "When you get to the point that you can no longer go on as a caregiver, and state that you can no longer go on, that you can't do it anymore, then the state has to step in and take charge and find alternative arrangements. You say baldly that you can no longer cope, they have to take them in, it's that simple."

And that's the reason they're on the waiting list now. That's the reason that the care manager has been on the phone to Chris this morning, saying that permission will almost certainly be granted for a council-sponsored permanent placement at the respite home, though they have to go through the motions of soliciting a local place first.

Chris calls his father and is relieved to find him remarkably cheery.

"I hear you are thinking of staying on, Dad."

"Yes, thinking about it, yes."

"I think that's great news for you, really good news, if the two of you are happy and settled there. I think you should go for it, Dad. Stay on. We'll make all the arrangements."

"Right, son."

"So you'll be staying on?"

"I'm coming round to that way of thinking, yes."

Chapter 31

*Only the paradox comes anywhere near to comprehending
the fullness of life.*

—C. G. JUNG

THE BOOK—AND PARTICULARLY, THE AMERICAN VER-
sion of The Book—says that taking up the nursing
home place is just the beginning of a new life for both
of you, the dementia sufferer and also the caregiver. The Book
doesn't seem to want caregivers to have any sense of relief or
liberation when caregiving comes to an end. That might be
unseemly, mightn't it? Being glad. Being glad is taboo. The
Book envisages that the caregiver will live close enough to the
home to visit every day—though this might involve moving.
The nursing home staff will be glad to see you popping in and
out, The Book says. The nursing home staff will be glad to
share tasks and to devolve some of them. You (the caregiver)
can help with dressing, and feeding, and bathing, and care,
quite apart from providing a face that still might be familiar and
all its resonances of love and family. Quite apart from providing
outings.

Interestingly, career nursing home managers with expertise in
dementia often feel differently. Those I've come across, at least.
Some of them, at least, are prepared to speak up for the wisdom
of letting go. Having spent a good many months immersed in
the online Alzheimer's community, I find that one common
experience shines out: that at some point along the dementia
journey, the fact that the caregiver is close to the person stops

helping them and starts hindering. So often, people find that it's their own interactions with the dementia sufferer that are triggering their senile anxiety, however unwittingly. Sometimes people see this and remark on it. Sometimes they don't and it's only the outsider who sees.

The caregiver hates leaving their demented relative at the home, which is, after all, an institution, and may jar aesthetically on the nerves of the healthy, with its hospital look, its easy-clean surfaces and perceived lack of comforts. But then they discover that the demented one's health and morale improve at the home. They find this hard to believe, because when they visit, all they see is unhappiness. The caregiver speaks to the staff about this—about their loved one's unhappiness—and may be told tactfully that actually the outbursts only happen when the caregiver visits, and possibly it might be better for the dementia sufferer to be left to get on with this new phase of life undisturbed. That's a hard thing to be told, and even harder to accept. After all, we think of ourselves as essential. We have been essential to the person for months and years, day in and day out without pause. Part of what disturbs us about leaving them at the nursing home is that we are missing from that environment; family and personal history are missing, and no one, surely, could be better off without those. The truth is that sometimes they are. Sometimes family and history exert too much pressure, provoking a chaotic mental state that can't deal with the presence of pieces of the old life, things sparked in a damaged brain that dementia can't make sense of.

TWO THINGS APPEAR to be true.

1. When Alzheimer's sufferers get to the point of constant unhappiness at home, they are ready to leave. Nothing you do or try will make any difference to this.

2. All that matters, at this advanced stage of the disease, is that they are as happy as they can be, even if that means your having restricted access to them. If they can be got through the day with minimal fear, anxiety, rage, then that's a good day.

It's time to stop reading the dementia books. There's a shelf full, the books placed there in acquisition order. They start at the left with the how-to caregiver books, proceed into the more medical tomes, the more specialized, soften abruptly into memoir, then take a swerve into American publishers, books of alien sizes and typefaces, titles dredged for and blundered into on Amazon. Some of these are rather wacky. Some I'm not sure what to make of. I meet a retired neuroscientist on a bus, a stranger, who sees what I'm reading and strikes up a conversation. He agrees with the basic premise of the book in my hands, one I'd taken to be eccentric, that Alzheimer's disease is a myth. "There isn't really any such thing, you know," he says, eyes twinkling. "It's just that some people age faster than others." This brings me up short. But do the two camps really have to be at odds, normal aging versus abnormal event? Isn't it possible that a condition that presents itself as the acceleration of brain aging is itself a disease? In any case, what about the 115-year-old woman, in the news recently, whose brain showed no signs of dementia at autopsy and was said to be as healthy as that of someone fifty years her junior? If she was merely an exception, how many exceptions are there? Are we two kinds of human, those who do and those who don't experience brain failure, the key to the mystery mundanely genetic?

Members of the Alzheimer's backlash, the dissenters like the writers of this "myth" book, have to admit that early-onset dementia is a disease. But like the neuroscientist on the bus, they regard late-onset dementia as a human-condition condition, one that will never find a cure. They cite the work of scientists at

Harvard University in pinpointing the disintegration of my-elin (our white matter) in the brain, which makes electrical signals between neurons weak and diffuse, as just as likely to explain *senility*. They point out that plaques may be beneficial—something, of course, that the pro-tau research body would also agree with. They point out that some dementia autopsy brains show neither plaques nor tangles, and that some autopsy brains of people who didn't suffer from dementia are plaque riddled. Alzheimer's as a disease, they say, is a myth fostered by pharmaceutical companies. I find others sympathetic to these ideas in the online community: those who think that labeling people as having dementia is a form of bone pointing (an Ab-original idea, in which the subject toward whom the bone is pointed convinces himself he is doomed, and dies accord-ingly); others who claim there's no actual loss of self entailed in the progress of dementia, other than for that imposed by society, which conditions the ill culturally and socially to be-have in a demented manner.

If some or all of this is bonkers, there's no doubt that the way healthy humans regard those with brain illnesses, brain damage, brain disability is in general shockingly uncivilized. I find myself averting my eyes in the supermarket as a woman with dementia of some kind rants and accosts passersby, all of whom avert their gaze in turn, and begin to create a margin as they pass, a collusive semicircle of safety. We're embarrassed by dementia. I'm embarrassed by dementia. The unpredict-ability of how somebody may act, what they may say to you—these are factors. I smile at an old lady with dementia on the bus and she shouts at me for the rest of the journey home. It's safer to keep your distance. In addition, there's the shame of being old, your body failing. We treat the old with contempt, their weakness provoking bullying by the healthy. Is it because they rub our noses in our own mortality? Because we see mortality as a failing, after all? Perhaps subconsciously we feel

the bone's been pointed, and that we should keep ourselves
clear. Mortality is contagious; we catch it from our parents. It's
hard to treat somebody with failing thinking and language
skills as a person as fully human as yourself. You may not think
so. Every instinct in you might insist otherwise. In the supermarket, though—how are you then, when the old lady thanks
you for finding the jar of mayonnaise, then smashes it on the
ground, hits you with her basket, calls you her daughter, tells
the checkout staff and everyone on the street outside that you're
taking her home? It's so much worse if the person is haphaz-
ardly dressed, dirty, smells; it's so much harder to treat them
like an equal.

These may sound like accusations but in fact I'm trying to
excuse the behavior of people toward the demented, which
tends to be awkward at best, unkind, and thereafter progresses
on a sliding scale into savagery. It's untrained. It's untrained,
certainly, though should the behavior of humans toward others need training to be fair? If it does, it can only be because
some unfortunate *ghost in the machine* has survived, subconsciously, in our own minds, that marks out brain afflictions as
dehumanizing and dehumanizes accordingly. This is the only
way I can account for the behavior of the many doctors, specialists, and consultants written about in dementia forums who
are on the record as having treated those with Alzheimer's so
badly and so dismissively. And how else can we explain the
treatment of the elderly in nursing homes (some elderly, in some
nursing homes), who are talked to like bad children, neglected,
ill fed, abused, or even—as in a recent case in the newspapers—
tied onto their chairs?

The old woman on the bus who shouted—she was real.
But the woman in the supermarket—I made her up. Or rather
my brain did, while I was sleeping. The thing is, she was me,
the woman in the dream, the Barbour bag lady in thirty

years' time. She wasn't like me, she was me. It was me. All that separated us was time, and the dementia roll of the dice that will determine whether in 2040 I'll be one of the 90 million, or not.

It's time to stop reading the dementia books.

Chapter 32

Things that were hard to bear are sweet to remember.

—SENECA

THIS IS WHAT MIGHT HAPPEN TO OLD PEOPLE WHO GO into nursing homes. They have secure, dull lives looked after by gentle Eastern Europeans in easy-care aprons. Their families ring when they get around to it. Their tidy, institutional bedrooms with the matching floral duvet and curtains show little sign of life, other than for the book and glasses by the bed, and the two propped cards that have arrived from old friends.

It's two hours' journey from the house to the home, which is a ranch-style bungalow, purpose-built, U-shaped with deep wings and a steeply pitched hipped roof. Inside it's warm, draft-proof, with tight modern windows, wide carpeted corridors, jolly pine furnishings, and chain-store chandeliers.

We go to visit at Easter; our holiday route almost passes the door. There has been excited anticipation of our visit. Nancy and Morris are washed, pressed, have had their hair cut that very morning. Because we are en route and in a rush, we anticipate we'll be there for less than an hour, but that seems to have been forgotten. Nancy and Morris's lunch has been delayed indefinitely in our honor. As it turns out, we're running late and spend twenty-seven minutes in the building. Chris speaks to the manager and asks where we can have our meeting. He doesn't use the word *meeting,* of course, but that's what this feels like, a hurried business conversation in a motel conference facility. We use an alcove designed for the purpose just by the front doors, a cubbyhole furnished with three chairs.

Morris isn't around. He's wheeled himself off to his room to get a birthday card for Caitlin, one that we bought and mailed to him in readiness. I go into the dayroom and see an old lady there. She's sitting alone in a winged armchair, rubbing her hands energetically together and muttering.

"Oh, and she said, she said it was all right, so I suppose it is. It must be if she says so. She knows everything."

Nancy. In some bizarre unexpected way I have been missing her. Her eyes are fixed unblinking on the table twenty feet away, where six residents and two staff are sitting having a conversation, desultorily engaged in nursing home activities. Playing cards. Sticking down a magazine cutout collage. I stop at her chair and stoop to touch her arm and her face shifts from its blankness briefly to a look of alarm and then into a great beaming smile.

"Oh! Hello! What on earth are you doing here?"

She seems genuinely to recognize me. Chris had this experience last month, when he came to see that they'd settled in, and his mother greeted him with "So how is the family?" Her improvement since she's been here has been quite remarkable, say the staff. That's why the social workers have already let it be known that they wouldn't let her out to live in the civilian world again. Morris, a couple of weeks ago, was on the phone to Chris to say that he was thinking about returning to live with us, and Chris had had to tell him so.

"I've come to visit you," I say, kissing her and offering an armful of supermarket tulips. "Look, flowers for your room. And a box of Dairy Milk, your favorites."

"Oooh, thank you," she says. "Gimme gimme!" Making playful grabbing motions.

"Your grandchildren are just round the corner, in the visitor chairs," I say to her. "Do you want to come and see them?"

"Oh no. No, thank you. I don't think so. Not today."

"Come and see them. Just for a minute." I hold my hand out and she takes it, getting up and toddling after me. "Well, all right, then. Seems like I don't have any choice. As usual."

Nineteen minutes left. I look covertly at my watch. Morris arrives in his chair with Chris, all smiles, looking well.

"Here he is," Nancy says. She seems to know who Morris is. She tells him off when he starts talking about their new life: "Oh, hold your wheesht, you," slapping him flirtily on the knee. We talk about our trip south, and ask about the home. They have a pretty good social life, it seems, though Morris has been reprimanded for preferring to sit with a book than join in, he tells me. He's reading about Hitler's last days in the bunker. He urges me to visit his room and see his certificates and there they are, thumbtacked to the wall. One is for winning at the Beetle drive, the other for being placed third in carpet bowls. The children don't say much and neither does Nancy, but she smiles at everybody and her teeth are clean. She is altogether immensely clean, her fingernails white and her silver bob immaculate. Morris has no complaints, he says, other than about being kept waiting for meals once they're seated in the dining hall. Their timekeeping here isn't that impressive and it's annoying having to wait. The food's pretty good, though. And he has television in his room.

"How's she been?" I whisper to Morris, while Chris is chatting to his mother.

"Pretty good," he says. "She's in this part of the home with me some of the time . . . but the rest of the time she's in the Alzheimer's wing, locked up." He looks embarrassed.

"What's it like through there?" I ask, looking toward the security doors.

"Just like this side, a bit smaller, but otherwise a mirror image of here," he tells me.

Nancy has gone through the looking glass.

"She wanders into other people's rooms, apparently," Chris tells me later. "Ignores them, goes and looks out of the window and then leaves without saying anything."

It's time to go.

Nancy tries to follow us out of the building.

"Will you be back soon?" she asks, anxious, trying to grasp at my hands.

"Yes," I say. "Very soon," nudging at her arms so I can close the door.

Morris is barking instructions at her. She turns to him and she says, "Just wait till I get you home."

ALMOST EXACTLY A year later, Morris died at the home from kidney failure. During his last illness he spent a lot of time anxious about Nancy, unwilling to stay in bed. She might be up to something. He ought to be there. He couldn't rest.

Nancy didn't understand or mark his passing and his funeral service was held in Edinburgh as he wished. Nancy was judged too ill to make the journey, which would have entailed spending most of a day on the train south, a night in the city, and another day on the train back. In some ways she's very ill, and in others amazingly robust. Physically, she continues to be good for her age. The nursing home staff speak about her with touching protectiveness. She remains somebody who wants to be doing things and busy and finds it hard to sit still. If she's awake, she's usually on the move. She's prone to aggression; there are long gaps between haircuts as they have to pick the right day to embark. Haloperidol (Haldol), an antipsychotic, is administered in small doses, a half teaspoon two or three times a week, on an ad hoc basis of need, and doesn't appear to slow her down. She's unaware who anybody is, but keen to be included in the group, despite her communication difficulties. Shrunken, but insistent on wearing favorite old trousers, she gathers spare fabric bunched up at the waistband with one hand as she shuffles about. She looks like a very old lady now. Having rejected, finally, the wearing of false teeth, her food's mashed up for her; she eats only with her fingers, and can be insistent about keeping moving, eating a little on each circuit of the home. Often she hasn't the patience for dealing with food at all, and steals a neighbor's tea biscuits later. She gets dietary supplement drinks. On a good day she'll react positively to the photographs in her room, though she can't put a face to a name. She talks to staff about her parents sometimes. Occasionally she mentions a man she used to know, a man in a wheelchair.

As for me, I've arrived, already, at a state of self-protective forgetting. People are good at that, at moving on, dwindling the past into a story we tell ourselves, into parables, and choosing the future over the past. It's true that every now and then mistakes that I made rear up in memory, like splinters surfacing out of a finger. Memories of bad days, revisited synaptically in sound and vision, far outweigh the good. But it's also true that, as Oscar Wilde put it, "The great events of life often leave one unmoved; they pass out of consciousness, and, when one thinks of them, become unreal. Even the scarlet flowers of passion seem to grow in the same meadow as the poppies of oblivion."

Additional Reading

Online Resources

Useful resources on the Internet divide into two main types: those that offer information, and those that offer support. I can't urge you strongly enough, if you are a caregiver of someone with dementia, to join a forum community and share your day-to-day struggles, concerns, and questions. "Talking" online to others who have just the same kind of issues and crises is invaluable. There is a lot of genuine companionship and good advice out there. Just to have an ongoing conversation with others in a similar situation to yourself, and to forge friendships, is immensely helpful and can vastly improve caregiver morale.

www.alz.org
The Alzheimer's Association. Education, advice, publications, and support. A guide to your rights and options. A very popular forum, where you can "talk" via message to other caregivers and sufferers. Twenty-four-hour toll-free advice on the phone.

www.alzfdn.org
Alzheimer's Foundation of America. Practical advice about the technicalities of caring for and supporting someone with dementia. A not-for-profit organization that acts as an umbrella for 1,200 other organizations. A useful list of government organizations to contact, under caregivers' tips/government/federal resources.

forum.alzheimers.org.uk
"Talking Point," a useful, busy caregivers' forum hosted by the Alzheimer's Society in the United Kingdom. Though the drug names and care procedures and legislation may be different, you'll find British caregivers have many of the same kinds of problems and solutions.

www.alzheimersreadingroom.com

A useful digest of Alzheimer's stories in the news, and articles on aspects of dementia and dementia care, edited by a caregiver.

www.alzinfo.org/forum

A forum for those affected by Alzheimer's, hosted by the Fisher Center for Alzheimer's Research Foundation (www.alzinfo.org).

www.caps4caregivers.org

CAPS—Children of Aging Parents. A nonprofit charitable organization that aims to offer support and information for caregivers to the elderly. There is also an online support group.

www.caregiver.org

Family Caregiver Alliance. Campaigning on behalf of caregivers, providing education and support. State-by-state navigator for care options. You can sign up to "talk" to other caregivers online.

www.caregiving.com

Information, personal stories, resources.

www.caregiving.org

National Alliance for Caregiving. A nonprofit coalition of national organizations focusing on issues surrounding family caregiving. An advocacy group.

www.ehealthforum.com

Hosts forums for a whole list of illnesses. Choose "Alzheimer's" from the menu. Post problems and get feedback. This Web site says that medical personnel can give feedback also; you need to sign up for this.

www.eldercare.gov

A search facility that puts Americans in touch with finding the organizations in their own area that can help and advise about home-based and community care.

www.thefamilycaregiver.org

The National Family Caregivers Association. Information and advocacy: giving a voice to the vast silent army of caregivers in the United States. The Family Caregiver Forum has message boards where you can post your problems and solutions and share with others.

www.healthboards.com
Forums for all sorts of illnesses: Go to the message board index and choose Alzheimer's and Dementia, or put "Alzheimer's" into the search box.

www.helpguide.org
Navigate via the Seniors & Aging link, to Alzheimer's/Dementia. The "Support for Caregivers" section has good advice.

www.mayoclinic.com
The Mayo Clinic's own information pages about Alzheimer's (follow the links) offer good basic guidance. The blog strives to be positive and can-do. There is a chance to comment; the comments from caregivers present an interesting contrast.

www.nia.nih.gov
National Institute on Aging Web site. Click on Alzheimer's Disease Information. Clear and simply written information on diagnosis, treatment, and caregiving.

www.tangledneuron.info
"A layperson reports on memory loss, Alzheimer's and dementia." A useful digest of dementia news.

Blogs

More and more caregivers are beginning to use the Internet to post diaries of their thoughts and experiences. You may find some of the following blogs useful, though be warned that sometimes their sadness and courage can prove overwhelming.

www.alzheimersdad.blogspot.com
www.alzheimersspeaks.wordpress.com
www.acaregiversjournal.com
www.eldercarecafe.blogspot.com
blog.seattlepi.com/witnessingalzheimers
www.mindingoureldersblogs.com
www.ajourneywithalzheimers.blogspot.com
www.knowitAlz.com
www.thelastofhismind.com
www.killingmyfather.com

Popular Books About Dementia and Alzheimer's

The Alzheimer's Action Plan, by P. Murali Doraiswamy and Lisa P. Gwyther—A guide that looks at what can be done about MCI and early stages of dementia.

Alzheimer's from the Inside Out, by Richard Taylor—Essays written by a psychologist and early-onset-dementia sufferer, observing his own deterioration.

The Brain That Changes Itself: Stories of Personal Triumph from the Frontiers of Brain Science, by Norman Doidge—An interesting book about brain plasticity, its ability to rewire itself.

A Caregiver's Guide to Alzheimer's Disease: 300 Tips for Making Life Easier, edited by Patricia R. Callone—A very practical guide popular with caregivers.

Creating the Good Will, by Elizabeth Arnold—A comprehensive guide to financial end-of-life planning.

Dementia Diary: A Care Giver's Journal, by Robert Tell—An account by a son of his mother's slow descent into disease.

Elder Rage, or Take My Father . . . Please! by Jacqueline Marcell—A popular and cathartic howl of frustration by a child looking after a difficult aged parent.

Learning to Speak Alzheimer's, by Joanne Koenig Coste—Personal experience and person-centered home-based-care advice from the wife of an Alzheimer's sufferer.

Losing My Mind, by Thomas DeBaggio—An account of his own decline, by an early-onset-Alzheimer's sufferer.

Mothering Mother: A Daughter's Humorous and Heartbreaking Memoir, by Carol O'Dell—Another account of a mother with dementia being taken into her child's home and life and the struggles that ensued.

Still Alice, by Lisa Genova—A bestselling novel about a psychology professor with early-onset Alzheimer's.

The 36-Hour Day, by Nancy L. Mace and Peter V. Rabins—The best-known of the how-to-care guides for family and home-based caregivers.

Acknowledgments

Introduction
Luis Buñuel, *My Last Sigh,* translated by Abigail Israel, published by Alfred A. Knopf, a division of Random House, Inc. A paperback edition is published by University of Minnesota Press.

Chapter 2
Aaron Copland quotation reprinted by permission of the publisher from *Music and Imagination: The Charles Eliot Norton Lectures 1951–52* by Aaron Copland. Harvard University Press, Cambridge, Mass. Copyright © 1952 by the President and Fellows of Harvard College, Copyright © renewed 1980 by Aaron Copland.

Chapter 5
Philip Larkin, "Best Society," from *Collected Poems by Philip Larkin.* Copyright © 1988, 2003 by the Estate of Philip Larkin. Reprinted by permission of Farrar, Straus, and Giroux, LLC.

Philip Larkin, "Aubade," from *Collected Poems by Philip Larkin.* Copyright © 1988, 2003 by the Estate of Philip Larkin. Reprinted by permission of Farrar, Straus, and Giroux, LLC.

Ludwig Wittgenstein, aphorism 109, from *Philosophical Investigations,* 1953. New edition edited by Hacker and Schulter, and published by Wiley-Blackwell.

Ludwig Wittgenstein, *Tractatus Logico-Philosophicus,* 1922. New edition translated by Pears and McGuinness, and published by Routledge Classics.

Chapter 16
Antonio Damasio, *The Feeling of What Happens,* 2000, published by Harvest Books.

Chapter 18

C. G. Jung and W. Pauli, *The Interpretation of Nature and the Psyche,* 1955. Translated by R. F. C. Hull and published by Routledge.

Sigmund Freud, *Civilisation and Its Discontents,* 1930, translated by David McLintock, published by Penguin Modern Classics.

R. D. Laing, *The Facts of Life,* 1976, published by Allen Lane. Reproduced with kind permission of the R. D. Laing Estate.

Chapter 20

Elizabeth Bowen, *Vogue* magazine interview, September 1955. Reproduced with permission of Curtis Brown Group Ltd, London, on behalf of the Estate of Elizabeth Bowen. © Elizabeth Bowen 1955.

Chapter 22

T. S. Eliot, "The Hollow Men," from *Collected Poems, 1909–1962,* © 1936 by Harcourt, Inc. and renewed 1964 by T. S. Eliot. Reprinted by permission of Houghton Mifflin Harcourt Publishing Company.

John Bayley, *Iris,* 1998, published by Duckworth.

Chapter 23

Henry Miller, *Black Spring.* Reproduced with permission of Curtis Brown Group Ltd, London, on behalf of the Estate of Henry Miller. © Henry Miller 1936.

Douglas Adams, *The Hitchhiker's Guide to the Galaxy,* 1979, published by Macmillan.

Chapter 25

Louis MacNeice, "Snow," from *Collected Poems,* 2007, published by Faber & Faber.

Chapter 26

Wallace Stevens, "Man and Bottle," from *The Collected Poems of Wallace Stevens,* 1990, published by Vintage Books, a division of Random House, Inc.

Chapter 27

C. G. Jung, *Children's Dreams, Notes from the Seminars Given in 1936–40,* translated by Ernst Falzeder and Tony Woolfson, published 2007 by Princeton University Press.

Chapter 28

Philip Larkin, "Long Last," from *Collected Poems by Philip Larkin*. Copyright © 1988, 2003 by the Estate of Philip Larkin. Reprinted by permission of Farrar, Straus, and Giroux, LLC.

Chapter 31

C. G. Jung, *Psychology and Alchemy,* translated R. F. C. Hull, and published by Routledge.

Keeper

Reader's Guide

About This Book

Keeper is an account of a crisis in a family's life: a long drawn-out crisis without simple boundaries or solutions. When Nancy comes to live with her son and daughter-in-law and their children, along with her husband, Morris, she brings her Alzheimer's disease with her. They move together to a romantic mansion out on a headland in remote northern Scotland, expecting life to be easier for Nancy and manageable for the rest of them. But Alzheimer's is a ticking clock, building to a sustained emotional explosion. When Nancy no longer knows who she is, when her autobiography has been whittled away by brain disease, the learning curve is steeper than anyone could have imagined. *Keeper* takes the form of interweaving a vivid diary of Nancy's day-to-day unraveling with the author's own research into what Alzheimer's is and what it means for us as human souls.

About This Guide

Dear Reader:

Here are some questions that seem obvious to me, as the author of the book. They're the questions I ask myself, now that I read it again, given the benefit of some distance from the events described.

My best to you,
Andrea Gillies

Discussion Questions

1. Did Andrea and Chris have any real choice when they offered to take Nancy and Morris into their home? Where would another choice have led the family as a whole?

2. On what basis does the author rationalize the choice she's made to care for Nancy herself? Is her reasoning sound, or based on idealism and ignorance?

3. To what extent does the romantic setting—the landscape surrounding the house and the beauty of the house itself—become metaphorical and emblematic of the progress of the story?

4. How do Nancy's and the author's "journeys" (in terms of mood and state of mind) come to mirror each other?

5. Why do the other characters, particularly the author's husband and children, play so small a part in the book?

6. What's Morris's role in the progression of Nancy's dementia?

7. What's the turning point in the story, and why? When does it become clear that the experiment isn't going to work?

8. How successful is the author in explaining how a disease can affect a personality? Were you convinced that, as the author comes to believe, memory is the same thing as identity and that "self" is a biological entity?

9. Can the author's getting aggressive and indifferent with Nancy be justified? And if so, how?

10. At the end of the book, when change comes, do Andrea and Chris make the right decision for Morris and Nancy? Should they have taken this course of action at the beginning?

About the Author

ANDREA GILLIES is a writer and journalist. *Keeper,* her first book, won the 2009 Wellcome Trust Book Prize for the best book on a medical topic published in the United Kingdom. She lives with her family in Edinburgh, Scotland, and has just completed her first novel.